T0141439

Trends in Functional Programming
Volume 7

Edited by
Henrik Nilsson
The University of Nottingham

intellect Bristol, UK / Chicago, USA

First Published in the UK in 2007 by
Intellect Books, PO Box 862, Bristol BS99 1DE, UK

First published in the USA in 2007 by
Intellect Books, The University of Chicago Press, 1427 E. 60th Street, Chicago,
IL 60637, USA

A catalogue record for this book is available from the British Library.

Cover Design: Gabriel Solomons

ISBN 978–1-84150–188-8

Printed and bound by Gutenberg Press, Malta.

Contents

Preface

This is Volume 7 of Trends in Functional Programming (TFP). It contains the Refereed Proceedings of TFP 2006: the Seventh Symposium on Trends in Functional Programming. TFP is an international forum for researchers with interests in all aspects of functional programming. Its goal is to provide a broad view of current and future trends in functional programming in a lively and friendly setting. Consequently, talks are accepted to the TFP symposia through submission of extended abstracts. These are screened by the Programme Committee to ensure they are within the scope of the symposium. After the symposium, the speakers are invited to submit full-length versions of their papers. These are refereed to international conference standards by the Programme Committee, and the best ones are selected for publication in the Refereed Proceedings.

TFP 2006 took place Nottingham, UK, 19–21 April, hosted by the School of Computer Science and Information Technology, the University of Nottingham. TFP 2006 was co-located with Types 2006 and the 2006 Spring School on Datatype-Generic Programming.

The TFP symposia are the successors to the Scottish Functional Programming Workshops. Prior to Nottingham, the last few TFP symposia were held in Edinburgh, Scotland in 2003, in Munich, Germany in 2004, and in Tallinn, Estonia in 2005. For further general information about TFP, see http://www.tifp.org.

In all, 33 talks were given at TFP 2006, including talks in a joint Types/TFP session and an invited talk by Simon Peyton Jones, Microsoft Research. 52 people from 11 nations and 4 continents (Asia, Australia, Europe, and North America) attended the Symposium (not counting session-hopping delegates from the co-located events). 25 full-length papers were eventually submitted for consideration for the present volume of refereed proceedings, and 13 of these where finally selected after careful refereeing and an electronic programme committee meeting in September 2006. The selection covers a diverse mix of topics, from implementation to application of functional languages, from debugging to depended types, and from applied to theoretical.

TFP pays special attention to research students, acknowledging that they are almost by definition part of new subject trends. One manifestation of this is the TFP prize for the best student paper. This prize is awarded by the TFP Programme Committee as a part of the post-symposium refereeing. To qualify, the work described in a paper must mostly be that of a student or students, and the paper itself must mainly be written by that student or those students. The TFP 2006 Programme Committee decided to reward *two* papers that were judged to be equally worthy of recognition:

- *When Is an Abstract Data Type a Functor?* by Pablo Nogueira

- *Extensible and Modular Generics for the Masses* by Bruno C. d. S. Oliveira (main author), Ralf Hinze, and Andres Löh.

The chapters in this volume appear in the order they were presented at TFP 2006 in Nottingham.

ACKNOWLEDGMENTS

Making TFP 2006 happen was very much a team effort. First of all, I would like to thank the TFP speakers and the authors of the papers in the present volume for their contributions. Thanks to you, TFP 2006 covered a wide range of current topics. Then I would like to thank the programme committee for all their help with promoting TFP 2006, screening abstracts, and the post-symposium refereeing. A special thank you to Graham Hutton for very helpful advice and support, and another special thank you to Jeremy Gibbons and Hans-Wolfgang Loidl for typesetting and LaTeX advice. Thanks also to May Yao and Holly Spradling, Intellect, for help with the copy-editing and publication of this book. An event like TFP involves a lot of down-to-earth organisation and plain hard work. Thanks to the co-location and close cooperation with Types 2006, we got a lot of help with practical matters. Thus a big thank you to the Types Team: Thorsten Altenkirch, James Chapman, Conor McBride, Peter Morris, and Wouter Swierstra. And last, but most certainly not the least, another big thank you to Joel Wright, who was responsible for the local arrangements of TFP 2006 and did a splendid job mostly behind the scenes to make everything work. TFP 2006 was an APPSEM-affiliated event, and we gratefully acknowledge the support from APPSEM-II.

Henrik Nilsson
Programme Chair and Editor
Nottingham, January 2007

TFP 2006 ORGANISATION

Symposium Chair:	Marko van Eekelen	Radboud Universiteit Nijmegen
Programme Chair:	Henrik Nilsson	University of Nottingham
Treasurer:	Greg Michaelson	Heriot-Watt University
Local Arrangements:	Joel Wright	University of Nottingham

TFP 2006 PROGRAMME COMMITTEE

Kenichi Asai	Ochanomizu University
Gilles Barthes	INRIA, Sophia Antipolis
Olaf Chitil	University of Kent
Catherine Dubois	IIE, Evry
Marko van Eekelen	Radboud Universiteit Nijmegen
Jeremy Gibbons	Oxford University
Kevin Hammond	University of St Andrews
Zoltán Horváth	Eötvös Loránd University
Frank Huch	Christian-Albrechts-Universität zu Kiel
Johan Jeuring	Universiteit Utrecht
Greg Michaelson	Heriot-Watt University
Henrik Nilsson	University of Nottingham
Ricardo Peña	Universidad Complutense de Madrid
Morten Rhiger	Roskilde University
Colin Runciman	University of York
Carsten Schürmann	IT University of Copenhagen
Zhong Shao	Yale University
Phil Trinder	Heriot-Watt University

Chapter 1

Proving Termination Using Dependent Types: the Case of Xor-Terms

Jean-François Monin[1], Judicaël Courant[1]

Abstract: We study a normalization function in an algebra of terms quotiented by an associative, commutative and involutive operator (logical xor). This study is motivated by the formal verification of cryptographic systems, relying on a normalization function for xor-terms. Such a function is easy to define using general recursion. However, as it is to be used in a type theoretic proof assistant, we also need a proof of its termination. Instead of using a mixture of various rewriting orderings, we follow an approach involving the power of Type Theory with dependent types. The results are to be applied in the proof of the security API described in [14].

1.1 INTRODUCTION

This work originates in the verification of a cryptographic system in the Coq proof assistant [14]. In the course of this verification, we modelized plaintext and encrypted data as first-order sorted terms[2]. For instance, a typical term could be $\{K_1 \oplus K_2\}_{H(KM,H(EXP,KP))}$ where $\{x\}_y$ denotes encryption of x using a key y, $H(x,y)$ denotes the fingerprint (cryptographic checksum) of the pair (x,y), $x \oplus y$ denotes the bitwise exclusive or of x and y. The cryptographic primitives $\{\_\}_\_$ and H are commonly supposed to be perfect, and can thus be treated as free constructors. On the contrary, we need to deal with the equational theory of the exclusive or

---

[1] VERIMAG, Université Joseph Fourier, Grenoble;
E-mail: {jean-francois.monin|judicael.courant}@imag.fr

[2] Such a model is known as the *symbolic model* ; by contrast the other, much less automated, mainstream approach, known as the *computational model*, modelizes data as strings of binary digits.

function as many (potential or effective) attacks are based on its algebraic properties [20, 6, 8, 10].

Deduction in presence of a non-trivial equational theory in the general case is notoriously difficult: [15] shows that the matching problem in the presence of an associative-commutative (AC) function symbol is NP-complete, even in very restricted cases, and AC matching is still an active research topic. In order to solve our particular problem, we only needed a way to define a canonical form for closed terms and a proof of existence of a canonical form for each term. More precisely, we needed a canonicalization function putting any term into its canonical form. On paper, we would use results from term rewriting theory in order to prove the existence of a normalization function with respect to some rewriting system. Unfortunately, the formalization of these results in Coq is only partial yet. Therefore we tried to apply the methods of terms rewriting theory to our problem but stopped when we realized the amount of work needed to complete the definition of the normalization function (section 1.2).

Then we observed that the existence of such a normalization function could be reduced to the existence of a normalization function for terms built over $\oplus$ and 0 only. In other words, we can layer our terms into alternating levels of free and non-free constructors, and normalization of the overall term can be deduced from the normalization of all layers (section 1.3).

We formalized such a proof in Coq (section 1.4). Our results are to be applied in our proof of security of an API [14]. However, the approach investigated here is not tied to the specific term algebra of this case study. We reflected this at several places in our formal development, by stating some key definitions and lemmas in an abstract setting, independently of any specific application.

1.2 BACKGROUND

1.2.1 The Need for a Canonicalization Function

In order to reason of our cryptographic system, we need to define some functions or properties over terms. In order to be consistent, we must ensure that these definitions are compatible with the equational theory E induced by commutativity, associativity and cancelation laws of $\oplus$ and 0. We can define such a property P using one of the following ways:

- We define P on the whole set of terms (for instance by structural induction). We check afterwards that P is indeed compatible with equality, that is, we check that $\forall t_1\ t_2\ \ t_1 =_E t_2 \Rightarrow P(t_1) \iff P(t_2)$.

- We give a canonicalization function N for terms, *i.e.* a function N from terms to terms such that $\forall t_1\ t_2\ \ t_1 =_E t_2 \iff N(t_1) = N(t_2)$. Then we define P *over canonical forms only* and extend it in the only compatible way. More formally, we first define some auxiliary predicate P' over terms (for instance by structural induction) and $P(t)$ is defined as $P'(N(t))$. Thus P is compatible with E by construction.

In our case, the latter approach looks the only reasonable one. For instance, we needed to check whether some secret constant appears in a given term. Let us consider an example: it is clear that KM does not appear in $\{K_1\}_{H(\text{EXP,KEK})}$. But checking that it does not appear in $KM \oplus \{K_1\}_{H(\text{EXP,KEK})} \oplus KM$ is a bit more difficult, as you have to notice that, although KM syntactically is a subterm of this latter term, the occurences of KM have no semantic significance here because of the self-cancelation law. We therefore do not see how to give a definition for this notion by structural induction on the whole set of terms. On the other hand, once we applied all possible simplication rules (self-cancelation and neutral element cancelation, modulo associativity and commutativity), we just need to check a syntactical occurence of KM.

Therefore, we need to define a canonicalization function N over terms which is also a simplification function, *i.e.* it ensures that for all term t, no simplification rule applies to $N(t)$.

1.2.2   What Term Rewriting Theory Says

The equational theory of $\oplus$ and 0 can be described by the following equations:

Commutativity:	$x \oplus y \simeq y \oplus x$	(1.1)
Associativity:	$(x \oplus y) \oplus z \simeq x \oplus (y \oplus z)$	(1.2)
Neutral element:	$x \oplus 0 \simeq x$	(1.3)
Involutivity:	$x \oplus x \simeq 0$	(1.4)

Term rewriting theory modulo associativity and commutativity (AC), as described in [18] would say that this equational theory is generated by the following rewrite system, where $\oplus$ is an associative-commutative symbol:

$$0 \oplus x \quad \rightarrow \quad x \qquad (1.5)$$
$$x \oplus x \quad \rightarrow \quad 0 \qquad (1.6)$$

If this system is terminating and critical pair converge, the existence of a unique normal form is ensured up to associativity and commutativity. In order to get a unique normal form, one just has to sort repeated applications of $\oplus$ according to a given arbitrary total ordering.

Tools for automatically checking termination and critical pair convergence have been developed for years by the term rewriting community. For instance, the tool CiME [11, 18] checks these properties instantaneously (code figure 1.1).

1.2.3   Applicability to Type Theory

However, formally giving such a normalization function in Type Theory and formally proving its correctness is much more challenging.

The first show-stopper is termination. In Type Theory, all functions are total and terminating by construction. This means that general fixpoints are not

```
operators                                    │ axioms
  + : AC                                      │   0+x = x;
  0 : constant                                │   x+x = 0;
  H, E : binary                               │ order
  K1,K2,IMP,EXP,DATA,KEK : constant           │   rpo(+>0)
  x,y,z : variable                            │ end
```

FIGURE 1.1. CiME code for xor-terms

allowed for defining functions. In order to achieve this fundamental property while keeping a good expressive power, Type Theory *limits recursion* to higher-order primitive recursion, and structural recursion over all inductively defined types. The theory and support tools automatically provide combinators for naturals numbers, lists and user-defined inductive types, which are enough in most cases. Alternatively, in recent versions of Coq, the user can define a function recursively, provided she points out to the system a parameter of this function which structurally decreases at each recursive call. A special and very important case is well-founded recursion: the decreasing argument is a proof, formalized as an inductive object, witnessing that a given value is accessible for some binary relation. In complex cases, the latter approach is by far more convenient. But there is no such thing as a free lunch: while type-checking ensures totality and strong normalization, the user has to design the right types and provide the right arguments. Of course, standard libraries about well-founded relations may help here. Besides, one can consider additional tools or methodology such as those developed by Bertot and Balaa, or Bove and Capretta [3, 7].

In the case of our canonicalization function, using standard rewriting arguments is surprisingly difficult in a proof assistant such as Coq [19, 4]:

- Although some theoretical work addresses the addition of rewriting to the Calculus of Constructions [5], this is yet to be implemented.

- Some work provides ways to define tactics for reasonning over associative-commutative theories [2], but they only provide ways to normalize given terms, not to define a normalization function.

We therefore tried to define our own specific rewriting relation corresponding to the defining equations of $\simeq$, but found this approach really costly:

- We had to give a well-founded ordering. As neither recursive path ordering nor lexicographic path ordering library was available in Coq, we used the lexicographic combination of a partial ordering $\leq_1$ with a total ordering $\leq_2$, where $\leq_1$ is a polynomial ordering, and $\leq_2$ is a lexicographic ordering. Although $\leq_2$ is not well-founded, the set of terms having a given weight for the polynomial defining $\leq_1$ is finite, therefore we could prove in Coq that the lexicographic combination of $\leq_1$ and $\leq_2$ is finite.

- Then we defined a rewriting relation $\triangleright$. The difficult part here is to take into account commutativity and associativity. In order to avoid AC-matching issues, we decided to add a rewriting rule for associativity and a conditionnal rewriting rule for commutativity ($x \oplus y$ would rewrite to $y \oplus x$ if and only if x is smaller than y). Moreover, we had to complete our rewriting system in order to close critical pairs such as $x \oplus x \oplus y$, which could be rewritten to y or to $x \oplus (x \oplus y)$.

- We still had to define the normalization function. As mentioned above, the definition of such a function using well-founded induction in Coq is difficult. Therefore we stopped there and used another approach instead.

- Once this would be done, we would still have to prove that the transitive closure of our rewriting relation is irreflexive, that our normalization function is sound with respect to it, and that it computes normal forms. Essentially, the main results to prove here would be $\forall t \; t \not\rhd^+ t$, $\forall t \; t \rhd^\star norm(t)$ and $\forall t_1 \forall t_2 \; t_1 \rhd t_2 \Rightarrow norm(t_1) = norm(t_2)$.

1.3   OUR APPROACH

1.3.1   Intuitive Presentation

Although implementing normalization in Coq is hard in general, it is much easier in some particular cases. For instance consider the term $t_1 \overset{\text{def}}{=} K_1 \oplus K_2 \oplus K_1$. In the examples considered here, K_1 and K_2 are constants (they are taken from our crytographic application). Normalizing t_1 is easy as it contains only constants and the exclusive or function. Such terms can easily be normalized as follows: we first compute the list of the constants it contains, here we get $[K_1 ; K_2 ; K_1]$, then we sort this list with respect to some total ordering on these constants, here we get, say, $[K_2 ; K_1 ; K_1]$. Then we easily detect repeated elements and apply self-cancelation: we therefore get the list $[K_2]$ hence the normalized form of $K_1 \oplus K_2 \oplus K_1$ is K_2.

Consider now the following term t_2, where EXP and KM are two other constants, while E is a free binary constructor – $E(u, v)$ stands for the encryption of u by v, usually denoted by $\{u\}_v$:

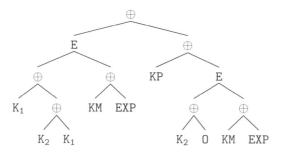

We first normalize the subterms $K_1 \; \oplus \; K_2 \; \oplus \; K_1$ and $K_2 \; \oplus \; 0$. Replacing them in the initial term, we get:

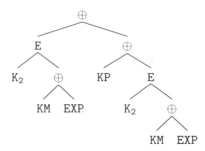

Now, both occurrences of $\{K_2\}_{KM\oplus EXP}$ behave as constants with respect to normalization. Indeed, they are in normal form and moreover the applications of the function symbols E at their heads act as a barrier preventing their subterms from any interaction with outside subterms with respect to rewriting. Therefore, we can normalize the whole term t_2 as previously for t_1 by sorting the list
$\left[\{K_2\}_{KM\oplus EXP}; KP; \{K_2\}_{KM\oplus EXP}\right]$ with respect to some total ordering, then detect repeated elements, apply self-cancelation and get KP as normal form.

We generalize this approach to all terms as follows, using typical features of Type Theory. In a first stage, the term to be normalized is layered in such a way that each level is built up from terms belonging to the previous level. These levels alternate between layers built up using only $\oplus$ constructors and layers built up using only other constructors, as lasagnas alternate between pasta-only layers and sauce layers (mixed up to your taste of tomato, meat, and cheese – in fact anything but pasta). At the term level, this stage is nothing else than constructor renaming. In a second stage, layers are normalized bottom-up. Normalizing a $\oplus$-layer only requires us to sort a list and remove pairs of identical items, while normalization of a non-$\oplus$-layer is just identity.

The second stage is easy, although we had to avoid some pitfalls (see section 1.4.3). Surprisingly, the first stage requires more work than expected: the new version of a term has a much more precise type whose computation turns out to be non-trivial (see section 1.4.2). In the whole development, we need the full power of programming with polymorphic dependent types: each layer owns its specific ordering relation, which depends on the ordered structure of the previous layer.

1.3.2   Layering Types

Let us now outline our approach in more detail. We call $\mathcal{T}$ the first-order inductive type of terms to be normalized. Let $\{\oplus, 0\} \uplus \mathcal{N}$ be the set of constructors of $\mathcal{T}$. For instance, in our application, we have $\mathcal{N} = \{PC, SC, E, Hash\}$ with

$$PC : \texttt{public\_const} \to \mathcal{T} \qquad\qquad E : \mathcal{T} \to \mathcal{T} \to \mathcal{T}$$
$$SC : \texttt{secret\_const} \to \mathcal{T} \qquad\qquad Hash : \mathcal{T} \to \mathcal{T} \to \mathcal{T}$$

where `public_const` and `secret_const` are suitable enumerated types[3].

---

[3]In our application, `public_const` contains 8 constants, including KP and EXP, while `secret_const` contains 5 constants, including K_1 and K_2. In the examples of

As explained in section 1.3.1, we want to split a $\mathcal{T}$-term into layers. Moreover, we have to state and prove a number of functions and lemmas for each layer. For modularity reasons, it is better to handle each layer separately. Each layer provides a data type, a comparison function and a sorting function on this type, as well as correctness lemmas. Intuitively, it could be seen as a module in the sense of Harper, Lillibridge and Leroy [16, 17], or better: a functor, because each layer relies on the interface of the previous layer. HLL modules have been adapted to the Calculus of Inductive Constructions [12, 13] and implemented in Coq [9]. But our case is out of their scope, because here the number of layers is a dynamic notion which depends on a piece of data, namely the term we normalize. Therefore we only use the features of basic CIC, which are dependent, polymorphic and inductive types.

In a first stage, we introduce two polymorphic inductive types $\mathcal{T}_x(\alpha)$ and $\mathcal{T}_n(\alpha)$ respectively called the *xor layer type* (pasta) and the *non-xor layer type* (sauce). The constructors of $\mathcal{T}_x(\alpha)$ are (copies of) $\oplus$ and 0 while the constructors of $\mathcal{T}_n(\alpha)$ are (copies of) those belonging to $\mathcal{N}$. Moreover, $\mathcal{T}_x(\alpha)$ (respectively $\mathcal{T}_n(\alpha)$) has an additional injection $U_x : \alpha \to \mathcal{T}_x(\alpha)$ (respectively $U_n : \alpha \to \mathcal{T}_n(\alpha)$). Precise definitions of $\mathcal{T}_x$, $\mathcal{T}_n$, U_x and U_n will be given in section 1.4.1. It is intuitively clear that we can recast any term t from $\mathcal{T}$ to either the type $\mathcal{T}_x(\mathcal{T}_n(\mathcal{T}_x(\dots(\emptyset))))$ or the type $\mathcal{T}_n(\mathcal{T}_x(\mathcal{T}_n(\dots(\emptyset))))$, according to the top constructor of t.

In a second stage, normalizing t can be defined as bottom-up sorting in the following way. We say that a type α is *sortable* if it is equipped with a decidable equality $=$ and a decidable total irreflexive and transitive relation $<$. We could take a decidable total ordering as well, but the above choice turns out to be more convenient. Every sortable type α enjoys the following properties:

- $\mathcal{T}_n(\alpha)$ is sortable;

- the multiset of α-leaves of any inhabitant t of $\mathcal{T}_x(\alpha)$ can be sorted (with deletion of duplicates) into a list $N_\alpha(t)$, such that $t_1 \simeq t_2$ iff $N_\alpha(t_1)$ is syntactically equal to $N_\alpha(t_2)$;

- $\text{list}(\alpha)$ is sortable (*i.e.* can be equipped with suitable equality and comparison relation);

- given a property P, $\{x : \alpha \mid P\,x\}$ is sortable once equipped with the equality and comparison relation over α.

Formally, we define the type *sortable* as a dependent structure made of a *Set* α, two binary relations $=_\alpha$ and $<_\alpha$ on α, and of proofs that $=_\alpha$ and $<_\alpha$ have the properties just mentionned. If A is a *sortable*, the underlying *Set* is denoted by $|A|$.

Let A be a sortable structure, then by the above remarks we can construct the following sortable structures:

---

section 1.3.1, K_1 should actually be replaced with $SC(K_1)$, and so on, but there is nothing essential here.

- $\mathcal{R}_u(A)$, such that $|\mathcal{R}_u(A)| = \mathcal{T}_n(|A|)$;

- $\mathcal{R}_x(A)$, such that $|\mathcal{R}_x(A)| = \texttt{list}(|A|)$;

- $\mathcal{S}_x(A)$, such that $|\mathcal{S}_x(A)| = \{l : \texttt{list}(|A|) \mid \textit{sorted } l\}$.

For $=_{|\mathcal{R}_u(A)|}$ (respectively $=_{|\mathcal{R}_x(A)|}$), take the congruent extensions of $=_{|A|}$ on the constructors of $\mathcal{T}_n$ (respectively $\texttt{list}$). For $<_{|\mathcal{R}_u(A)|}$ and $<_{|\mathcal{R}_x(A)|}$, take a lexicographic ordering based on $<_{|A|}$. Proving that $=_{|\mathcal{R}_u(A)|}$, $=_{|\mathcal{R}_x(A)|}$, $<_{|\mathcal{R}_u(A)|}$ and $<_{|\mathcal{R}_x(A)|}$ have the required properties is standard. For $\mathcal{R}_x(A)$, it is done once for all. For $\mathcal{R}_u(A)$, the proofs follow a systematic scheme – and this is the only step which depends on the definition of $\mathcal{T}$.

Then, we can define a local normalizing function from $|\mathcal{T}_x(A)|$ to $|\mathcal{R}_x(A)|$ or even better, to $|\mathcal{S}_x(A)|$. Note that thanks to polymorphism, we deal with each layer in a modular way.

Then we can normalize any term of type $\dots \mathcal{T}_x(\mathcal{T}_n(\mathcal{T}_x(\emptyset)))$ to a term of type $\dots \mathcal{R}_x(\mathcal{R}_u(\mathcal{R}_x(\emptyset)))$, or better $\dots \mathcal{S}_x(\mathcal{R}_u(\mathcal{S}_x(\emptyset)))$, by induction on the number of layers. This step does not depend on $\mathcal{T}$ either.

1.4 FORMALIZATION

1.4.1 Stratified Types

Defining xor and non-xor Layers

The types for xor and non-xor layers mostly partition $\mathcal{T}$, as mentioned in the previous section. However, in order to unfold sequences of $\oplus$, we want to avoid artificial separation of $\oplus$ layers like $x \oplus U_x(U_n(y \oplus z))$. Therefore, we want to be able to forbid constructions like $U_x(U_n(a))$.

A layer is said trivial when it consists only of a term $U_x(a)$ or $U_n(a)$. Hence we distinguish between potentially trivial layers and non-trivial layers, by parameterizing the xor layer type $\mathcal{T}_x$ by a Boolean telling us whether trivial layers are included or not; we call this parameter the *tolerance*:

Section sec_x.
Variable $\alpha : Set$.
Inductive $\mathcal{T}_x : bool \rightarrow Set :=$
  | $\text{Unit}_x : \forall b, Is\_true\ b \rightarrow \alpha \rightarrow \mathcal{T}_x\ b$
  | $0_x : \forall b, \mathcal{T}_x\ b$
  | $\text{Xor}_x : \forall b, \mathcal{T}_x\ true \rightarrow \mathcal{T}_x\ true \rightarrow \mathcal{T}_x\ b$
.

Definition $U_x := \text{Unit}_x\ true\ I$.

The predicate Is_true is defined by case analysis on its argument: $Is\_true\ \texttt{true}$ reduces to the trivially verified $True$, while $Is\_true\ \texttt{false}$ reduces to the absurd proposition $False$. In the definition of U_x, I denotes the (unique) inhabitant of $True$. Therefore, for any a in α, $U_x\ a$ is an inhabitant of $\mathcal{T}_x\ \alpha\ true$, as expected.

By contrast, in a consistent context, the constructor Unit_x cannot be used for building an element of type $\mathcal{T}_x\,\alpha\,\text{false}$.

Likewise the inductive sauce layer type $\mathcal{T}_n$ (non-xor terms) is parameterized by a Boolean tolerance telling whether trivial layers are included or not.

Section sec_nx.
Variable α : Set.
Inductive $\mathcal{T}_n$: $bool \to Set$:=
   | Unit_n : $\forall\, b, Is\_true\, b \to \alpha \to \mathcal{T}_n\, b$
   | PC_n : $\forall\, b, public\_const \to \mathcal{T}_n\, b$
   | SC_n : $\forall\, b, secret\_const \to \mathcal{T}_n\, b$
   | E_n : $\forall\, b, \mathcal{T}_n\, \text{true} \to \mathcal{T}_n\, \text{true} \to \mathcal{T}_n\, b$
   | Hash_n : $\forall\, b, \mathcal{T}_n\, \text{true} \to \mathcal{T}_n\, \text{true} \to \mathcal{T}_n\, b$
.

Definition U_n := $\text{Unit}_n\, \text{true}\, I$.

Zero-one Types

We distinguish *zero-one*[4] propositions (*ZO* for short), inductively characterized as follows:

Inductive ZO : $Prop \to Type$:=
   | ZO_True : $ZO\, True$
   | ZO_False : $ZO\, False$
   | ZO_conj : $\forall\, p\, q, ZO\, p \to ZO\, q \to ZO\, (p \wedge q)$
   | ZO_disj : $\forall\, p\, q, ZO\, p \to ZO\, q \to (p \to q \to False) \to ZO\, (p \vee q)$
.

Such propositions are decidable and have at most one inhabitant.

Lemma dec_ZO : $\forall\, p, ZO\, p \to \{p\} + \{\tilde{}p\}$.
Lemma $unique\_ZO$: $\forall\, p, ZO\, p \to \forall\, x\, y\colon p, x = y$.

Proof: by induction on $ZO\, p$.

ZO is lifted to predicates and binary relations.

Definition $pred\_ZO\, \alpha\, (P\colon \alpha{\to}Prop)$:= $\forall\, (x\colon \alpha), ZO\, (P\, x)$.
Definition $rel\_ZO\, \alpha\, (R\colon \alpha{\to}\alpha{\to}Prop)$:= $\forall\, (x\, y\colon \alpha), ZO\, (R\, x\, y)$.

For the predicates we used in our development, we found that proving that they were zero-one was as easy as proving that they were decidable. Moreover, once we prove a predicate to be zero-one, lemma *unique_ZO* automatically gives us proof irrelevance. Therefore, we could avoid some pitfalls with dependent types such as $\{x : \alpha \mid P\,x\}$: thanks to proof irrelevance, two inhabitants of this type, say $\langle x_1, p_1 \rangle$ and $\langle x_2, p_2 \rangle$ are equal if and only if $x_1 =_\alpha x_2$.

Sortable Structures

The complete definition of a sortable structure is as follows. It is made of a carrier set X, two binary relations *ueq* and *ult* on X and seven properties telling us that

---

[4]This notion has no connection with Kolmogorov's zero-one law in probability theory.

ueq and *ult* can indeed be used for sorting.

Record *sortable* : *Type* := *mksrt* {

  X : *Set*;

  ueq : $X \to X \to Prop$;
  ult : $X \to X \to Prop$;

  ueq_ZO : *rel_ZO ueq*;
  ueq_equal : *is_equal ueq*;
  ueq_refl : *reflexive ueq*;

  ult_ZO : *rel_ZO ult*;
  ult_ueq_False : *incompatible ult ueq*;
  ult_trans : *transitive ult*;
  ult_total : *total ult*

}.

The simplest example of a sortable is when X is empty. We get a structure called $\mathcal{R}_\emptyset$. Given a sortable A, we define two binary relations on list $|A|$ as follows:

Fixpoint *ueq_lnxor* ($l_1 \, l_2$: *lnxor*){*struct l_1*} : *Prop* :=
  match l_1, l_2 with
  | nil, nil $\Rightarrow$ *True*
  | $x_1 :: l_1, x_2 :: l_2 \Rightarrow$ *ueqA* $x_1 \, x_2 \wedge$ *ueq_lnxor* $l_1 \, l_2$
  | _, _ $\Rightarrow$ *False*
  end.

Fixpoint *ult_lnxor* ($l_1 \, l_2$: *lnxorA*) {*struct l_1*} : *Prop* :=
  match l_1, l_2 with
  | _, nil $\Rightarrow$ *False*
  | nil, _ :: _ $\Rightarrow$ *True*
  | $x_1 :: l_1, x_2 :: l_2 \Rightarrow$ *ultA* $x_1 \, x_2 \vee$ (*ueqA* $x_1 \, x_2 \wedge$ *ult_lnxor* $l_1 \, l_2$)
  end.

Then we can prove the seven required lemmas, so that applying *mksrt* to list $|A|$, *ueq_lnxor*, *ult_lnxor* and these lemmas yields a sortable $\mathcal{R}_x A$, with $|\mathcal{R}_x A| =$ list $|A|$. Using similar steps, we get another sortable $\mathcal{R}_u A$, with $|\mathcal{R}_u A| = \mathcal{T}_n |A|$.

We define a generic construction of a new sortable from a sortable A and a decidable predicate P on $|A|$:

Definition *relativize_sortable* :
  $\forall$ (A: *sortable*) (P: $|A| \to Prop$), *pred_ZO P $\to$ sortable*.

Given a sortable A and a list $l \stackrel{\text{def}}{=} [x_1; \ldots x_n]$ of elements of $|A|$, we say that l is *sorted* iff $x_1 <_A \ldots x_n$, where $<_A$ stands for *ultA*. To put it otherwise, *sorted l* tells us that l is sorted and has no duplicates. As *sorted l* reduces to a finite conjunction of zero-one propositions, we have:

Theorem *sorted_ZO* : *pred_ZO sorted*.

Proof: Show $\forall l, ZO(sorted \, l)$ by induction on l.

We then define $S_x A \stackrel{\text{def}}{=}$ *relativize_sortable* ($\mathcal{R}_x A$) *sorted sorted_ZO*.

Maps over Layers

Given a function f from $\alpha : Set$ to $\beta : Set$, we define a map_x (resp. map_n) function lifting f to functions from $\mathcal{T}_x \alpha$ to $\mathcal{T}_x \beta$ (resp. from $\mathcal{T}_n \alpha$ to $\mathcal{T}_n \beta$).

Fixpoint map_x $(f{:}\alpha{\rightarrow}\beta)$ b $(x{:}\mathcal{T}_x$ α $b)$ $\{struct\ x\}$: $\mathcal{T}_x$ β b :=
    match x in $(\mathcal{T}_x$ _ $b)$ return $(\mathcal{T}_x$ β $b)$ with
    | $\mathtt{Unit}_x$ b it $n \Rightarrow \mathtt{Unit}_x$ b it $(f\ n)$
    | $\mathtt{O}_x$ $b \Rightarrow \mathtt{O}_x$ b
    | $\mathtt{Xor}_x$ b x_1 $x_2 \Rightarrow \mathtt{Xor}_x$ b $(map_x f\ \mathtt{true}\ x_1)$ $(map_x f\ \mathtt{true}\ x_2)$
    end.

The definition of map_n is similar. Moreover, given an evaluation function $f : \alpha \rightarrow \mathcal{T}$, we can lift it to the domain $\mathcal{T}_x \alpha$ (resp. $\mathcal{T}_n \alpha$) by interpreting copies of $\oplus$ and $\mathtt{O}$ (resp. of constructors belonging to $\mathcal{N}$) as the corresponding constructors of $\mathcal{T}$, and $\mathtt{U}_x$ (resp. $\mathtt{U}_n$) as the application of f to its argument.

Stacking Layers

Building a stack of k layers now essentially amounts to building the type $(\mathcal{T}_x \circ \mathcal{T}_n)^{k/2}(\emptyset)$ or $\mathcal{T}_n(\mathcal{T}_x \circ \mathcal{T}_n)^{k/2}(\emptyset)$, depending on the parity of k. In a more type-theoretic fashion, we define two mutually inductive types *alte* and *alto*, denoting even and odd natural numbers respectively: the constructors of *alte* are $\mathtt{O}_e$ and $\mathtt{S}_{o \rightarrow e}$, the successor function from odd to even numbers, whereas *alto* has only one constructor, $\mathtt{S}_{e \rightarrow o}$, the successor function from even to odd numbers. We also define *parity* as either $\mathtt{P}_e$ or $\mathtt{P}_o$. We then build the function

$$
\begin{array}{rcl}
type\_of\_par : parity & \rightarrow & Set \\
\mathtt{P}_e & \mapsto & alte \\
\mathtt{P}_o & \mapsto & alto
\end{array}
$$

Lasagnas

The types of lasagnas are defined using mutual recursion on their height.

Fixpoint $\mathcal{L}_{\mathcal{T}x}$ $(e{:}alte)$: Set :=
    match e with
    | $\mathtt{O}_e \Rightarrow empty$
    | $\mathtt{S}_{o \rightarrow e}$ $o \Rightarrow \mathcal{T}_x$ $(\mathcal{L}_{\mathcal{T}n}\ o)$ $\mathtt{false}$
    end
with $\mathcal{L}_{\mathcal{T}n}$ $(o{:}alto)$: Set :=
    match o with
    | $\mathtt{S}_{e \rightarrow o}$ $e \Rightarrow \mathcal{T}_n$ $(\mathcal{L}_{\mathcal{T}x}\ e)$ $\mathtt{false}$
    end.

The pair of types for normalized terms is defined similarly, but their realm is *sortable* instead of *Set*:

Fixpoint $\mathcal{L}_{Sx}$ (e:$alte$) : $sortable$:=
  match e with
  | $0_e \Rightarrow \mathcal{R}_\emptyset$
  | $S_{o \to e}\ o \Rightarrow S_x\ (\mathcal{L}_{Sn}\ o)$
  end
with $\mathcal{L}_{Sn}$ (o:$alto$) : $sortable$:=
  match o with
  | $S_{e \to o}\ e \Rightarrow \mathcal{R}_a\ (\mathcal{L}_{Sx}\ e)$ `false`
  end.

1.4.2   Stratifying a Term

Lifting a Lasagna

The intuitive idea we have about lasagnas is somewhat misleading, because the number of pasta and sauce layers is uniform in a whole lasagna dish, while the number of layers of subterms which are rooted at the same depth of a given term are different in the general case. However, any lasagna of height n can be lifted to a lasagna of height $n + e$, where e is even, because the empty type at the bottom of types such as $\mathcal{T}_x(\mathcal{T}_n(\mathcal{T}_x(\dots(\emptyset))))$ can be replaced with any type. Formally, the lifting is defined by structural mutual induction as follows, using map combinators:

Fixpoint *lift_lasagna_x* $e_1\ e_2$ {struct e_1} : $\mathcal{L}_{Tx}\ e_1 \to \mathcal{L}_{Tx}\ (e_1 + e_2)$:=
  match e_1 return $\mathcal{L}_{Tx}\ e_1 \to \mathcal{L}_{Tx}\ (e_1 + e_2)$ with
  | $0_e \Rightarrow$ fun $emp \Rightarrow$ match emp with end
  | $S_{o \to e}\ o_1 \Rightarrow map_x\ (lift\_lasagna\_n\ o_1\ e_2)$ `false`
  end
with *lift_lasagna_n* $o_1\ e_2$ {struct o_1} : $\mathcal{L}_{Tn}\ o_1 \to \mathcal{L}_{Tn}\ (o_1 + e_2)$:=
  match o_1 return $\mathcal{L}_{Tn}\ o_1 \to \mathcal{L}_{Tn}\ (o_1 + e_2)$ with
  | $S_{e \to o}\ e_1 \Rightarrow map_n\ (lift\_lasagna\_x\ e_1\ e_2)$ `false`
  end.

Counting Layers of a $\mathcal{T}$-term

Given a $\mathcal{T}$-term t, the type of the corresponding lasagna depends on the number $l(t)$ of its layers, which has to be computed first.

At first sight, we may try to escape the problem by computing a number $u(t)$ which is known to be greater or equal to $l(t)$ (a suitable u is the height). However, we would then have to provide proofs that the proposed number $u(t)$ does provide an upper bound on $l(t)$. Such proofs have to be constructive, because they provide a bound on the number of recursive calls in the computation of the layering of a $\mathcal{T}$-term. Then they embark the difference between $u(t)$ and $l(t)$, in a hidden way. So it is unclear that $u(t)$ would really help us to simplify definitions, and we chose to stick to an accurate computation of $l(t)$ as follows.

We define the maximum of two natural numbers n and m as $n - m + m$. It is easy to check that this operation is commutative, hence the lasagnas of two immediate subterms of a $\mathcal{T}$-term can be lifted to lasagnas of the same height, using the lifting functions described above.

A further difficulty is that the arguments of a constructor occurrence in t are heterogeneous, i.e. some of them can be $\oplus$ and the others can be in $\mathcal{N}$. Of course, we may use appropriate injections U_x or U_n, however, their use is controlled (see section 1.4.1): they can be used only at the borderline between two different layers. Therefore, in general, we do not compute the lasagna of height n of a given term, that is, a $\mathcal{L}_{\mathcal{T}x} n \stackrel{\text{def}}{=} \mathcal{T}_x (\mathcal{L}_{\mathcal{T}n} (n{-}1)) \texttt{false}$ or a $\mathcal{L}_{\mathcal{T}n} n \stackrel{\text{def}}{=} \mathcal{T}_n (\mathcal{L}_{\mathcal{T}x} (n{-}1)) \texttt{false}$, but, for any Boolean tolerance b, a *lasagna candidate* $C_{\mathcal{T}x} (n{-}1) b$ or $C_{\mathcal{T}n} (n{-}1) b$ of height only $n-1$, where $C_{\mathcal{T}x} n \stackrel{\text{def}}{=} \mathcal{T}_x (\mathcal{L}_{\mathcal{T}n} n)$ and $C_{\mathcal{T}n} n \stackrel{\text{def}}{=} \mathcal{T}_n (\mathcal{L}_{\mathcal{T}x} n)$. When the tolerance is $\texttt{true}$, the lasagna candidate is a *true lasagna candidate*.

The previously defined lifting functions are easily generalized to lasagna candidates.

The height of a term, given as an argument to a lasagna candidate, is computed for any given parity p by a function called *alt_of_term_par*:

Definition *inj_odd_parity p* : *alto* $\rightarrow$ *type_of_par p* :=
     match *p* return *alto* $\rightarrow$ *type_of_par p* with
     | $P_e \Rightarrow S_{o \rightarrow e}$
     | $P_o \Rightarrow$ fun $o \Rightarrow o$
     end.

(The function *inj_even_parity* is defined similarly.)

Fixpoint *alt_of_term_par* $(t{:}\mathcal{T})$: $\forall p$, *type_of_par p* :=
     match *t* return $\forall p$, *type_of_par p* with
     | Zero $\Rightarrow$ fun $p \Rightarrow$ *inj_odd_parity p* $(S_{e \rightarrow o} 0_e)$
     | Xor $x\ y \Rightarrow$
         let o_1 := *alt_of_term_par x* P_o in
         let o_2 := *alt_of_term_par y* P_o in
         fun $p \Rightarrow$ *inj_odd_parity p* $(max\_oo\ o_1\ o_2)$

     | PC $x \Rightarrow$ fun $p \Rightarrow$ *inj_even_parity p* 0_e
     | SC $x \Rightarrow$ fun $p \Rightarrow$ *inj_even_parity p* 0_e
     | E $x\ y \Rightarrow$
         let e_1 := *alt_of_term_par x* P_e in
         let e_2 := *alt_of_term_par y* P_e in
         fun $p \Rightarrow$ *inj_even_parity p* $(max\_ee\ e_1\ e_2)$
     [Similarly for other constructors]
     end.

Computing the Lasagna

The main recursive function computes a true lasagna candidate. The type of its result depends on the desired parity, and is computed by the following function:

Definition $kind\_lasagna\_cand\_of\_term$ $(t{:}\mathcal{T})$ $(p{:}\ parity)$: Set :=
  match p with
  | $P_e \Rightarrow C_{Tn}\ (alt\_of\_term\_par\ t\ P_e)$ true
  | $P_o \Rightarrow C_{Tx}\ (alt\_of\_term\_par\ t\ P_o)$ true
  end.

    Its body introduces injections as required. Here is its definition:

Fixpoint $lasagna\_cand\_of\_term$ $(t{:}\mathcal{T})$:
  $\forall\ p, kind\_lasagna\_cand\_of\_term\ t\ p$:=
  match t return $\forall\ p, kind\_lasagna\_cand\_of\_term\ t\ p$ with
  | Zero $\Rightarrow$
      fun $p \Rightarrow$ match p return $kind\_lasagna\_cand\_of\_term$ Zero p with
      | $P_e \Rightarrow U_n\ (0_x$ false$)$
      | $P_o \Rightarrow 0_x$ true
      end
  | Xor $t_1\ t_2 \Rightarrow$
      let $l_1 := lasagna\_cand\_of\_term\ t_1\ P_o$ in
      let $l_2 := lasagna\_cand\_of\_term\ t_2\ P_o$ in
      fun $p \Rightarrow$ match p return $kind\_lasagna\_cand\_of\_term$ (Xor $t_1\ t_2$) p with
      | $P_e \Rightarrow U_n\ (bin\_xor$ Xor$_x\ l_1\ l_2)$
      | $P_o \Rightarrow bin\_xor$ Xor$_x\ l_1\ l_2$
      end

  | PC $x \Rightarrow$
      fun $p \Rightarrow$ match p return $kind\_lasagna\_cand\_of\_term$ (PC x) p with
      | $P_e \Rightarrow PC_n$ true x
      | $P_o \Rightarrow U_x\ (PC_n$ false $x)$
      end
  [Similarly for other constructors in $\mathcal{N}$].

    The above definition uses a function bin_xor mapping a constructor of $\mathcal{T}_x$ to an operation on lasagna candidates having arbitrary heights o_1 and o_2 and returning a lasagna candidate having an arbitrary tolerance b. Parameters o_1, o_2 and b are implicit (inferred from the context). For instance, the tolerance of the first (resp. second) occurrence bin_xor above is false (resp. true). This is the place where lifting is used.

Definition bin_xor
  $(bin : \forall\ \alpha\ b, \mathcal{T}_x\ \alpha$ true $\rightarrow \mathcal{T}_x\ \alpha$ true $\rightarrow \mathcal{T}_x\ \alpha\ b)\ o_1\ o_2\ b$
  $(l_1 : C_{Tx}\ o_1$ true$)\ (l_2 : C_{Tx}\ o_2$ true$) : C_{Tx}\ (max\_oo\ o_1\ o_2)\ b$:=
  $bin\ (\mathcal{L}_{Tn}\ (max\_oo\ o_1\ o_2))\ b$
    $(lift\_lasagna\_cand\_x$ true $o_1\ (o_2 - o_1)\ l_1)$
    $(coerce\_max\_comm\ (lift\_lasagna\_cand\_x$ true $o_2\ (o_1 - o_2)\ l_2))$.

    Note the essential use of the conversion rule in the typing of bin_xor: the type of the lifted version of l_1, i.e. $C_{Tx}\ (o_1 + (o_2 - o_1))$ true, is convertible with $\mathcal{T}_x\ (\mathcal{L}_{Tn}(max\_oo\ o_1\ o_2))$ true, and similarly for l_2; and the type of the result, i.e. $C_{Tx}\ (max\_oo\ o_1\ o_2)\ b$, is convertible with $\mathcal{T}_x\ (\mathcal{L}_{Tn}\ (max\_oo\ o_1\ o_2))\ b$.

Finally, we define the function *lasagna_of_term*. We force the parity to depend on the constructor at the root:

Definition *alt_of_term t* := *alt_of_term_par t* (*parity_of_term t*).

Definition *lasagna_of_parity p* : *type_of_par p* $\to$ *Set* :=
  match *p* return *type_of_par p* $\to$ *Set* with
  | P_e $\Rightarrow$ $\mathcal{L}_{Tx}$
  | P_o $\Rightarrow$ $\mathcal{L}_{Tn}$
  end.

Definition *lasagna_of_term* (*t*:$\mathcal{T}$) :
  lasagna_of_parity (*parity_of_term t*) (*alt_of_term t*) :=
  match *t* return *lasagna_of_parity* (*parity_of_term t*) (*alt_of_term t*) with
  | Zero $\Rightarrow$ 0_x false
  | Xor t_1 t_2 $\Rightarrow$
    let l_1 := *lasagna_cand_of_term* t_1 P_o in
    let l_2 := *lasagna_cand_of_term* t_2 P_o in
    bin_xor Xor$_x$ l_1 l_2

  | PC *x* $\Rightarrow$ PC$_n$ false *x*
  [Similarly for other constructors in $\mathcal{N}$].

1.4.3   Normalizing

We define a pair of normalization functions N_x : $\forall e, \mathcal{L}_{Tx} e \to |\mathcal{L}_{Sx} e|$ and N_n : $\forall o, \mathcal{L}_{Tn} o \to |\mathcal{L}_{Sn} o|$ by structural mutual recursion. The latter does nothing, while the core of the former is $\lambda x.$ *fold_insert* (*map_xor* (N_n *o*) *false x*) []$.

However, things are more complicated: normalizing a list may produce a one-element list, which behaves exactly as U_x, as explained in 1.4.1. In order to force the removing of such fake layers, we eventually replace the type list α in $\mathcal{R}_x$ with a type n1_list α of lists having either no element (N1_0), or two elements at least (N1_2 *x y l*). Then, when sorting an inhabitant of $\mathcal{T}_x |A|$ the normalization function for lasagnas returns a value in a type with two options: either a n1_list $|A|$, or an element of $|A|$ lifted as an element of $\mathcal{R}_u(\mathcal{S}_x |A|)$.

Using this lifting requires some work: we have to show that it is monotonic, and that the various map functionals preserve monotony.

1.4.4   Back to $\mathcal{T}$

We recover ordinary terms from normalized terms using two mutually recursive functions. We first need to translate a n1_list to a xor term (for instance, [$x; y; z$] will be translated as $x \oplus y \oplus z$).

Fixpoint *xor_of_nelist* (*x*: α) (*l*: *list* α) {*struct l*} : $\mathcal{T}_x$ α true :=
  match *l* with
    | nil $\Rightarrow$ U_x *x*
    | *y* :: *l* $\Rightarrow$ Xor$_x$ true (U_x *x*) (*xor_of_nelist y l*)
  end.

Definition xor_of_nl b (l: nl_list) : $\mathcal{T}_x$ α b :=
  match l with
    | N1_0 $\Rightarrow$ O_x b
    | N1_2 x y l $\Rightarrow$ Xor$_x$ b (U$_x$ x) (xor_of_nelist y l)
  end.

Fixpoint $term\_of\_sortagna\_x$ (e:$alte$) : $|\mathcal{L}_{Sx}$ $e| \rightarrow \mathcal{T}$:=
  match e return $|\mathcal{L}_{Sx}$ $e| \rightarrow \mathcal{T}$ with
  | 0_e $\Rightarrow$ fun em $\Rightarrow$ match em with end
  | S$_{o \rightarrow e}$ o $\Rightarrow$ fun x $\Rightarrow$ let (l, sl) := x in
    map_xor_term ($term\_of\_sortagna\_n$ o) false (xor_of_nl _ false l)
  end
with $term\_of\_sortagna\_n$ (o:$alto$) : $|\mathcal{L}_{Sn}$ $o| \rightarrow \mathcal{T}$:=
  match o return $|\mathcal{L}_{Sn}$ $o| \rightarrow \mathcal{T}$ with
  | S$_{e \rightarrow o}$ e $\Rightarrow$ map_nx_term ($term\_of\_sortagna\_x$ e) false
  end.

1.4.5 Current Results

We formalized the correctness of the sorting function (with self-cancelation). The whole normalization function is defined and typechecks. We claim that syntactic equality in the type of its output (up to the number of layers) corresponds exactly to the equivalence of its input wrt algebraic laws of $\oplus$. We did not formalize this latest claim yet, but are quite confident since we carefully designed the normalization function to this end.

1.5 CONCLUSION

The Epigram project [1] already advocates the definition of functions using dependent types. They mostly aim at ensuring partial correctness properties (such as a balancing invariant in the case of *mergesort*).

The present paper shows how dependent types can help for ensuring termination too. We showed that an alternate path to termination orderings can be followed in some situations. We considered here a theory containing one AC and involutive symbol. Note that AC normalizing can be considered as a special case. Alternatively, a direct and somewhat simplified development could be provided as well (e.g. sorting is simpler and complications solved with nl_list in 1.4.3 don't appear).

While our approach is certainly less general, it relies on more elementary arguments. As a consequence, we can get a better insight into the reasons why the normalization process terminate: it indeed is a (mutual) induction on the implicit structure of terms. Like approaches advocated by Epigram, the overall approach consists in finding dependent types that render this implicit structure explicit.

Our work is available from http://www-verimag.imag.fr/~monin/.

REFERENCES

[1] Thorsten Altenkirch, Conor McBride, and James McKinna. Why dependent types matter. Manuscript, available online at http://www.cs.nott.ac.uk/ txa/publ/ydtm.pdf, April 2005.

[2] C. Alvarado and Q. Nguyen. ELAN for equational reasoning in Coq. In J. Despeyroux, editor, *Proc. of 2nd Workshop on Logical Frameworks and Metalanguages. Institut National de Recherche en Informatique et en Automatique, ISBN 2-7261-1166-1*, June 2000.

[3] Antonia Balaa and Yves Bertot. Fix-point equations for well-founded recursion in type theory. In M. Aagaard and J. Harrison, editors, *Proc. of 13th Int. Conf. on Theorem Proving in Higher Order Logics, TPHOLS'00, Portland, OR, USA, 14–18 Aug. 2000*, volume 1689, pages 1–16. Springer-Verlag, Berlin, 2000.

[4] Yves Bertot and Pierre Castéran. *Interactive Theorem Proving and Program Development. Coq'Art: The Calculus of Inductive Constructions*, volume XXV of *Texts in Theoretical Computer Science. An EATCS Series*. Springer, 2004. 469 p., Hardcover. ISBN: 3-540-20854-2.

[5] Frédéric Blanqui. Definitions by rewriting in the calculus of constructions. In *Logic in Computer Science*, pages 9–18, 2001.

[6] Mike Bond. *Understanding Security APIs*. PhD thesis, University of Cambridge Computer Laboratory, June 2004.

[7] Ana Bove and Venanzio Capretta. Modelling general recursion in type theory. *Mathematical Structures in Computer Science*, 15(4):671–708, August 2005.

[8] Yannick Chevalier, Ralf Küsters, Michaël Rusinowitch, and Mathieu Turuani. An np decision procedure for protocol insecurity with xor. *Theor. Comput. Sci.*, 338(1-3):247–274, 2005.

[9] Jacek Chrząszcz. Implementation of modules in the coq system. In David Basin and Burkhart Wolff, editors, *Theorem Proving in Higher Order Logic*, volume 2758 of *LNCS*, pages 270–286, sep 2003. Roma, Italy.

[10] H. Comon-Lundh and V. Cortier. New decidability results for fragments of first-order logic and application to cryptographic protocols. In *Proc. 14th Int. Conf. Rewriting Techniques and Applications (RTA'2003)*, volume 2706 of *Lecture Notes in Computer Science*, pages 148–164. Springer, 2003.

[11] Evelyne Contejean and Claude Marché. CiME: Completion modulo E. In Harald Ganzinger, editor, *RTA*, volume 1103 of *Lecture Notes in Computer Science*, pages 416–419. Springer, 1996.

[12] Judicaël Courant. A Module Calculus for Pure Type Systems. In *Typed Lambda Calculi and Applications 97*, Lecture Notes in Computer Science, pages 112 – 128. Springer-Verlag, 1997.

[13] Judicaël Courant. $\mathcal{M}C_2$: A Module Calculus for Pure Type Systems. *The Journal of Functional Programming*, 2006. To appear.

[14] Judicaël Courant and Jean-François Monin. Defending the bank with a proof assistant. In Dieter Gollmann and Jan Jürjens, editors, *Sixth International IFIP WG 1.7 Workshop on Issues in the Theory of Security*, pages 87 – 98, Vienna, March 2006. European Joint Conferences on Theory And Practice of Software.

[15] Steven Eker. Single elementary associative-commutative matching. *J. Autom. Reason.*, 28(1):35–51, 2002.

[16] Robert Harper and Mark Lillibridge. A type-theoretic approach to higher-order modules with sharing. In *POPL '94: Proceedings of the 21st ACM SIGPLAN-SIGACT symposium on Principles of programming languages*, pages 123–137, New York, NY, USA, 1994. ACM Press.

[17] Xavier Leroy. A modular module system. *J. Funct. Program.*, 10(3):269–303, 2000.

[18] Claude Marché. Normalized rewriting: an alternative to rewriting modulo a set of equations. *Journal of Symbolic Computation*, 21(3):253–288, 1996.

[19] The Coq Development Team. *The Coq Proof Assistant Reference Manual Version 8.0.* Logical Project, January 2005.

[20] Paul Youn, Ben Adida, Mike Bond, Jolyon Clulow, Jonathan Herzog, Amerson Lin, Ronald L. Rivest, and Ross Anderson. Robbing the bank with a theorem prover. Technical Report UCAM-CL-TR-644, University of Cambridge, Computer Laboratory, August 2005.

Chapter 2

Proving the Correctness of Algorithmic Debugging for Functional Programs

Yong Luo, Olaf Chitil[1]

Abstract: This paper presents a formal model of tracing for functional programs based on a small-step operational semantics. The model records the computation of a functional program in a graph which can be utilised for various purposes such as algorithmic debugging. The main contribution of this paper is to prove the correctness of algorithmic debugging for functional programs based on the model. Although algorithmic debugging for functional programs is implemented in several tracers such as Hat, the correctness has not been formally proved before. The difficulty of the proof is to find a suitable induction principle and a sufficiently general induction hypothesis.

2.1 INTRODUCTION

Usually, a computation is treated as a black box that performs input and output actions. However, we have to look into the black box when we want to see how the different parts of the program cause the computation to perform the input/output actions. The most common need for doing this is debugging: When there is a disparity between the actual and the intended semantics of a program, we need to locate the part of the program that causes the disparity. Traditional debugging techniques are not well suited for declarative programming languages such as Haskell, because it is difficult to understand how programs execute (or their procedural meaning). Algorithmic debugging (also called declarative debugging) was invented by Shapiro [8] for logic programming languages. Later

---

[1]Computing Laboratory, University of Kent, Canterbury, Kent, UK
Email: {Y.Luo, O.Chitil}@kent.ac.uk

the method was transferred to other programming languages, including functional programming languages. A question of an algorithmic debugger must fully describe a subcomputation; hence algorithmic debugging works best for purely declarative languages, which do not use side effects but make all data and control flow explicit. As Haskell is a purely functional programming language that even separates input/output operations from the rest of the language, it is particularly suitable for algorithmic debugging. There exists three algorithmic debuggers for Haskell: Freja [4], Hat [11] and Buddha/Plargleflarp [7].

In contrast to this advance of algorithmic debugging in practise and the relative simplicity of the underlying idea, there are few theoretical foundations and no proofs that these debuggers do actually work correctly. We need a full understanding of algorithmic debugging for functional languages to determine its limits and to develop more powerful extensions and variations. That is the problem we address in this paper. We shall give a direct and simple definition of *trace* that will enable us to formally relate a view to the semantics of a program. The *evaluation dependency tree (EDT)* will be generated from a computation graph. We can correctly locate program faults, and the correctness will be formally proved. This is a non-trivial proof since the simple induction principle, the size of graph, does not work.

In the next section we give a brief overview of algorithmic debugging. Related work is also discussed. In section 2.3, some basic definitions and the *augmented redex trail* (ART) are formally presented. In section 2.4, we show how to generate an EDT from an ART. In section 2.5, we prove the properties of an EDT, in particular, the correctness of algorithmic debugging. Future work will be discussed in the last section.

2.2 ALGORITHMIC DEBUGGING

Algorithmic debugging can be thought of searching a fault in a program. When a program execution has produced a wrong result an algorithmic debugger will ask the programmer a number of questions about the computation. Each question asks whether a given subcomputation is correct, that is, whether it agrees with the intentions of the programmer. After a number of questions and answers the algorithmic debugger gives the location of a fault in the program.

For example, for an execution of the Haskell program

```
main = implies True False
implies x y = not y || x
```

a session with an algorithmic debugger might be as follows, with answers given by the programmer in italics:

```
1) main = True ?                      no
2) implies True False = True ?  no
3) not False = True ?                 yes
4) True || True = True ?         yes
Fault located. The definition of 'implies' is faulty.
```

The principle of algorithmic debugging is relatively simple. From the computation that produces the wrong result a *computation tree* is built; each node of the computation tree is labelled with a question about a subcomputation:

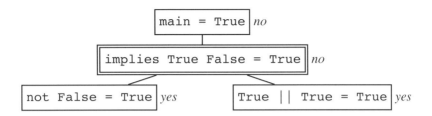

An algorithmic debugger traverses the computation tree asking the questions of the nodes until it locates a so-called *faulty node*, that is, a node whose computation is erroneous according to the programmer's intentions, but the computations of all its children are correct. The algorithmic debugger reports the definition of the function reduced in the faulty node as the fault location.

Naish [3] gives an abstract description of algorithmic debugging, independent of any particular programming language. He proves that algorithmic debugging is *complete* in the sense that if the program computation produces a wrong result, then algorithmic debugging will locate a fault. No such general proof exists for the *soundness* of algorithmic debugging, that is, the property that the indicated fault location is indeed faulty. Soundness depends on the exact definition of the computation tree. Programming languages with different semantics, for example logic languages vs. functional languages, require different definitions of the computation tree. Even for a single programming language several definitions are possible. For lazy functional programming languages Nilsson and Sparud [6, 5, 9] introduced the evaluation dependency tree (EDT) as computation tree. The EDT has the property that the tree structure reflects the static function call structure of the program and all arguments and results are in their most evaluated form. The example computation tree given above is an EDT. The algorithmic debuggers Freja, Hat and Buddha/Plargleflarp are based on the EDT. The construction of an EDT during the computation of a program is non-trivial, because the structure of the EDT is very different from the structure of the computation as determined by the evaluation order.

For a lazy functional logic language Caballero et al. [1] give a formal definition of an EDT and sketch a soundness proof of algorithmic debugging. However, this approach relies on the EDT being defined through a high-level non-deterministic big-step semantics[2]. Thus this definition of the EDT is far removed from any real implementation of an algorithmic debugger.

---

[2]Non-determinism is essential for this approach, irrespective of whether the programming language has logical features or not.

2.3 FORMALISING THE AUGMENTED REDEX TRAIL

An augmented redex trail (ART) is a graph that represents a computation of a functional program. A graph enables sharing of subexpressions which is the key both to a space efficient trace structure and closeness to the implementations of functional languages. The one essential difference to standard graph rewriting of functional language implementations is that ART rewriting does not overwrite a redex with its reduct, but adds the reduct to the graph, keeping the reduct and thus the computation history.

In this section we give some basic definitions which will be used throughout the paper, and we describe how to build an ART.

Definition 2.1. *(Atoms, Terms. Patterns, Rewriting rule and Program)*

- *Atoms consist of function symbols and constructors.*

- *Terms: (1) an atom is a term; (2) a variable is a term; (3) MN is a term if M and N are terms.*

- *Patterns: (1) a variable is a pattern; (2) $cp_1...p_n$ is a pattern if c is a constructor and $p_1,..., p_n$ are patterns, and the arity of c is n.*

- *A rewriting rule is of the form $f \ p_1...p_n = R$ where f is a function symbol and $p_1,..., p_n \ (n \geq 0)$ are patterns and R is a term.*

- *A program is a finite set of rewriting rules.*

Example 2.2. $id \ x = x$, $not \ True = False$, $map \ f \ (x : xs) = f \ x \ : \ map \ f \ xs$ and $ones = 1 : ones$ are rewriting rules.

Note that we only allow disjoint patterns if there is more than one rewriting rule for a function. We also require that the number of arguments of a function in the left-hand side must be the same. For example, if there is a rewriting rule $f \ c_1 = g$, then $f \ c_2 \ c_3 = c_4$ is not allowed. The purpose of disjointness is to prevent us from giving different values to the same argument when we define a function. Disjointness is one of the ways to guarantee the property of Church-Rosser. In many programming languages such as Haskell the requirement of disjointness is not needed, because the patterns for a function have orders. If a closed term matches the first pattern, the algorithm will not try to match the rest patterns. We also require that all the patterns are linear because conversion test is difficult sometimes. Many functional programming languages such as Haskell only allow linear patterns.

Now, we define computation graphs and choose a particular naming scheme to name the nodes in a computation graph. The letters f and a mean the function component and the argument component of an application respectively. The letter r means a small step of reduction.

Definition 2.3. *(Node, Node expression and Computation graph)*

- A **node** is a sequence of letters r, f and a, i.e. $\{r, f, a\}^*$.

- A **node expression** is either an atom, or a node, or an application of two nodes, which is of the form $m \circ n$.

- A **computation graph** is a set of pairs which are of the form (n, e), where n is a node and e is a node expression.

Example 2.4. We have a Haskell program:

$$g \, (Just \, x) = h \, x$$

$$h \, x \, y = y \, \&\& \, x$$

The following is a computation graph for the starting term $g \, (Just \, True) \, (id \, (not \, False))$.

$\{(r, rf \circ ra), (rf, rff \circ rfa), (rff, g), (rfa, rfaf \circ rfaa), (rfaf, Just), (rfaa, True),$
$(ra, raf \circ raa), (raf, id), (raa, raaf \circ raaa), (raaf, not), (raaa, False),$
$(rar, raa), (raar, True), (rfr, rfrf \circ rfaa), (rfrf, h), (rr, rrf \circ rfaa), (rrf, rrff \circ ra),$
$(rrff, \&\&), (rrr, True)\}$

It can be depicted as follows:

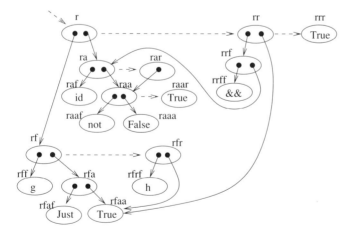

The dashed edges represent the computation steps. If a node mr is in a graph then there is a computation from the node m to mr. So, the pairs of the form (m, mr) are omitted in the formal representation of the graph. For example, (r, rr) and (rf, rfr) are not included in the above graph.

Notation: $dom(G)$ denotes the set of nodes in a computation graph G.

Pattern matching in a graph

The pattern matching algorithm for a graph has two different results, either a set of substitutions or "doesn't match".

- The final node in a sequence of reductions starting at node m, $last(G,m)$:

$$last(G,m) \quad = \quad \begin{cases} last(G,m\mathsf{r}) & \text{if } m\mathsf{r} \in dom(G) \\ last(G,n) & \text{if } (m,n) \in G \text{ and } n \text{ is a node} \\ m & \text{otherwise} \end{cases}$$

  The purpose of this function is to find out the most evaluated point for m. For example, if G is the graph in Example 2.4, then we have $last(G,\mathsf{r}) = \mathsf{rrr}$ and $last(G,\mathsf{ra}) = \mathsf{raar}$.

- The head of the term at node m, $head(G,m)$, where G is a graph and m is a node in G:

$$head(G,m) \quad = \quad \begin{cases} head(G,last(G,i)) & \text{if } (m,i \circ j) \in G \\ a & \text{if } (m,a) \in G \text{ and } a \text{ is an atom} \\ \text{undefined} & \text{otherwise} \end{cases}$$

  For example, if G is the graph in Example 2.4, then we have $head(G,\mathsf{r}) = h$ and $head(G,\mathsf{rf}) = g$.

- The arguments of the function at node m, $args(G,m)$:

$$args(G,m) \quad = \quad \begin{cases} \langle args(G,last(G,i)), j \rangle & \text{if } (m,i \circ j) \in G \\ \langle \rangle & \text{otherwise} \end{cases}$$

  Note that the arguments of a function are a sequence of nodes. For example, if G is the graph in Example 2.4, then we have $args(G,\mathsf{r}) = \langle \mathsf{rfaa},\mathsf{ra} \rangle$ and $args(G,\mathsf{ra}) = \langle \mathsf{raa} \rangle$.

Now, we define two functions $match_1$ and $match_2$ which are mutually recursive. The arguments of $match_1$ are a node and a pattern. The arguments of $match_2$ are a sequence of nodes and a sequence of patterns.

- $match_1$:

$$match_1(G,m,x) = [m/x] \text{ where } x \text{ is a variable}$$
$$match_1(G,m,cq_1...q_k)$$
$$= \begin{cases} match_2(G,args(G,m'),\langle q_1,...,q_k \rangle) & \text{if } head(G,m') = c \\ \text{does not match} & \text{otherwise} \end{cases}$$

  where $m' = last(G,m)$.

- $match_2$:

$$match_2(G,\langle m_1,...,m_n \rangle, \langle p_1,...,p_n \rangle)$$
$$= match_1(G,m_1,p_1) \cup ... \cup match_1(G,m_n,p_n)$$

where $\cup$ is the union operator. Notice that if $n = 0$ then

$$match_2(G, \langle \rangle, \langle \rangle) = [\ ]$$

If any m_i does not match p_i, $\langle m_1, ..., m_n \rangle$ does not match $\langle p_1, ..., p_n \rangle$. If the length of two sequences are not the same, they do not match. For example, $\langle m_1, ..., m_s \rangle$ does not match $\langle p_1, ..., p_{s'} \rangle$ if $s \neq s'$.

- We say that G at node m matches the left-hand side of a rewriting rule $f\, p_1...p_n = R$ with $[m_1/x_1, ..., m_k/x_k]$ if $head(G, m) = f$ and

$$match_2(G, args(G, m), \langle p_1, ..., p_n \rangle) = [m_1/x_1, ..., m_k/x_k]$$

In the substitution form $[m/x]$, m is not a term but a node. In Example 2.4, the graph at node r matches $h\, x\, y$ with $[\mathsf{rfaa}/x, \mathsf{ra}/y]$. The definition of pattern matching and its result substitution sequence will become important for making computation order irrelevant when we generate graphs. In Example 2.4, no matter which node is reduced first, ra or raa, the final graph will be the same.

Graph for label terms. During the computations all the variables in a term will be substituted by some nodes. When the variables are substituted by a sequence of shared nodes, it becomes a label term. For example, $(y \,\&\&\, x)[\mathsf{rfaa}/x, \mathsf{ra}/y] \equiv$ ra && rfaa is a label term. The function *graph* defined in the following has two arguments: a node and a label term. The result of *graph* is a computation graph.

$$graph(n, e) = \{(n, e)\} \quad \text{where } e \text{ is an atom or a node}$$

$$graph(n, MN) = \begin{cases} \{(n, M \circ N)\} & \text{if } M \text{ and } N \text{ are nodes} \\ \{(n, M \circ \mathsf{na})\} \cup graph(\mathsf{na}, N) & \text{if only } M \text{ is a node} \\ \{(n, \mathsf{nf} \circ N)\} \cup graph(\mathsf{nf}, M) & \text{if only } N \text{ is a node} \\ \{(n, \mathsf{nf} \circ \mathsf{na})\} \cup graph(\mathsf{nf}, M) & \text{otherwise} \\ \quad \cup graph(\mathsf{na}, N) \end{cases}$$

Building an ART

- For a start term M, the start ART is $graph(\mathsf{r}, M)$. Note that the start term has no nodes inside.

- *(ART rule)* If an ART G at m matches the left-hand side of a rewriting rule $f\, p_1...p_n = R$ with $[m_1/x_1, ..., m_k/x_k]$, then we can build a new ART

$$G \cup graph(m\mathsf{r}, R[m_1/x_1, ..., m_k/x_k])$$

- An ART is generated from a start ART and by applying the *ART rule* repeatedly. Note that the order in which nodes are chosen has no influence in the final graph.

Example 2.5. If the start term is $g\, (Just\, True)\, (id\, (not\, False))$ as in Example 2.4, then the start graph is

$$\{(\mathsf{r}, \mathsf{rf} \circ \mathsf{ra}), (\mathsf{rf}, \mathsf{rff} \circ \mathsf{rfa}), (\mathsf{rff}, g), (\mathsf{rfa}, \mathsf{rfaf} \circ \mathsf{rfaa}), (\mathsf{rfaf}, Just), (\mathsf{rfaa}, True),$$
$$(\mathsf{ra}, \mathsf{raf} \circ \mathsf{raa}), (\mathsf{raf}, id), (\mathsf{raa}, \mathsf{raaf} \circ \mathsf{raaa}), (\mathsf{raaf}, not), (\mathsf{raaa}, False)\}$$

The new parts built from r and ra are

$$graph(\text{rr}, (y \,\&\&\, x)[\text{rfaa}/x, \text{ra}/y])$$
$$= \;\; graph(\text{rr}, (\text{ra} \,\&\&\, \text{rfaa}))$$
$$= \;\; \{(\text{rr}, \text{rrf} \circ \text{rfaa}), (\text{rrf}, \text{rrff} \circ \text{ra}), (\text{rrff}, \&\&)\}$$

$$graph(\text{rar}, x[\text{raa}/x]) = \{(\text{rar}, \text{raa})\}$$

Note that the order of computation is irrelevant because the result of pattern matching at the node ra is always $[\text{raa}/x]$, no matter which node is computed first. The definition of pattern matching simplifies the representation of ART. Otherwise we would have several structurally different graphs representing the same reduction step. Multiple representations just cause confusion and would later lead us to give a complex definition of an equivalence class of graphs.

The following simple properties of an ART will be used later.

Lemma 2.6. *Let G be an ART.*

- *If $m \in dom(G)$ then there is at least one letter r in m.*

- *If $m\text{r} \in dom(G)$ then $m \in dom(G)$ or $m = \varepsilon$ where ε is the empty sequence.*

- *If $m\text{r} \in dom(G)$ then $(m, n) \notin G$ for any node n.*

Proof. The first and second are trivial. The third is proved by contradiction. If $(m, n) \in G$ then $head(G, m)$ is undefined. There cannot be a computation at m, i.e. $m\text{r} \notin G$.

2.4   GENERATING AN EVALUATION DEPENDENCY TREE

In this section we generate the *Evaluation Dependency Tree* (EDT) from a given ART.

The real Hat ART also includes so-called *parent edges*. Each node has a parent edge that points to the top of the redex that caused its creation. Parent edges are key ingredient for the redex trail view of locating program faults [10]. One may notice that there are no parent edges in the ART here. They need not be given explicitly because the way that the nodes are labelled gives us the parents of all nodes implicitly.

Definition 2.7. *(Parent edges)*

$$parent(n\text{f}) \;\; = \;\; parent(n)$$
$$parent(n\text{a}) \;\; = \;\; parent(n)$$
$$parent(n\text{r}) \;\; = \;\; n$$

Note that $parent(\text{r}) = \varepsilon$ where ε is the empty sequence.

Definition 2.8. *(children **and** tree) Let G be an ART, and $m\text{r}$ a node in G (i.e. $m\text{r} \in dom(G)$). children and tree are defined as follows.*

- *children:*

$$children(m) = \{n \mid parent(n) = m \text{ and } n\mathsf{r} \in dom(G)\}$$

The condition $n\mathsf{r} \in dom(G)$ is to make sure that only evaluated nodes become children.

- *tree:*

$$tree(m) = \{(m,n_1),...,(m,n_k)\} \cup tree(n_1) \cup ... \cup tree(n_k)$$

where $\{n_1,...,n_k\} = children(m)$

Example 2.9. If G is the graph in Example 2.4, then

$$tree(\varepsilon) = \{(\varepsilon,\mathsf{r}),(\varepsilon,\mathsf{ra}),(\varepsilon,\mathsf{raa}),(\varepsilon,\mathsf{rf}),(\mathsf{r},\mathsf{rr})\}$$

Notation: In the above definitions such as *children*, the ART G should be one of the arguments but it is omitted. For example, we write *children*(m) for *children*(G,m). We shall use this notation later when no confusion may occur.

Usually, a single node of a computation graph represents many different terms. We are particularly interested in two kinds of terms of nodes, the most evaluated form and the redex.

Definition 2.10. *(Most Evaluated Form) Let G be an ART. The most evaluated form of a node m is a term and is defined as follows.*

$$mef(m) = \begin{cases} mef(m\mathsf{r}) & \textit{if } m\mathsf{r} \in dom(G) \\ meft(m) & \textit{otherwise} \end{cases}$$

where

$$meft(m) = \begin{cases} a & (m,a) \in G \textit{ and } a \textit{ is an atom} \\ mef(n) & (m,n) \in G \textit{ and } n \textit{ is a node} \\ mef(i)\,mef(j) & (m,i \circ j) \in G \end{cases}$$

One may also use the definition of *last*(G,m) to define the most evaluated form.

Example 2.11. If G is the graph in Example 2.4, then

$$mef(\mathsf{r}) = mef(\mathsf{rr}) = meft(\mathsf{rrr}) = True$$

$$mef(\mathsf{ra}) = mef(\mathsf{rar}) = meft(\mathsf{rar}) = mef(\mathsf{raa}) = True$$

Definition 2.12. *(redex) Let G be an ART, and $m\mathsf{r}$ a node in G (i.e. $m\mathsf{r} \in dom(G)$). redex is defined as follows.*

- $redex(\varepsilon) = main$

- $redex(m) = \begin{cases} mef(i)\,mef(j) & \textit{if } (m,i \circ j) \in G \\ a & \textit{if } (m,a) \in G \textit{ and } a \textit{ is an atom} \end{cases}$

Note that the case $(m,n) \in G$ is not defined in this definition because $(m,n) \notin G$ for any node n by Lemma 2.6.

Example 2.13. If G is the graph in Example 2.4, then

$$redex(\mathsf{r}) = mef(\mathsf{rf})\ mef(\mathsf{ra}) = h\ True\ True$$

Now, we define the evaluation dependency tree of a graph.

Definition 2.14. *(Evaluation Dependency Tree) Let G be an ART. The evaluation dependency tree (EDT) of G consists of the following two parts.*

1. The set $tree(\varepsilon)$;

2. The set of equations; for any node in $tree(\varepsilon)$ there is a corresponding equation $redex(m) = mef(m)$.

Note that we write $mef(\varepsilon)$ for $mef(\mathsf{r})$.

Notation: For an EDT T, $dom(T)$ denotes the set of all the nodes in $tree(\varepsilon)$. We also say $(m,n) \in T$ if $(m,n) \in tree(\varepsilon)$.

$redex(m) = mef(m)$ represents an evaluation at node m from the left-hand side to the right-hand side. A pair (m,n) in an EDT represents that the evaluation $redex(m) = mef(m)$ depends on the evaluation $redex(n) = mef(n)$.

Example 2.15. The EDT for the graph in Example 2.4 is the following.

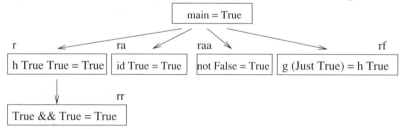

2.5   PROPERTIES OF THE EVALUATION DEPENDENCY TREE

In this section, we present the properties of the EDT and prove the correctness of algorithmic debugging.

The following theorems suggest that the EDT of an ART covers all the computation in the ART. Although two evaluations may rely on the same evaluation in an ART, every evaluation for algorithmic debugging only needs to be examined once.

Lemma 2.16. *Let G be an ART, and T its EDT. If there is a sequence of nodes $m_1, m_2, ..., m_k$ such that*

$$m \in children(m_1), m_1 \in children(m_2), ...,$$
$$m_{k-1} \in children(m_k), m_k \in children(\varepsilon)$$

then $m \in dom(T)$.

Proof. By the definition of $tree(\varepsilon)$.

Lemma 2.17. *Let G be an ART. If $m\mathsf{r} \in dom(G)$, then $m \equiv \varepsilon$ or there is a sequence of nodes $m_1, m_2, ..., m_k$ such that*

$$m \in children(m_1), m_1 \in children(m_2), ...,$$
$$m_{k-1} \in children(m_k), m_k \in children(\varepsilon)$$

Proof. By induction on the size of m, and by Lemma 2.6.

Since $m\mathsf{r} \in dom(G)$, by Lemma 2.6, we only need to consider the following two cases.

- If $m = \varepsilon$, the statement is obviously true.

- If $m \in dom(G)$, by Lemma 2.6, there is at least one letter r in m. We consider the following two sub-cases.

  · $m = \mathsf{r}n$, where there is no r in n. Since $m\mathsf{r} \in dom(G)$ and $parent(\mathsf{r}n) = \varepsilon$, we have $\mathsf{r}n \in children(\varepsilon)$.

  · $m \equiv m_1\mathsf{r}n$, where there is no r in n. Since $m\mathsf{r} \in dom(G)$ and $parent(m) = m_1$, we have $m \in children(m_1)$. Now, because m_1 is a sub-sequence of m, by induction hypothesis, there is a sequence of index numbers $m_2, ..., m_k$ such that

$$m_1 \in children(m_2), ..., m_{k-1} \in children(m_k), m_k \in children(\varepsilon)$$

  So, there is a sequence of index numbers $m_1, m_2, ..., m_k$ such that

$$m \in children(m_1), m_1 \in children(m_2), ..., m_k \in children(\varepsilon)$$

Theorem 2.18. *Let G be an ART, and T its EDT.*

If $m\mathsf{r} \in dom(G)$, then $m \in dom(T)$. In other word, T covers all the computations in G.

Proof. By Lemma 2.17 and 2.16.

Lemma 2.19. *Let G be an ART, and T its EDT.*

If $(m,n) \in T$, then $n \in children(m)$ and $parent(n) \equiv m$.

Proof. By the definition of *tree*.

Theorem 2.20. *Let G be an ART, and T its EDT.*

If $(m,n) \in T$ and $m \not\equiv k$, then $(k,n) \notin T$.

Proof. By Lemma 2.19.

The above theorem suggests that every evaluation for algorithmic debugging only needs to be examined once although two evaluations may rely on the same evaluation. For example, g is defined as $g\,x = (not\,x, not\,x, not\,x)$. When we compute $g\,(not\,True)$, the equation $not\,True = False$ only appears once in the EDT.

In the algorithmic debugging scheme, one needs to answer several questions according to the EDT and intended semantics in order to locate a faulty node.

Notations: $M \simeq_I N$ means that M is equal to N with respect to the semantics of the programmer's intention. If the evaluation $M = N$ of a node in an EDT is in the programmer's intended semantics, then $M \simeq_I N$. Otherwise, $M \not\simeq_I N$ i.e. the node is erroneous.

Semantical equality rules are given in figure 2.1, which will be used in Lemma 2.27 later.

General semantical equality rules:

$$\frac{}{M \simeq_I M} \quad \frac{M \simeq_I N}{N \simeq_I M} \quad \frac{M \simeq_I N \quad M' \simeq_I N'}{MM' \simeq_I NN'} \quad \frac{M \simeq_I N \quad N \simeq_I R}{M \simeq_I R}$$

FIGURE 2.1.   **Semantical equality rules**

As mentioned in section 2.2, if a node in an EDT is erroneous but has no erroneous children, then this node is called *a faulty node*. The following figure shows what a faulty node looks like, where $n_1, n_2, ..., n_k$ are the children of m.

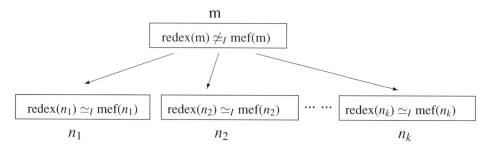

FIGURE 2.2.   *m* **is a faulty node**

Definition 2.21. *Suppose the equation* $f p_1 ... p_n = R$ *is in a program P. If there exists a substitution* σ *such that* $(f p_1 ... p_n)\sigma \equiv f b_1 ... b_n$ *and* $R\sigma \equiv N$, *then we say that* $f b_1 ... b_n \rightarrow_P N$.

If $f b_1 ... b_n \rightarrow_P N$ *but* $f b_1 ... b_n \not\simeq_I N$, *then we say that the definition of the function f in the program is faulty.*

$f b_1 ... b_n \rightarrow_P N$ means that it is a single-step computation from $f b_1 ... b_n$ to N according to one of the rewriting rules in the program P, and there is no computation in $b_1, ..., b_n$.

CORRECTNESS OF ALGORITHMIC DEBUGGING

Definition 2.22. *If the following statement is true, then we say that algorithmic debugging is correct.*

- *If the equation of a faulty node is $fb_1...b_n = M$, then the definition of the function f in the program is faulty.*

For a faulty node m, we have $redex(m) \not\simeq_I mef(m)$. We shall find a term N and prove $redex(m) \rightarrow_P N \simeq_I mef(m)$. In order to define N, we need other definitions.

Definition 2.23. *Let G be an ART and m a node in G. $reduct(m)$ is defined as follows.*

$$reduct(m) = \begin{cases} a & \text{if } (m,a) \in G \text{ and } a \text{ is an atom} \\ mef(n) & \text{if } (m,n) \in G \text{ and } n \text{ is a node} \\ reduct(m\mathsf{f}) \ reduct(m\mathsf{a}) & \text{if } (m, m\mathsf{f} \circ m\mathsf{a}) \in G \\ reduct(m\mathsf{f}) \ mef(j) & \text{if } (m, m\mathsf{f} \circ j) \in G \text{ and } j \neq m\mathsf{a} \\ mef(i) \ reduct(m\mathsf{a}) & \text{if } (m, i \circ m\mathsf{a}) \in G \text{ and } i \neq m\mathsf{f} \\ mef(i) \ mef(j) & \text{if } (m, i \circ j) \in G \text{ and } i \neq m\mathsf{f} \text{ and } j \neq m\mathsf{a} \end{cases}$$

reduct represents the result of a single-step computation. And we shall prove $redex(m) \rightarrow_P reduct(m\mathsf{r}) \simeq_I mef(m)$ for a faulty node m. Note that $mef(m) = mef(m\mathsf{r})$ and so we want to prove $reduct(m\mathsf{r}) \simeq_I mef(m\mathsf{r})$. In order to prove this, we prove a more general result $reduct(m) \simeq_I mef(m)$ for all $m \in dom(G)$ (see Lemma 2.27 for the conditions).

We define *branch* and the reduction principle *depth* in order to prove this general result.

Definition 2.24. *(branch **and** branch')* *We say that n is a branch node of m, denoted as $branch(n,m)$, if one of the following holds.*

- *$branch(m,m)$;*

- *$branch(n\mathsf{f},m)$ if $branch(n,m)$;*

- *$branch(n\mathsf{a},m)$ if $branch(n,m)$.*

Let G be an ART.

$$branch'(m) = \{n \mid n\mathsf{r} \in dom(G) \text{ and } branch(n,m)\}$$

Note that $branch'(m)$ is the set of all evaluated branch nodes of m.

Lemma 2.25. *Let G be an ART.*

- *If $n \in branch'(m\mathsf{f})$ or $n \in branch'(m\mathsf{a})$ then $n \in branch'(m)$.*

- *If $m\mathsf{r} \in dom(G)$ then $children(m) - branch'(m\mathsf{r})$.*

Proof. By the definitions of *children* and *branch'*.

Definition 2.26. *(depth) Let m be a node in an ART G.*

$$depth(m) = \begin{cases} 1 + max\{depth(m\text{f}), & if\ (m, m\text{f} \circ m\text{a}) \in G \\ \quad depth(m\text{a})\} & \\ 1 + depth(m\text{f}) & if\ (m, m\text{f} \circ j) \in G\ and\ j \neq m\text{a} \\ 1 + depth(m\text{a}) & if\ (m, i \circ m\text{a}) \in G\ and\ i \neq m\text{f} \\ 1 & if\ (m, i \circ j) \in G\ and\ i \neq m\text{f}\ and\ j \neq m\text{a} \\ 0 & otherwise \end{cases}$$

Lemma 2.27. *Let G be an ART and m a node in G. If $redex(n) \simeq_I mef(n)$ for all $n \in branch'(m)$, then $reduct(m) \simeq_I mef(m)$.*

Proof. By induction on $depth(m)$.

When $depth(m) = 0$, we have $(m, e) \in G$ where e is a node or an atom.

- If e is a node, then $m\text{r} \in G$ by Lemma 2.6. Then by the definitions of *reduct* and *mef*, we have $reduct(m) = mef(e)$ and $mef(m) = meft(m) = mef(e)$.

- If e is an atom, we have $reduct(m) = e$. Now, we consider the following two cases. If $m \in branch'(m)$, then we have $m\text{r} \in dom(G)$ and $mef(m) \simeq_I redex(m) = e$. If $m \notin branch'(m)$, then we have $m\text{r} \notin dom(G)$ and $mef(m) = meft(m) = e$.

For the step cases, we proceed as follows.

- If $m \in branch'(m)$, then we have $m\text{r} \in dom(G)$ and $redex(m) \simeq_I mef(m)$. And we need to prove $redex(m) \simeq_I reduct(m)$.
  Let us consider only one case here. The other cases are similar. Suppose $(m, m\text{f} \circ j) \in G$ and $j \neq m\text{a}$, then by the definitions we have

$$\begin{aligned} redex(m) &= mef(m\text{f})\ mef(j) \\ reduct(m) &= reduct(m\text{f})\ mef(j) \end{aligned}$$

  Since for any $n \in branch'(m\text{f})$, by Lemma 2.25, we have $n \in branch'(m)$ and hence $redex(n) \simeq_I mef(n)$. By the definition of *depth*, we also have $depth(m\text{f}) < depth(m)$. Now, by induction hypothesis, we have $reduct(m\text{f}) \simeq_I mef(m\text{f})$. And hence we have $redex(m) \simeq_I reduct(m)$ by the semantical equality rules in figure 2.1.

- If $m \notin branch'(m)$, then $m\text{r} \notin dom(G)$.
  Let us also consider only one case. The other cases are similar. Suppose $(m, m\text{f} \circ j) \in G$ and $j \neq m\text{a}$, then by the definitions we have

$$\begin{aligned} mef(m) &= mef(m\text{f})\ mef(j) \\ reduct(m) &= reduct(m\text{f})\ mef(j) \end{aligned}$$

The same arguments as above suffice.

Corollary 2.28. *Let G be an ART and $m\mathfrak{r}$ a node in G (i.e. $m\mathfrak{r} \in dom(G)$). If $redex(n) \simeq_I mef(n)$ for all $n \in children(m)$, then $reduct(m\mathfrak{r}) \simeq_I mef(m)$.*

Proof. By Lemma 2.25 and 2.27.

The condition, $redex(n) \simeq_I mef(n)$ for all $n \in children(m)$, basically means that m does not have any erroneous child nodes as in figure 2.2.

Lemma 2.29. *Let G be an ART and $m\mathfrak{r}$ a node in G (i.e. $m\mathfrak{r} \in dom(G)$). Then $redex(m) \rightarrow_P reduct(m\mathfrak{r})$.*

Proof. Since there is a computation at the node m, we suppose G at node m matches the left-hand side of the rewriting rule $f p_1...p_n = R$ with $[m_1/x_1,...,m_k/x_k]$. We need to prove that there exists a substitution σ such that $redex(m) = (f p_1...p_n)\sigma$ and $reduct(mt) = R\sigma$. In fact $\sigma = [mef(m_1)/x_1,...,mef(m_k)/x_k]$.

   Now, we need to prove that $redex(m) = (f p_1...p_n)\sigma$ and $reduct(mt) = R\sigma$. For the first, we proceed by the definition of $redex$ and pattern matching. For the second, we proceed by the definition of $reduct$ and $graph$.

A similar result as in the above lemma is proved in [2].

   Now, we come to the most important theorem, the correctness of algorithmic debugging.

Theorem 2.30. *(Correctness of Algorithmic Debugging) Let G be an ART, T its EDT and m a faulty node in T. If the equation for the faulty node m is $f b_1...b_n = M$, then the definition of f in the program is faulty.*

Proof. By Lemma 2.29 and Corollary 2.28, we have $redex(m) \rightarrow_P reduct(m\mathfrak{r})$ and $reduct(m\mathfrak{r}) \simeq_I mef(m)$. Since $f b_1...b_n \equiv redex(m) \not\simeq_I mef(m) \equiv M$, we have $f b_1...b_n \rightarrow_P reduct(m\mathfrak{r})$ and $f b_1...b_n \not\simeq_I reduct(m\mathfrak{r})$. The computation from $f b_1...b_n$ to $reduct(m\mathfrak{r})$ is a single-step computation, but $f b_1...b_n$ is not semantically equal to $reduct(m\mathfrak{r})$. So the definition of f in the program must be faulty.

2.6   CONCLUSION AND FUTURE WORK

In this paper, we have formally presented the ART and EDT. The ART is an efficient and practical trace, and it is a model of a real implementation (i.e. Hat). The EDT is directly generated from the ART. We proved the most important property of Hat, the correctness of algorithmic debugging. What the theorem proves is the consistency between the answers given be the user and the detection of the faulty node made by the debugging algorithm. Many other related properties of the ART and EDT are also proved.

   However, there is still more work that needs to be done. Currently we are studying three extensions of the ART model, and the resulting EDT.

   1. Replace the unevaluated parts in an ART by underscore symbols (i.e. _). An unevaluated part in an ART intuitively means the value of this part is irrelevant to any reduction in the graph.

2. Add error messages to an ART when there is a pattern matching failure.

3. Add local rewriting rules (or definitions) to the program.

How these three extensions will affect the EDT and algorithmic debugging needs further study.

ACKNOWLEDGMENTS

The work reported in this paper was supported by the Engineering and Physical Sciences Research Council of the United Kingdom under the grant EP/C516605/1.

REFERENCES

[1] Rafael Caballero, Francisco J. López-Fraguas, and Mario Rodríguez-Artalejo. Theoretical foundations for the declarative debugging of lazy functional logic programs. In Herbert Kuchen and Kazunori Ueda, editors, *Functional and Logic Programming, 5th International Symposium, FLOPS 2001, Tokyo, Japan, March 7-9, 2001, Proceedings*, LNCS 2024, pages 170–184. Springer, 2001.

[2] Olaf Chitil and Yong Luo. Structure and properties of traces for functional programs. To appear in ENTCS 2006.

[3] Lee Naish. A declarative debugging scheme. *Journal of Functional and Logic Programming*, 1997(3), 1997.

[4] Henrik Nilsson. *Declarative Debugging for Lazy Functional Languages*. PhD thesis, Linköping, Sweden, May 1998.

[5] Henrik Nilsson and Peter Fritzson. Algorithmic debugging for lazy functional languages. *Journal of Functional Programming*, 4(3):337–370, July 1994.

[6] Henrik Nilsson and Jan Sparud. The evaluation dependence tree as a basis for lazy functional debugging. *Automated Software Engineering: An International Journal*, 4(2):121–150, April 1997.

[7] B. Pope and Lee Naish. Practical aspects of declarative debugging in Haskell-98. In *Fifth ACM SIGPLAN Conference on Principles and Practice of Declarative Programming*, pages 230–240, 2003.

[8] E. Y. Shapiro. *Algorithmic Program Debugging*. MIT Press, 1983.

[9] Jan Sparud and Henrik Nilsson. The architecture of a debugger for lazy functional languages. In Mireille Ducassé, editor, *Proceedings of AADEBUG'95*, Saint-Malo, France, May, 1995.

[10] Jan Sparud and Colin Runciman. Tracing lazy functional computations using redex trails. In H. Glaser, P. Hartel, and H. Kuchen, editors, *Proc. 9th Intl. Symposium on Programming Languages, Implementations, Logics and Programs (PLILP'97)*, pages 291–308. Springer LNCS Vol. 1292, September 1997.

[11] Malcolm Wallace, Olaf Chitil, Thorsten Brehm, and Colin Runciman. Multiple-view tracing for Haskell: a new Hat. In *Preliminary Proceedings of the 2001 ACM SIGPLAN Haskell Workshop*, UU-CS-2001-23. Universiteit Utrecht, 2001. Final proceedings to appear in ENTCS 59(2).

Chapter 3

Systematic Synthesis of Functions

Pieter Koopman[1], Rinus Plasmeijer[1]

Abstract: In this paper we introduce a new technique to synthesize functions matching a given set of input-output pairs. Using techniques similar to defunctionalisation the abstract syntax tree of the candidate functions is specified at a high level of abstraction. We use a recursive data type to represent the syntax tree of the candidate functions. The test system G∀ST is used for the systematic synthesis of candidate functions and the selection of functions matching the given condition. The representation of candidate functions as data structures gives us full control over them and the transformation of the syntax tree to the actual function is straight forward. Instances of the syntax tree are generated by a generic algorithm that can be tailored easily to specific needs. This yields a very flexible system to synthesize clear (recursive) function definitions efficiently.

3.1   INTRODUCTION

At TFP'05 Susumu Katayama [7] presented an intriguing system that was able to synthesize a general function that fits a number of argument result pairs. For instance, if we state f 2 = 2, f 4 = 24, and f 6 = 720, we expect a factorial function like f x = **if** (x≤0) 1 (x*f (x-1)). There are of course thousands of functions that match the given condition, but by generating candidate functions in an appropriate order and form, the system should find the above recursive solution first. Katayama's work is one of the latest steps in a long research effort to synthesize pure functional programs from examples. Some key steps are Summers 1977 [16], Banerjee 1987 [1], and Cypher 1993 [4].

Programming by example is not only a curious toy, but it is used within areas like adaptive user interfaces [4, 5] and branches of AI-like rule learning for

---

[1]Nijmegen Institute for Computer and Information Science, Radboud University Nijmegen, The Netherlands; E-mail: pieter@cs.ru.nl, rinus@cs.ru.nl

planning [8, 18]. Using proof checkers one has sometimes to invent a function matching given conditions. Jeuring et al. [6] use our approach as an inspiration to generate generic functions that perform a task defined by some typical examples. The goal of all these programming by example systems is not to replace programming in general, but to have a tool that within some limited area is able to synthesize a function that is a generalization of the input-output behavior specified by a (small) number of input-output pairs. In this paper we extend this to a small number of expressions containing an application of the function. Since we have the synthesized candidate function available as a data structure representing its abstract syntax tree, it is easy to do symbolic manipulations of the synthesized candidate functions (like selecting or eliminating functions of some kind, or determination of the derivative of the candidate function).

There are various approaches in the generation of functions matching the given input result pairs. The research based on *computation traces* [16, 4] orders the examples in a lattice and synthesizes the desired function by folding the steps in these computation traces. The main problem with this approach is the construction of the lattice from individual examples. It is far from easy to generate a usable lattice for the example above. The *genetic programming* approach [15, 17] maintains a set of "promising functions". By heuristic exchange and variation of subexpressions one tries to synthesize a matching function. The main topics in this approach are sensible variations of the candidate functions and the determination of their fitness. A third approach uses the *exhaustive enumeration* of candidate functions. The challenge here is to generate a candidate function matching the given examples in reasonable time. Katayama [7] generates candidate functions as λ-expressions of the desired type. Apart from the usual abstraction, application and variables, his anonymous λ-expressions contain a small number of predefined functions. These predefined functions from the component library provide also the necessary recursion patterns. A dynamic type system is used to generate λ-expressions with the desired type. A detailed comparison between his work and this paper is given in section 3.7.

In this paper we show how the exhaustive generation of candidate functions can be improved. Instead of λ-expressions, we generate functions that can be directly recursive. These functions are not composed of λ-expressions, but their structure is determined by the type of their abstract syntax trees. This syntax tree is represented as a data structure in a functional programming language. The test system G∀ST [9] is used to generate instances of this data type in a systematic way [10] and to judge the suitability of the generated candidates.

Existing test systems like QUICKCHECK [2] and G∀ST have limited capabilities for the generation of functions. The generation of a function of type $\sigma \rightarrow \tau$ is done in two steps. First the argument of type σ is transformed to an integer. In the second step this integer is used to select an element of type τ. Either a value is selected from a list of values, or the integer is used as seed for the pseudo random generator. In QUICKCHECK the function $\sigma \rightarrow$ int has to be provided by the user as an instance of the class `coarbitrary`, in G∀ST it was[2] derived automatically by the generic generation algorithm. A multi-argument function of type $\sigma \to \tau \to \upsilon$ is transformed to a function $\tau \to \upsilon$ by providing a pseudo randomly generated element of type σ. In this way all information of all arguments is encoded in a single integer. This approach is not powerful enough for more complex functions, and has as drawback that it is impossible to print these functions. By its nature the system will never generate a decent (recursive) algorithm. Due to these limitations this generic generation is not suitable for the problem treated in this paper and it has been removed from G∀ST.

In this paper we show how the generation and print problems are solved by defining the grammar as a data type and a simple translation from instances of this data type to the corresponding functions. For the generation of instances of the data type the existing generic capabilities of our test system G∀ST are used. In [11] we have used basically the same technique, but in a less sophisticated way, to test properties over higher-order functions. There was the goal to test a (universally quantified) property of a higher-order function by generating a huge number of functions as test arguments. Here we are interested in the synthesized function obeying the restrictions given by some applications of the function. This can be viewed as the mirror image of testing universal quantified properties: there the goal is to find arguments that falsify the property.

It turns out that a similar representation of functions by data types is used at different places in the literature. The technique is called *defunctionalisation*, and the function transforming the data type is usually called *apply*. This technique was introduced by Reynolds [14], and repopularized by Danvy [3]. Defunctionalisation is a program transformation to turn higher-order programs into first-order ones. It has been proven to be meaning preserving. The basic idea is to replace every lambda abstraction with a data constructor that will carry the environment needed, and replace every application of the higher-order function with an apply function that will interpret the data structure. Here we will generate a list of instances of a recursive type representing the grammar of the candidate functions. This implies that each and every function is generated as a data structure. Whenever desired this data structure is transformed to the function it represents by the corresponding instance of the class `apply`.

The key contributions of this paper are the use of data structures to guide the synthesis of candidate functions in a flexible and controlled way, and the use of a general test system to find the functions matching the given input-output pairs. The use of a test system seems rather surprising since it is geared towards finding counterexamples and here we need functions that match the given predicate. The key step is a rephrasing of the property: if we state that such a function does not exist, the counterexamples produced by the test system are exactly the functions we are looking for.

---

[2]For technical reasons the mapping of values to integers had to be integrated in the generic generation algorithm. Since this slows down the generic generation algorithm, the increased memory consumption and the limited use of functions generated in this way, this feature has been removed from G∀ST.

In the next section we will show how such a function is found by our test system. First we will limit our system to functions of type Int → Int. We illustrate the power of our approach with a number of examples. The ways to control the synthesis of candidate functions are discussed in section 3.3. In section 3.4 we illustrate how this approach can handle multi-argument functions. The generation of functions handling other types, like lists, is covered in section 3.5. Section 3.6 illustrates that this approach enables more powerful properties than just matching input-output pairs. Section 3.7 provides a comparison of our work with Katayama's system. Finally we draw some conclusions.

3.2 FUNCTION GENERATION

In this section we will show how functions of type Int → Int can be generated using a grammar. The grammar specifies the syntax tree of the candidate functions. Our test system uses the type to generate candidate functions. The restriction to functions of type Int → Int in this section is by no means a conceptual restriction of the described approach. We use it here just to keep the explanations simple; a similar approach can be used for any type.

In section 3.2.1 we review the basic operations of the automatic test system G∀ST. In 3.2.2 we state the function synthesis problem as a test problem. The rest of this section covers the generation and manipulation of the data structures used to represent the syntax tree of the candidate functions synthesized.

3.2.1 Basic verification by automatic testing

First we explain the basic architecture of the logical part of our test system G∀ST. The logical expression $\forall t : T.P(t)$ is tested by evaluating $P(t)$ for a large number of values of type T. In G∀ST the predicate P is represented by a function of type T → Bool. The potentially infinite list of all possible values of type T is used as test suite. In order to obtain a test result in finite time, a given fixed number N (say 1000) of tests are done. There are three possible test results. The result *Proof* indicates that the test succeeded for all values in the test suite. This can only be achieved for a type with less than N values. The result *Pass* indicates that no counterexamples are found in the first N tests. The result *Fail* indicates that a counterexample was found during the first N tests.

The result of testing in G∀ST will be represented by the data type Verdict:

```
:: Verdict = Proof | Pass | Fail | Undefined
```

The function testAll implements the testing of universally quantified predicates:

```
testAll :: Int (t→Bool) [t] → Verdict
testAll n p []   = Proof
testAll 0 p list = Pass
testAll n p [x:r]
    | p x        = testAll (n-1) p r
    | otherwise = Fail
```

The list of values of type T is the test suite. It can be specified manually, but is usually derived fully automatically from the type T by the generic algorithm described in [10]. G∀ST also reports any counterexample found (if any), handles properties over multiple variables, and has a complete set of logical operators.

A similar test function exists for existentially quantified logical expression of the form $\exists t : T . P(t)$. The test system returns *Proof* if a test value is found that makes $P(t)$ true. The result is *Fail* if none of the values of type T makes the predicates true. If none of the first N values makes the predicate true, the result is *Undefined*. The result *Undefined* means that within the given bounds G∀ST was neither able to find a counterexample, nor a value that makes this predicate hold. Hence, its value is undefined.

A typical example is the rule that the absolute value of any number is greater than or equal to zero, $\forall i . \mathrm{abs}(i) \geq 0$. In G∀ST we have to choose a type for the number in order to allow the system to generate an appropriate test suite. Using integers as test suite this property reads:

```
propAbs :: Int → Bool
propAbs i = abs i ≥ 0
```

This property can be tested by executing the start rule `Start = test propAbs`. The function `test` provides the number of tests and the test suite as additional arguments to `testAll`. The test suite is obtained as instance of the generic class `ggen` [10]. G∀ST almost immediately finds the counterexample -2147483648, which is the minimal integer that can be represented in 32 bit numbers. This value is one of the common border values that are in the front of any test sequence of integers, other border values are `-1`, `0`, `1` and `maxint`.

3.2.2   The function selection problem as a predicate

In this section we will show how G∀ST can be used to synthesize candidate functions and to select functions obeying the desired properties. It is not difficult to state a property about functions that expresses that it should obey the given input-output pairs. For our running example, `f 2 = 2`, `f 4 = 24` and `f 6 = 720`, we state "$P(f) = f(2) = 4 \wedge f(4) = 24 \wedge f(6) = 720$". Using a straightforward approach, the property to test becomes $\exists f . P(f)$. Test systems like QUICKCHECK and G∀ST are geared towards finding counterexamples. This implies that testing yields just *Proof* if such an f is found, and yields *Undefined* if such a function is not found in the given number of tests. Here we want a function that makes the predicate true. Changing the test system such that it reports successes in an existentially quantified predicate is not very difficult, but undesirable from a software engineering point of view.

We search for a function by stating that a function matching the given examples does not exist $\neg \exists f . P(f)$ or more conveniently for testing $\forall f . \neg P(f)$. Counterexamples found by G∀ST are exactly the desired functions. Now these functions are counterexamples and will be shown by the test system. We state in G∀ST:

```
prop0 :: (Int→Int) → Bool
prop0 f = ~ (f 2 == 2 && f 4 == 24 && f 6 == 720)
```

where ∼ is the negation operator. Any counterexample found by G∀ST is a function that matches the given input-output pairs. As outlined in the introduction, functional test systems like QUICKCHECK and G∀ST are not very good in generating functions and printing them. Instead of prop0 we use a property over the data type Fun. The type Fun represents the grammar of candidate functions, see 3.2.3. The function apply, see 3.2.5, turns an instance of this data type in the actual function.

```
prop1 :: Fun → Bool
prop1 d = ~(f 2 == 2 && f 4 == 24 && f 6 == 720) where f = apply d
```

This predicate can be tested by executing a program with Start = test prop1 as starting point. Our system yields the following result:

```
Counterexample 1 found after 30808 tests: f x = if (x≤0) 1 (x*f (x-1))
Execution: 1.02  Garbage collection: 0.15  Total: 1.17
```

This counterexample is exactly the general primitive recursive function we are looking for, the well-known factorial function. More examples will be given below. In the next subsection we treat the structure of the type Fun and the synthesis of instances.

3.2.3   A grammar for candidate functions

In the generation of candidate functions we have to be very careful to generate only terminating functions. If one of the generated functions happens to be nonterminating for one of the examples, testing can become nonterminating as well. Termination can either be guaranteed by an upper limit on the number of recursive calls (if the candidate function does not terminate in N calls, it is rejected), or by only generating functions that are terminating by construction.

We will construct only terminating (primitive recursive) functions. For the integer domain, these functions either do not recurse, or use as stop criterion a conditional of the form $x \leq c$, where x is the function argument and c is some small integer constant. The then-part is an expression containing no recursive calls. The else-part contains only recursive calls of the form f (x–d), where d is a small positive number. Since we want to generate only primitive recursive functions, recursive calls are not nested.

The body of a function is either a non-recursive expression, or a recursive expression of the described form. An expression is either a variable, an integer constant or a binary operator applied to two expressions. This is captured by the following grammar.

$$
\begin{aligned}
Fun &= \mathbf{f}\,\mathbf{x} = (Expr \mid RFun) \\
RFun &= \mathbf{if}\,(\mathbf{x} - IConst)\,Expr\,Expr2 \\
IConst &= \text{positive\_integer} \\
Expr &= \text{Variable} \mid \text{integer} \mid BinOp\,Expr \\
BinOp\,e &= e + e \mid e - e \mid e * e
\end{aligned}
$$

The expression in an else-part is either a variable, a constant or a binary operator over a variable, a constant, or a recursive function application:

$$
Expr2 \;=\; \text{Variable} \mid \text{integer} \mid BinOp\,(\text{Variable} \mid \text{integer} \mid \mathbf{f}\,(\mathbf{x} - \text{integer}))
$$

Note that the grammar rule for *BinOp* is parameterized by the arguments for the binary operators. This is convenient since we can now use this rule for *Expr* as for *Expr2*. This reuse of data types carries over directly to the implementation. Although the principle of parameterizing grammar rules is not completely standard, it is known as two level grammar, or Van Wijngaarden grammar, and is at least as old as the Algol 68 report.

This grammar is directly mapped to a data type in CLEAN [13]. We use the type OR to mimic the choice operator, |, used in the grammar.

```
:: OR s t = L s | R t
```

The composition of types allows us to use a choice between types. This saves us from the burden of defining a tailor-made type for each choice.

In the definition of the data types representing the grammar we represent only the variable parts of the grammar. Literal parts of the grammar (like **f x** =) are omitted (as in any abstract syntax tree). Constructors like IConst are introduced in order to make the associated integer a separate type, this is necessary in order to generate values of this type in a different way than standard integers.

Constructs that behave similarly are placed in the same type (like BinOp). A separate type is used for recursive parts in the grammar, parts that are used at several places, or for clarity.

```
:: IConst  = IConst Int
:: BinOp x = OpPlus x x | OpMinus x x | OpTimes x x
:: Var     = X
:: Expr    = Expr (OR (OR Var IConst) (BinOp Expr))
:: FunAp   = FunAp Int
:: TermVal = TermVal Int
:: RFun    = RFun TermVal Expr
                  (OR (OR Var IConst) (BinOp (OR (OR Var IConst) FunAp)))
:: Fun     = Fun (OR Expr RFun)
```

These data types are used to represent recursive functions as illustrated above. The design of these types controls the shape of the candidate functions. It is very easy to add additional operators like division or power.

3.2.4   Generating candidate functions

The generic algorithm ggen [10] used by G∨ST generates a list of all instances of a
(recursive) type from small to large. The only thing to be done is to order CLEAN
to derive the generic generation for these types.

derive ggen OR, BinOp, Var, Expr, RFun, Fun

For the constants we do not use the ordinary generation of integers. A much
smaller set of values is used to speed up the synthesis of matching candidates
functions. After studying many examples of recursive functions in textbooks and
libraries the values 0..2 appear to be commonly used as termination value. The
occurring recursive calls for integer functions are usually of the form $f(x-1)$
or $f(x-2)$. The occurring integer constants are in the range 0..5. These values
are used in the following tailor-defined instances of the corresponding types in
CLEAN. The variables n and r can be used to make a pseudo random change in
the order of the values. This is not needed nor wanted here.

```
ggen {|TermVal|}  n r = map TermVal [0..2]
ggen {|FunAp|}    n r = map FunAp   [1..2]
ggen {|IConst|}   n r = map IConst  [0..5]
```

None of these upper limits is critical. Making the maximum IConst 50 (or even
unbounded) instead of 5 slows the discovery of most functions down by a factor
of 2. Using 3 as maximum, instead of 5, usually gives a speedup of a factor of 2.
Using a maximum that is too small prevent the desired function from being found.
Katayama uses only $f(x-1)$ in his recursion pattern.

3.2.5   Transforming data structures into functions

Until now we generate the syntax trees representing candidate functions, but for
the determination of the fitness of a candidate function we need the function corresponding to this syntax tree. The class apply will be used to transform a syntax
tree into the corresponding actual function. Although apply can also be defined
in a generic way, we prefer an ordinary class here. The generic definition is not
shorter, and the ordinary class is more efficient. The class apply contains only the
function apply. The class is parameterized by the data type d to be transformed,
the environment e, and the type of value v to be generated[3].

class apply d e v :: d → e → v

We will use two different environments. The first type of environment contains
only the integer used as function argument. The second type of environment is a
tuple containing the recursive function and the function argument.

  The interesting cases using the environment are:

instance apply Var Int   Int **where** apply x = λi.i

---

[3]In Haskell one would have to write
class apply d e v **where** apply :: d → e → v instead of this shorthand notation.

```
instance apply Var (x,Int) Int where apply x = λ(_,i).i
instance apply FunAp (Int→Int,Int) Int
where apply (FunAp d) = λ(f,i).f (i-d)
```

In the definition of a recursive function, RFun, an environment containing the integer argument is transformed into an environment containing the recursive function and the argument. The recursion is constructed by the cycle in the definition of f.

```
instance apply RFun Int Int
where apply rf=:(RFun (TermVal c) then else) = f
    where f i = if (i≤c) (apply then i) (apply else (f,i))
```

Note that the transformation of the syntax tree into the corresponding function is done only once for all recursive applications of the function (the generated function f is passed in the environment of the else-part). This more sophisticated implementation results in a faster execution than repeated interpretation of the data structure for recursive calls (by passing rf to the recursive calls).

The definition of the apply for expressions of type Expr is somewhat smart. Expressions do not contain calls of the recursive function. Hence it is superfluous to pass it to all nodes of the syntax tree.

```
instance apply Expr Int Int where apply (Expr f) = apply f
instance apply Expr (x,Int) Int where apply (Expr f) = λ(_,i).apply f i
```

The instance of apply for binary operators takes care of the computations. The instance of apply for BinOp x requires that there is an instance of apply for x and this environment e and result of type v. Moreover, it is required that the operators +, −, and * are defined for type v.

```
instance apply (BinOp x) e v | apply x e v & +, −, * v
where apply (OpPlus  x y) = λe.apply x e + apply y e
    apply (OpMinus x y) = λe.apply x e − apply y e
    apply (OpTimes x y) = λe.apply x e * apply y e
```

The other instances of apply just pass the environment to their children, e.g:

```
instance apply (OR x y) b c | apply x b c & apply y b c
where apply (L x) = apply x
    apply (R y) = apply y
```

3.2.6 Pretty printing generated functions

If we would derive showing of candidate functions in the generic way, we would obtain the following representation for the factorial function from section 3.2.2.

```
Fun (R (RFun (TermVal 0) (Expr (L (R (IConst 1))))
                    (R (OpTimes (L (L X)) (R (FunAp 1))))))))
```

Although this data structure represents exactly the recursive factorial function listed above, it is harder to read. Instead of deriving generic instances of the print

given examples	generated function	tests	time
f 1 = 1	f x = 1	1	0.01
f 1 = 1, f 2 = 4	f x = x*x	69	0.02
f 1 = 1, f 2 = 5	f x = if (x≤1) 1 5	160	0.02
f 2 = 2, f 6 = 720, f 4 = 24	f x = if (x≤0) 1 (x*f (x-1))	30808	1.17
f 4 = 5, f 5 = 8	f x = if (x≤1) 1 (f (x-2)+f (x-1))	2791	0.16
f (-2) = 2, f 5 = 5, f (-4) = 4	f x = if (x≤0) (0-x) x	678	0.05

TABLE 3.1.   Input-output pairs and the synthesized functions.

routines for the data types representing the grammar, we use tailor-made definitions in order to obtain nicely printed functions instead of the data structures
representing them.

The generic function genShow yields a list of strings to be printed. It has a sep-
arator sep as argument that is used between constructors. The second argument,
p, is a Boolean indicating whether parentheses around compound expressions are
needed. The third argument is the object to be printed. The last argument, rest, is
a continuation. This continuation is the list of strings representing the rest of the
result of genShow.

The dull code below just takes care of the pretty printing of candidate functions. It just adds the constant parts of the grammar not represented in the syntax
tree and removes some constructors. We list some typical examples.

```
genShow {|OR|}  f g sep p (L x)        rest = f sep p x rest
genShow {|OR|}  f g sep p (R y)        rest = g sep p y rest
genShow {|IConst|}  sep p (IConst c)   rest = [toString c:rest]
genShow {|Var|}     sep p X            rest = ["x":rest]
genShow {|Expr|}    sep p (Expr e)     rest = genShow {|*|} sep p e rest
genShow {|RFun|}    sep p (RFun c t e) rest
 = ["if (x≤":genShow {|*|} sep False c
    [") ":genShow {|*|} sep True t [" ": genShow {|*|} sep True e rest]]]
genShow {|BinOp|}  f sep p (OpPlus x y) rest
 = [if p "(" "": f sep True x ["+": f sep True y [if p ")" "":rest]]]
```

3.2.7   Examples

In order to demonstrate the power of our approach we list some examples in table
3.1. The first column of the table contains the input-output pairs the function has
to match. The next columns contain the first matching function found, the number
of tests and the time needed (in seconds) to generate this function. We used a 1
GHz AMD PC running Windows XP and the latest versions of CLEAN and G∀ST.

These examples show that a small number of examples are sufficient to generate many well-known functions. >From top to bottom these functions are known
as: the constant one, square, a simple choice, factorial, fibonacci, and absolute
value.

Depending on the amount of memory (32 – 64 M) and the details of the generated functions, our implementation generates 10 to 25 thousand candidate func-

tions per second. Private communication with Katayama indicates that our implementation is more than one order of magnitude faster then Katayama's. When lists are excluded from his implementation it needs 25 seconds on Katayama's faster (3 GHz Pentium 4) machine for the factorial function. His solution for[4] $f\,0 = 1, f\,1 = 1, f\,2 = 2, f\,3 = 6, f\,4 = 24$ is

λa.nat_para a (λb.inc b) (λb c d.c (nat_para b d (λe f.c f))) zero

Using the paramorphism [12] nat_para, twice, as recursion pattern. The first occurrence of nat_para handles the recursion in the factorial function. The second instance of nat_para implements multiplication by repeated addition.

```
nat_para :: Int a (Int a → a) → a
nat_para 0 x f = x
nat_para i x f = f (i-1) (nat_para (i-1) x f)
```

Comparison with our running example, repeated as the fourth example in the table above, indicates that our system generates functions that are better readable. In addition our approach synthesizes a matching function faster, and the generated function is more efficient. Moreover, Katayama's system needs more input-output pairs to generate the desired factorial function. Katayama's system can be improved by adding primitive functions, like addition and multiplication, to the library.

3.3 CONTROLLING THE CANDIDATE FUNCTIONS

The generation of candidate functions can be controlled in three ways. In this section we will discuss these ways, and show their effect by searching for functions matching f 1 = 3, f 2 = 6, and f 3 = 9. The three different ways to control the synthesis of functions are:

Designing types By far the most important way to control the synthesis of candidate functions is the design of the data types used to represent the candidate functions. Only candidate functions that can be represented can be generated and will be considered.

In this paper we used this to guarantee that candidate functions are either non-recursive, i.e. the function body is an arithmetic expression, or the candidate function is primitive recursive containing an appropriate stop condition.

Generating instances of types The test system G∀ST generates instances of these types in its struggle to prove or falsify the statement that there is no function obeying the given input-output pairs. One of the advantages of G∀ST is that the generation of instances for types can be done by the generic algorithm ggen. The instance of ggen for a specific type just yields the list of candidate values.

---

[4]Katayama's system needs more input-output pairs to find the factorial functions. With the pairs used as running example his system finds another function. This is just an effect of the order of generation of candidate functions.

property	execution time (S)	candidates tested	candidates rejected
pExpr	0.02	180	0
pFun	0.03	429	0
pFit	0.21	1525	2860
pExpr2	0.12	2126	0

TABLE 3.2.   Generating 10 matching functions in different ways.

This implies that one can decide to specify a list of values by hand instead of deriving them by the generic algorithm.

We used this in the generation of constants. Although there is no conceptual limitation to leaves of the syntax trees to be generated, it is convenient to use it only there. One can use a general type for constants and easily control the actual constants used. It is possible to use this also for types with arguments, but that brings the burden of controlling the order of generating instance back to the user.

Selection of generated instances Finally, G∀ST has the possibility to apply a predicate to candidate functions, or actually their syntax tree, before they are used. If the predicate does not hold, the test value is not used. In fact it is not even counted as a test.

This is often used for partial functions. A typical example is the square root function that is only defined for nonnegative numbers. For these numbers we can state that the square of the square root of any nonnegative rational number should be equal to that number: $\forall r . r \geq 0 \Rightarrow sqrt(r)^2 = r$. This can be expressed directly in G∀ST as:

```
pSqrt :: Real → Property
pSqrt r = r ≥ 0.0 ⟹ (sqrt r)^2.0 = r
```

Using this mechanism we can eliminate undesirable candidate functions from the tests, and hence from the synthesis of matching functions.

These techniques are demonstrated by synthesis of functions matching f 1 = 3, f 2 = 6, and f 3 = 9. G∀ST searches for non-recursive solutions by testing:

```
pExpr :: Expr → Bool
pExpr d = ~(f 1 = 3 && f 2 = 6 && f 3 = 9)
where f = apply d
```

G∀ST quickly finds functions like $fx = 0 + ((x+x) + x)$, $fx = (x-x) + ((x+x) + x)$, and $fx = x + (x+x)$. In the property pFun we replace the type Expr of pExpr by Fun. When G∀ST tests this property, it will also generate recursive candidate functions. In table 3.2 we see that it takes longer to generate 10 matching functions for pFun than for pExpr. Since the synthesized recursive functions do not match the given condition, pFun has a lower success rate.

In order to get rid of redundant expressions like x-x or x+0 in the generated functions, we filter them with the predicate fit:

```
pFit :: Fun → Property
pFit d = fit d ⟹ ∼(f 1 == 3 && f 2 == 6 && f 3 == 6) where f = apply d
```

The predicate `fit` is implemented as a class. The instance for binary operators is given as an example. A subtraction is fit if the arguments are unequal and each of the arguments is fit. An addition is fit if both arguments are unequal to the constant zero, checked by `is0`, and fit. A multiplication is fit if both arguments are unequal to 0 and 1 and fit.

```
class fit a :: a → Bool
```

```
instance fit (BinOp x) | gEq {|*|} x & isConst, fit x
where fit (OpMinus x y) = x =!= y && ∼(is0 y) && fit x && fit y
      fit (OpPlus x y)  = ∼(is0 x) && ∼(is0 y) && fit x && fit y
      fit (OpTimes x y) = ∼(is01 x) && ∼(is01 y) && fit x && fit y
```

Defining a type without these redundant expressions is somewhat tricky, but doable. The key step is to define operators as a separate type with different type-arguments as left and right arguments:

```
:: Sub x y = Sub x y
:: Es = Es (OR (Sub Var NConst) (Sub IConst Var))
```

In table 3.2 we see that it takes considerably more time to generate 10 matching functions if we filter redundant expressions. This is not surprising since also the rejected candidates are generated and all candidates are tested. Using more sophisticated types is more efficient since no fitness tests and generation of redundant expressions occurs, but requires more programmer insight.

3.4   GENERATION OF MULTI-ARGUMENT FUNCTIONS

All generated functions above are of type `Int→Int`. This was chosen deliberately to keep things as simple as possible, but it is not an inherent limitation of the approach. To demonstrate this we show how to handle functions with `Arity`, e.g. 2, integer arguments. The type for variables is changed such that it represents a numbered argument.

```
:: VarN = VarN Int
```

The environment in `apply` will now contain a list of values.

```
instance apply VarN [Int] Int where apply (VarN n) = λ l.l !! n
```

The instance of `ggen` takes care that only valid argument numbers are generated.

```
ggen {|VarN|} n r = map VarN [0..Arity-1]
```

In the next section we will show functions having a list and an integer as example.

3.5   SYNTHESIS OF FUNCTIONS OVER OTHER DATA TYPES

The manipulation of other types than integers can be handled by defining a suitable abstract syntax tree for these functions, and the associated instances of `ggen`,

given example	generated function	tests	time
g [1,2,3] = [1,2,3]	g y = y	1	0.01
g [1,2,3] = [1,4,9]	g y = map f y where f x = x*x	34	0.05
g [1,2,5] = [1,2,120]	g y = map f y where f x = if (x≤1) x (f (x-1)*x)	67573	3.89

TABLE 3.3.   Input-output pairs of type [Int]→[Int] and synthesized functions.

apply and genShow. We derive the generation of all types introduced in this section.

The synthesis of functions of type Real→Real with the same structure as the functions of type Int→Int used above is very simple, we only have to supply suitable instances of apply.

As a slightly more advanced example we show how function over lists of integers, that is, of type [Int]→[Int], can be handled that are either the identity function, or the map of a function of type Int→Int over the argument list.

:: LFun = ID | MAP Fun

instance apply LFun [Int] [Int]
where apply ID = λl.l
     apply (MAP f) = map (apply f)

Although these are very restricted functions and not all that interesting, it shows how data types generating function can be reused. Some examples of its use are listed in table 3.3.

In exactly the same way we can synthesize functions destructing recursive data types like lists and trees. As an example we let G∀ST synthesize product functions over a list of integers with the property:

pProduct :: ListFun → Property
pProduct d = fit d ⟹ ∼(f [1,2,3] = 6 && f [] = 1 && f [5] = 5)
where f = apply d

Note that by changing f [] = 1 to f [] = 0 we will obtain the sum rather than the product.

The key to success is of course an appropriate type for ListFun and the associated instances of apply and genShow. Direct recursive functions can be synthesized by:

```
:: LFUN = LFUN IConst LEx            // expressions for nil and cons
:: LEx  = LEx (OR (OR Var IConst) (OR Rec (BinOp LEx)))  // note the recursion
:: Rec  = Rec                        // recursive call

:: Env = Env ([Int]→Int) Int [Int]  // environment: function, head, and tail
```

instance apply LEx Env Int **where** apply (LEx lex) = apply lex
instance apply Var Env Int **where** apply X = λ(Env f x l) → x
instance apply Rec Env Int **where** apply Rec = λ(Env f x l) → f l

```
instance apply LFUN [Int] Int
where apply (LFUN nil cons) = f
      where f []    = apply nil 0
            f [x:l] = apply cons (Env f x l)
```

One often prefers functions over lists with an accumulator in order to reduce the stack space needed by the synthesized function. This requires just another data type for functions:

```
:: AFun = AFun IConst AEx     // initial accumulator and body for recursion
:: AEx  = AEx (OR (OR Var IConst) (OR A (BinOp AEx)))  // note the recursion
:: A    = A                   // accumulator

:: AEnv = AEnv Int Int        // environment: accumulator and head

instance apply AEx AEnv Int where apply (AEx ex) = apply ex
instance apply A   AEnv Int where apply A = λ(AEnv a x) → a
instance apply Var AEnv Int where apply X = λ(AEnv a x) → x
instance apply AFun [Int] Int
where apply (AFun c ex) = f (apply c 0)
      where f a [] = a
            f a [x:l] = f (apply ex (AEnv a x)) l
```

By choosing (OR AFun LFUN) for ListFun in the property above, G∀ST synthesizes both kinds of functions in one test. The first three matching functions are:

```
Counterexample 1 found after 8 tests:
f []    = 1
f [x:l] = (f l)*x
Counterexample 2 found after 677 tests:
f []    = 1
f [x:l] = x*(f l)
Counterexample 3 found after 1039 tests:
f l = g 1 l
where g a []    = a
      g a [x:l] = g (a*x) l
```

3.6   OTHER PROPERTIES

Having the candidate function available as a real function enables us to write also other conditions, like twice f 1 = 4 or f 1≠5.

However, there is no reason to stick to these simple predicates on the synthesized candidate functions. In this section we show some other kinds of properties that can be stated about the desired functions. One possibility is to use the fully fledged test system to specify for instance properties containing additional for-all operators. Another possibility is to use the availability of the functions as data structures for symbolic manipulation.

Using the capabilities of the test systems it is for instance possible to search for non-recursive functions that obey the rule $f0 = 0$ and $\forall x . 2f(x) = f(2x)$. This can directly be stated in G∀ST as:

```
pfExpr :: Expr → Property
pfExpr d = fit d ⟹ ~(f 0 = 0 ∧ ForAll (λx.2*f x = f (2*x)))
where f = apply d
```

Note that we limit the search to fit candidates. The system promptly synthesizes functions like f x = 0, f x = x, f x = x+((x+x)+x), f x = 0-(x+x).

If we also include recursive functions in the search space, we have to take care that the integers tried as arguments by G∀ST are not too large. Computing the result of synthesized primitive recursive functions, like factorial and Fibonacci, for a typical test value like maxint uses infeasible amounts of time and space. The numbers used in the tests can be limited by computing them modulo some reasonable upper bound, like 15, or by stating a range of values directly. A typical example is:

```
pfFun :: Fun → Property
pfFun d = fit d ⟹ ~(f 1 = 1 ∧ ((λx.(f x)/x = f (x-1)) For [1..10]))
where f = apply d
```

The factorial function f x = if (x≤0) 1 (f (x-1)*x) is synthesized quickly.

Since the syntax trees of the candidate functions are available, it is easy to manipulate the candidate functions. As an example we show how we can obtain the derivative of functions of type Real→Real and how it is used in properties. The derivative $\frac{d}{dx}$ of expressions is computed by the class ddx. The rules are taken directly from high school mathematics:

class ddx t :: t → Expr

```
instance ddx Var where ddx X = toExpr (IConst 1)
instance ddx IConst where ddx c = toExpr (IConst 0)
instance ddx (BinOp t) | ddx t & toExpr t
where ddx (OpPlus  s t) = toExpr (OpPlus (ddx s) (ddx t))
      ddx (OpMinus s t) = toExpr (OpMinus (ddx s) (ddx t))
      ddx (OpTimes s t)
       = toExpr (OpPlus (toExpr (OpTimes (ddx s) (toExpr t)))
                        (toExpr (OpTimes (toExpr s) (ddx t))))
```

This can be used in properties over a function f and its derivative f'. For example $f(0) = 1$ and $\forall x . f'(x) = 2x$. In G∀ST this is:

```
pddx :: Expr → Property
pddx d = ~(f 0.0 = 1.0 ∧ ForAll (λx. f' x = 2.0*x))
where f  = apply d; f' = apply (ddx d)
```

After 145 test cases G∀ST synthesizes the first matching function: f x = (x*x)+1.

These examples show that it pays to use a general test system for the synthesis of functions. The matching of given pairs nicely integrates with the general logical expressions. Having the candidate function available as a data structure also enables symbolic manipulations like computing the derivative.

3.7 RELATED WORK

This paper presents an application of the concept of systematic generation of functions to the area of programming by example. The basic idea to synthesize functions via the synthesis of a data structure representing their syntax tree is presented in [11]. There the functions generated are used for the automatic testing of higher-order functions. The generated functions serve only as test arguments for the properties to be tested. We were interested in the property over the higher-order function rather than the set of functions generated as test suite. The main quest was there to find errors in a library of continuation based parser combinators.

Here we are interested in the generated properties themselves, since the goal is to find a general function matching the given input-output pairs. The techniques of synthesizing functions is improved by the introduction of the type OR. This type allows us to model the choice of elements of two existing data types. The advantage is that data types, and hence the components of functions modeled by them, can be reused. Furthermore, this paper systematically shows what has to be done if the system generates undesirable (for instance non terminating) functions. The options are: 1) improve the data type such that the dangerous functions cannot be represented, 2) replace the generic generation of instances of this type by a tailor-made generation such that only the desired instances are generated (this is only attractive for non-recursive definitions), or 3) define a predicate over the data type that rejects unwanted candidates before they are tried.

In the area of programming by example through systematic synthesis of candidate functions and selecting a match candidate the most related work is [7] of Katayama. The main differences between our work and Katayama's approach are:

Type correctness of generated candidates The type system selects statically the grammar used to generate values of the desired function result, instead of a dynamic system that controls the generation of λ-expressions.

Recursion in the synthesized functions Our system is able to synthesize definitions of (primitive) recursive functions directly, instead of searching λ-expressions containing an instance of a paramorphism as recursion builder. Although our examples are primitive recursive functions, this is not an inherent limitation of the approach. By including a clause for a recursion builder, like fold for lists, in the grammar, the corresponding recursion pattern can be generated. In Katayama's system any recursion pattern wanted should be supplied as a (higher-order) function in the library.

Control of the synthesis In Katayama's system the candidate functions are synthesized from ordinary λ-expressions and a library of functions. The recursion pattern has to be supplied in this library, since the generation of λ-expressions is not capable to generate recursion (for instance by a Y-combinator). By default Katayama's library of primitive functions provides two paramorphisms: one recursion pattern for integers and one for lists (similar to a fold function).

This is sufficient since his system only handles recursive functions over integers and lists. Katayama's system generates type correct expressions in a breadth first way. The exact algorithm used is not revealed.

We use data types to control the generation of candidate functions. Using these types, the system becomes more open and much easier to adapt to special wishes. The generation of instances of these types is done by our general generic algorithm [10] instead of an ad-hoc algorithm. Using the techniques discussed in this paper the synthesis can be fine-tuned if necessary. Due to the tailor-made data types the functions synthesized are not restricted to integers and lists nor to specific recursion patterns. The price we have to pay for this flexibility is that we have to define new a data type and associated instance of `apply` for each new recursion pattern and data type. We have shown that it is possible to reuse (parts of) existing solutions.

In the recursion pattern we use here as an example for functions of type `Int`→`Int` we use various values as stop condition and step size in the recursive call. In Katayama's systems all of the desired combinations should be stated as separate recursion patterns, or the needed constants should be included as functions in the library. A consequence of that last action would be that these constants would be used in each and every position where the type fits. As shown above, this can be controlled very easily and accurately in our approach.

Tool support Our general test system is used to generate candidate functions, and to select and print matching functions. No changes of the tool are required whatsoever. Katayama uses a tailor-made tool.

The advantage of Katayama's system is that it is in principle able to generate any function over integers and lists. The system should be extended in order to handle other types, like trees. The advantage of our approach is that it works for any type and any kind of function wanted. Since it synthesizes only instances of the defined abstract syntax trees, it is usually faster. Moreover, it tends to require less input-output pairs to find nice (recursive) functions. The price to be paid is that we have to define new data types and associated instances of `apply` for new kinds of functions.

Jeuring et al. [6] generate generic functions that performs a task defined by some typical examples. They use Djinn to generate arms of a generic function for instances of the user-specified generic signature of the desired function on the type indices of generic functions. This is partly based on their misconception that our approach is not suited to generate higher-order functions[5]. The selection of candidate functions is very similar to our approach, although they use QUICKCHECK rather than G∀ST. In [11] we show how higher-order functions can be generated using this approach. It is interesting future work to find out of the generation of generic functions can be done based on our technique.

---

[5]Jeuring et al. state in their introduction: "..the approach of Koopman and Plasmeijer [15] does not seem to be able to generate higher-order functions.."

3.8   CONCLUSION

In this paper we have shown how functions matching given input-result pairs can be synthesized in a clear and flexible way. By defining an appropriate type for syntax trees as data structure, the user can control the structure of the synthesized functions. We have shown non-recursive functions as well as various recursion patterns. If other kind of functions are wanted (other data types and or recursion patterns) we just have to define a data type representing their syntax tree, derive their instantiation, and add an instance of `apply` that turns the syntax tree into the corresponding function.

Generating the instances of the data types representing the syntax tree and selecting the correct corresponding functions can be done very well with our general test system G∀ST. There are three ways in which the synthesis of functions is controlled. The first and most important control mechanism is the type of the syntax tree representing the functions. The second control mechanism is the generation of instances of these types. It is very convenient to derive the generation of instances from the generic algorithm of G∀ST, but that is not required. Any list of values can be used. We use this in the generation of constants: the type is very general, but the used instances of `ggen` generate only a small list of desired values. The third and final way to control which functions are used in the test is by using a predicate in the property. In this paper we used the predicate `fit` to eliminate candidates representing undesirable subexpressions (like x–x and 0+x instead of 0 and x). By defining more sophisticated types, the other ways to control the synthesis become superfluous. The user decides what is most convenient and effective.

The test system does most of the work and provides an excellent platform. For most functions a single page of additional CLEAN code is sufficient. This approach is more transparent, flexible and efficient than existing systems like [7]. Although the described system works excellently for many examples, synthesizing functions involving very large expressions or very large constants will take a very long time. This is due to the size of the search space and the systematic search.

ACKNOWLEDGMENTS

The authors thank the anonymous referees for their contributions to improve this paper.

REFERENCES

[1] Debasish Banerjee. A methodology for synthesis of recursive functional programs. *ACM Transactions on Programming Languages and Systems*, 9(3).

[2] K. Claessen and J. Hughes. Quickcheck: A lightweight tool for random testing of haskell programs. In *Proceedings of the 2000 ACM SIGPLAN International Conference on Functional Programming (ICFP '00)*, pages 268–279. ACM Press, 2000.

[3] Olivier Danvy and Lasse R. Nielsen. Defunctionalization at work. In *ACM SIGPLAN conference on Principles and Practice of Declarative Programming (PPDP)*, pages 162–174, 2001.

[4] Allen Cypher (editor). *Watch What I Do: Programming by Demonstration*. MIT Press, 1993.

[5] Henry Lieberman (editor). *Your Wish is My Command: Programming by Example*. Morgan Kaufmann, 2001.

[6] Johan Jeuring, Alexey Rodriguez, and Gideon Smeding. Generating generic functions. In *WGP '06: Proceedings of the 2006 ACM SIGPLAN workshop on Generic programming*, pages 23–32, New York, NY, USA, 2006. ACM Press.

[7] Susumu Katayama. Systematic search for lambda expressions. In *Proceedings Sixth Symposium on Trends in Functional Programming (TFP2005)*, pages 195–205, 2005.

[8] E. Kitzelmann and U. Schmid. Inductive synthesis of functional programs. In *AISC 2002 and Calculemus 2002*, volume 2385 of *LNCS*, pages 26–37. Springer, 2002.

[9] P. Koopman, A. Alimarine, J. Tretmans, and R. Plasmeijer. Gast: Generic automated software testing. In Ricardo Peña and Thomas Arts, editors, *The 14th International Workshop on the Implementation of Functional Languages, IFL'02, Selected Papers*, volume 2670 of *LNCS*, pages 84–100. Springer, 2003.

[10] Pieter Koopman and Rinus Plasmeijer. Generic Generation of Elements of Types. In *Proceedings Sixth Symposium on Trends in Functional Programming (TFP2005)*, Tallin, Estonia, Sep 23-24 2005.

[11] Pieter W. M. Koopman and Rinus Plasmeijer. Automatic testing of higher order functions. In *Fourth Asian Symposium on Programming Languages and Systems (APLAS)*, pages 148–164, 2006.

[12] Lambert Meertens. Paramorphisms. *Formal Aspects of Computing*, 4:413–424, 1992.

[13] Rinus Plasmeijer and Marko van Eekelen. *Concurrent CLEAN Language Report (version 2.0)*, December 2001. http://www.cs.ru.nl/~clean/.

[14] John C. Reynolds. Defunciitional interpreters for higher-order programming languages. *Higher-Order and Symbolic Computation*, 11(4):363–397, 1998. reprinted from the proceedings of the 25th ACM National Conference (1972).

[15] Ute Schmid and Jens Waltermann. Automatic synthesis of XSL-transformations from example documents. In M.H. Hamza, editor, *Artificial Intelligence and Applications Proceedings (AIA 2004)*, pages 252–257, 2004.

[16] Philip Summers. A methadology for LISP program construction from examples. *Journal of the ACM (JACM)*, 24(1):161–175, 1977.

[17] Malcolm Wallace and Colin Runciman. Recursion, lambda abstractions and genetic programming. In *Genetic Programming 1998: Proceedings of the Third Annual Conference*, pages 422–431, 1998.

[18] Fritz Wysotzki and Ute Schmid. Synthesis of recursive programs from finite examples by detection of macro-functions. *Forschungsberichte des Fachbereichs Informatik der TU Berlin Nr. 2001-2*, (2).

Chapter 4

A Purely Functional Implementation of ROBDDs in Haskell

Jan Christiansen[1], Frank Huch[1]

Abstract: This paper presents an implementation of the ROBDD data structure in Haskell. It shows that lazy evaluation can be used to improve the performance of some ROBDD algorithms. While standard implementations construct the whole structure no matter which parts are demanded we use lazy evaluation to provide a more demand-driven construction. To achieve this behavior we relax a property that guarantees that ROBDDs contain no redundant nodes. All measurements show that relaxing causes only a small number of additional nodes. Furthermore we present an equality check implementation that performs well although it does not make use of canonicity, which is lost because of the relaxing. The equality check implementation benefits highly from laziness.

4.1 INTRODUCTION

A Reduced Ordered Binary Decision Diagram (ROBDD) is a data structure to represent boolean expressions. It is a compact representation that provides efficient operations for its manipulation. All BDD Package implementations, i.e., the ROBDD data structure with a couple of operations that are used in practice are written in C or C++. This paper presents the implementation of a BDD Package in Haskell.

We investigate the use of lazy evaluation to save unnecessary computations. This idea was already mentioned by Bryant who introduced ROBDDs [5]: "One possibility would be apply the idea of 'lazy' or 'delayed' evaluation to OBDD-based manipulation. That is, rather than eagerly creating a full representation of

---

[1] Institute of Computer Science, Christian Albrechts University Kiel, Germany;
E-mail: `jac@informatik.uni-kiel.de,fhu@informatik.uni-kiel.de`

every function during a sequence of operations, the program would attempt to construct only as much of the OBDDs as is required to derive the final information desired." Even the idea of using Haskell was brought up by Launchbury et al. [6]: "An even more interesting question may be whether there's some way to play off of Haskell's strengths and take advantage of laziness." These two citations document the relevance behind the idea of this paper. To the best of our knowledge, despite these citations there is no approach to an implementation of a BDD Package that explicitly takes advantage of laziness.

The less memory is used by an ROBDD the larger ROBDDs can be handled. If some of the ROBDD parts are not needed at all we do not have to construct them. The implementation of this idea in a strict language would be very hard. In Haskell we get this feature for free. Even though we do not beat an up-to-date C implementation we show that the idea of lazy evaluation can be applied to the area of ROBDD manipulation. The insights presented in this paper can potentially be taken back to strict languages to improve standard implementations.

4.2 ROBDDS

Lee introduced a data structure called Binary Decision Diagram (BDD) [11] which was popularized by Akers [1]. A BDD is a directed acyclic graph (DAG) which consists of two types of nodes. There are leaves labeled 0 and 1 representing the boolean values *false* and *true* and there are variable nodes. These nodes are labeled with boolean variables. A variable node has two successors, its low and high successor. The BDD that is rooted at the low successor represents the boolean expression that is yielded by substituting *false* for the variable. The high successor represents the boolean expression that is yielded by substituting *true*. A BDD with a fixed variable order, i.e., the variables on all paths from the root node to a leaf occur in the same order is called Ordered BDD (OBDD). Figure 4.1 a) shows an OBDD for the expression $(x_1 \land x_2) \lor (x_1 \land x_3) \lor (x_2 \land x_3)$ and the variable order $x_1 < x_2 < x_3$. This OBDD is the OBDD of worst case size for this expression.

In the worst case OBDDs have exponential size with respect to the number of variables. There are various OBDDs of different sizes that represent the same boolean function. Bryant introduced two properties for OBDDs and called OBDDs that satisfy these properties Reduced OBDDs (ROBDDs) [4].

An OBDD can contain two nodes with the same variable, low and high successor. For example, the two centre nodes labeled x_3 in figure 4.1 a) are equal in this respect. If we redirect all edges that point to one of these nodes to the other one the resulting OBDD still represents the same function. Figure 4.2 a) illustrates this transformation. If no node of an OBDD can be simplified in this way the OBDD satisfies the *sharing* property.

An OBDD can contain nodes whose low and high edge point to the same node. In figure 4.1 a) both edges of the outermost nodes labeled x_3 point to the same node, namely the *zero* and *one* leaf respectively. The value of the whole boolean expression is independent of the value of this variable. If we redirect all edges that point to such a node to its successor the resulting OBDD still represents the same

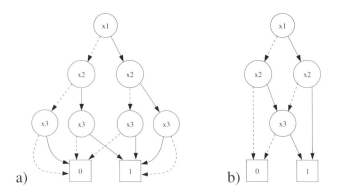

FIGURE 4.1. **An OBDD a) and an ROBDD b) for** $(x_1 \wedge x_2) \vee (x_1 \wedge x_3) \vee (x_2 \wedge x_3)$

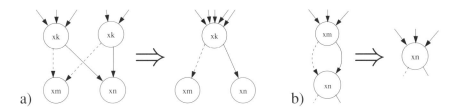

FIGURE 4.2. **Sharing Property a) and No-Redundancy Property b)**

function. Figure 4.2 b) illustrates this transformation. If no node of an OBDD can be simplified in this way the OBDD satisfies the *no-redundancy* property.

An OBDD that satisfies the *sharing* and the *no-redundancy* property is called ROBDD. For a boolean function f and a fixed variable order the ROBDD is the OBDD of minimal size of all OBDDs that represent f. The operation that takes an OBDD and yields the corresponding ROBDD is called *reduction*. Figure 4.1 b) shows an ROBDD for the boolean expression $(x_1 \wedge x_2) \vee (x_1 \wedge x_3) \vee (x_2 \wedge x_3)$. While the worst case OBDD for this expression has nine nodes the ROBDD has only six.

Bryant proved [4] that ROBDDs are canonical with respect to a variable order. That is, for a fixed variable order every boolean function is represented by exactly one ROBDD. All boolean expressions that are not satisfiable, i.e., the constant function *false* are represented by the same ROBDD namely the single *0* leaf. Similarly, all tautologies are represented by the same ROBDD namely the *1* leaf. Therefore, the satisfiability and the tautology check for ROBDDs are in $O(1)$. For a canonical representation the equality check is very simple because two ROBDDs are equal if and only if they are isomorphic. That is, they are structurally equal and the nodes are labeled with the same variable numbers.

Bryant presented operations for the efficient manipulation of ROBDDs. These operations have worst case behaviors that are linear in the number of nodes of the

ROBDD they are applied to. The operations are defined on the DAG that is formed
by an ROBDD.

4.3 ROBDD IMPLEMENTATION IN HASKELL

4.3.1 ROBDD Data Structure

The idea behind the implementation of the ROBDD data structure in Haskell is
to represent a directed acyclic graph by a tree with shared sub-trees. This sharing
is provided by Haskell and is used by the lazy evaluation mechanism to prevent
multiple evaluations of the same expression. We refer to this sharing as the implicit sharing because we have no access to information whether two terms are
shared. Later we additionally use explicit sharing.

The algebraic data type that implements the tree is called OBDD. There is one
constructor for the nodes that takes a variable of type Var and a nullary constructor for each leaf.

```
data OBDD = OBDD OBDD Var OBDD
          | Zero
          | One
```

To check whether a node is redundant we have to check whether the two
successors of the node are equal. The OBDD data structure represents a directed
acyclic graph by using implicit sharing. Therefore if the successors of a node are
equal they are implicitly shared. Haskell provides no mechanism to check pointer
equality of two terms, i.e., to check whether the two successors are shared. A comparison of whole sub-OBDDs would be inefficient. Thus we need explicit sharing
in addition to the implicit sharing to provide an efficient redundancy check.

We associate every node of an ROBDD with a unique identifier. These identifiers are integer values and we call them NodeIds. The NodeId of a node
uniquely determines the structure of a sub-ROBDD within an ROBDD. That is,
the root nodes of two sub-OBDDs have equal NodeIds if and only if these sub-
OBDDs are structurally equal. This is a standard way of making sharing explicit.
To check whether a node is redundant the NodeIds of the two successors of a
node are compared. If they are equal the node is redundant.

```
data OBDD = OBDD OBDD Var OBDD NodeId
          | RefOBDD OBDD Var OBDD NodeId
          | Zero
          | One
```

In this new implementation of OBDDs each node of the OBDD data type is enriched with a NodeId. The constructors for the leaves are not enriched with an
NodeId because they have the static NodeIds 0 and 1 respectively. Additionally
we mark references in the OBDD data structure. A node is a reference if it is shared
and the OBDD contains a node with the same NodeId that was constructed before.
Therefore an OBDD contains exactly one original node, i.e., one OBDD constructor

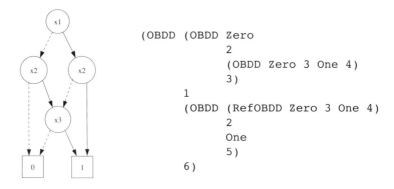

```
(OBDD (OBDD Zero
            2
            (OBDD Zero 3 One 4)
            3)
      1
      (OBDD (RefOBDD Zero 3 One 4)
            2
            One
            5)
      6)
```

FIGURE 4.3.   ROBDD and OBDD for the expression $(x_1 \wedge x_2) \vee (x_1 \wedge x_3) \vee (x_2 \wedge x_3)$

for every NodeId. All other nodes with the same NodeId are RefOBDD constructors. The original node is always the leftmost node of all nodes with the same NodeId in an OBDD. This decision is arbitrary but it has to be considered in the implementations of consumer functions.

All leaves are represented by the constructors Zero and One no matter whether they are a reference or not. Haskell shares constants, i.e., all Zero leaves are represented by the same piece of memory, which is the memory of one unary constructor. The same holds for all One leaves. We refer to a RefOBDD constructor as a reference node and to an OBDD constructor as an original node. The next section shows how the information whether a node is a reference can be used to save look-ups in the *reverse map* and improve the laziness of the construction. Figure 4.3 shows an ROBDD and the OBDD data structure for this ROBDD.

To preserve the *sharing* property we use a map that contains all constructed nodes. It maps triples consisting of the NodeIds of low and high successor and the variable number to the NodeId of the node. Because of the *sharing* property an ROBDD contains no two nodes with the same triple but different NodeIds. When a node is constructed it is looked up in this map. If the look-up is successful the new node is numbered with the yielded NodeId. This way two nodes with the same low and high successor and variable number get the same NodeId. Because the construction works bottom-up it preserves the *sharing* property. We do not only store NodeIds in this map but whole sub-OBDDs. That way equal sub-OBDDs are implicitly shared. Since this map is the reverse mapping of the structure of the ROBDD we refer to it as the *reverse map*.

```
data ROBDD = ROBDD OBDD RevMap
```

The ROBDD data type combines the OBDD and the *reverse map* which is implemented by the type RevMap. The RevMap data type provides the self-explanatory functions emptyRevMap, lookupRevMap and insertRevMap. Additionally it provides the function nextId which yields the smallest free NodeId. We use height-balanced search trees for the implementation of the RevMap.

4.3.2   Constructing an ROBDD

An ROBDD can be constructed by the use of the *Shannon Expansion*. The expression $t[x \mapsto 0]$ denotes the substitution of all occurrences of x in t by 0, i.e., *false*. The *Shannon Expansion* states that an expression can be decomposed by a case distinction of the truth value of one variable (x).

$$t \equiv (\neg x \wedge t[x \mapsto 0]) \vee (x \wedge t[x \mapsto 1])$$

By iterated use of this statement we can generate an ROBDD for every boolean expression. We have to use the *Shannon Expansion* once for every variable in the expression. The variables are substituted in the order that is provided by the ordering of the variables. The function `build` implements this procedure. We assume that the variable numbers are positive.

```
build :: BExp → ROBDD
build bexp = build' 1 bexp emptyRevMap


build' :: Var → BExp → RevMap → ROBDD
build' _ BFalse revmap = ROBDD Zero revmap

build' _ BTrue revmap  = ROBDD One revmap

build' i bexp revmap =
  let lowExp  = substitute bexp i BFalse
      highExp = substitute bexp i BTrue
      i' = succ i
      ROBDD low lowRevmap   = build' i' lowExp revmap
      ROBDD high highRevmap = build' i' highExp lowRevmap
  in
  rOBDD low i high highRevmap
```

The type `BExp` implements boolean expressions with variables and provides a `substitute` function. The ROBDDs for the expressions `BFalse` and `BTrue` are the single `Zero` and `One` leaf respectively. The ROBDD for an expression is a node labeled with the smallest variable that was not substituted. The low and high successor of this node are the ROBDDs where this variable is substituted by `BFalse` and `BTrue` respectively. The function `rOBDD` is a smart constructor for the ROBDD data structure. It takes a variable number, low and high successor, and the *reverse map* and yields the resulting ROBDD.

```
rOBDD :: OBDD → Var → OBDD → RevMap → ROBDD
rOBDD low var high revmap
  | getId low==getId high = ROBDD low revmap
  | otherwise =
    case lookupRevMap low var high revmap of
        Just obdd →  ROBDD obdd revmap
        Nothing   →  rOBDD2 low var high revmap
```

First it checks whether the node is redundant. This is the case if the `NodeIds` of the successors are equal. In this case the unchanged *reverse map* and the low

```
type Binding = [(Var,Bool)]
apply :: (Bool → Bool → Bool) → ROBDD → ROBDD → ROBDD
restrict :: ROBDD → Var → Bool → ROBDD
anySat :: ROBDD → Maybe Binding
allSat :: ROBDD → [Binding]
evaluate :: Binding → ROBDD → Bool
(==) :: ROBDD → ROBDD → Bool
```

TABLE 4.1.   Interface of a simple ROBDD implementation

successor are yielded. If the NodeIds are not equal we look up whether a node with these successors and variable number already exists. If the look-up succeeds an ROBDD is yielded that contains the shared OBDD and the *reverse map*. If the look-up fails the function rOBDD2 is applied.

```
rOBDD2 :: OBDD → Var → OBDD → RevMap → ROBDD
rOBDD2 low var high revmap =
  let obdd = OBDD low var high (nextId revmap)
  in
  ROBDD obdd (insertRevMap low var high (toRef obdd) revmap)
```

The function rOBDD2 constructs an OBDD with a new root node and inserts this OBDD into the *reverse map*. The function nextId yields the next free NodeId and increases the corresponding counter in the *reverse map*. All OBDDs in the *reverse map* are reference nodes. Therefore we apply the function toRef to the OBDD which replaces the outermost OBDD constructor by a RefOBDD constructor.

The ROBDD for a boolean expression can also be constructed by the use of the operation apply. The operation apply combines two ROBDDs with a boolean operator. The ROBDD for a boolean expression can be constructed by replacing all boolean operators in the expression by appropriate applications of apply. The negations in the expression are replaced by applications of apply with the boolean operator *xor* and the ROBDD for the boolean constant *true*. The ROBDDs for the constants *true* and *false* and single variables are simple to construct. This construction is more efficient than the one using build. We do not present the implementation of the function apply here. We want to focus on the laziness of the approach, for which the implementation of this function is not relevant.

Table 4.1 shows the functions of a simple BDD Package. We have implemented all these operations for the ROBDD data structure that is presented here. A Binding is an association list of variable numbers and boolean values. The operation restrict is equivalent to a substitution of a variable by *true* or *false* in the boolean expression. The consumer function allSat yields all satisfying bindings for an ROBDD while anySat yields only one binding. The operation evaluate takes a variable binding and an ROBDD and yields the boolean value that results from substituting all variables by *true* or *false* according to the given binding. Additionally, there is an equality check for ROBDDs.

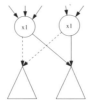

FIGURE 4.4.   Situation before a node is shared

4.4 LAZINESS

To check the laziness of this ROBDD implementation we observe which parts of
the OBDD are evaluated when applying the function anySat. This function is a
good check because it visits only a small number of nodes of the ROBDD. The
operation anySat yields one satisfying Binding for an ROBDD. It uses a depth
first traversal from left to right to find a *one* leaf.

Figure 4.4 illustrates the situation in which a node can be shared. Low and
high edge of the right node point to the same sub-ROBDDs as low and high edge
of the left node. In the OBDD data structure the successors of the right node are
reference nodes. If one of the two successors of the right node were not a reference
the node itself could not be a reference. That is, if at least one successor of a node
is not a reference the node is not a reference, too.

```
anySat :: ROBDD → Maybe Binding
anySat (ROBDD obdd _) = anySat' obdd
 where
  anySat' Zero = Nothing

  anySat' One  = Just []

  anySat' (OBDD low var high _) =
    case (anySat' low, anySat' high) of
         (Just path, _)  → Just ((var,False):path)
         (_, Just path)  → Just ((var,True):path)
```

The function anySat visits all nodes on the path to the leftmost *one* leaf and
left of it. The ROBDD is constructed from left to right and bottom up. The
predecessor of the leftmost *one* leaf cannot be shared because the *reverse map*
does not contain a node whose successor is a *one* leaf. Otherwise there would be
a *one* leaf that is left of the leftmost *one* leaf. All predecessors of this node are no
references because one of their successors is no reference. Therefore all nodes on
the path to the leftmost *one* leaf are original nodes. That is, anySat does not visit
a reference node at all. No rule for the RefOBDD constructor is needed.

4.4.1 Full No-Redundancy

We apply `anySat` to the ROBDD for the expression $(x_1 \wedge x_2) \vee (x_1 \wedge x_3) \vee (x_2 \wedge x_3)$ as shown in figure 4.1. This application yields the binding `[(1,False),` `(2,True), (3,True)]`. To detect which parts of a data structure are evaluated we use the Hood observer [9]. This tool illustrates which parts of a data structure are evaluated in a run of a program. After the run Hood prints the data structures that were observed indicating unevaluated parts by underscores. Figure 4.5 shows two observations made by the Hood observer.

The left observation in figure 4.5 results from observing the OBDD data structure when applying `anySat` to the corresponding ROBDD. The right observation shows the same application for an OBDD that fulfills neither the *sharing* nor the *no-redundancy* property. Without the two properties only the path to the leftmost

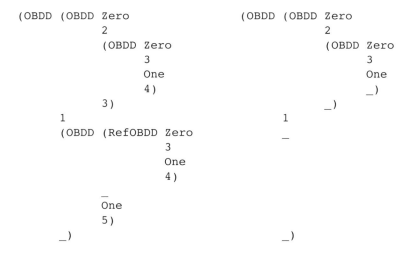

FIGURE 4.5. Observations when applying `anySat`

`One` leaf and all parts left of it are evaluated. With the properties almost the whole OBDD structure is evaluated. Although `anySat` does not pattern match against the `NodeIds` all identifiers except for the one of the root node are evaluated.

To check whether a node is redundant we compare the `NodeIds` of the two successors of a node when it is constructed. To determine the `NodeIds` of the successors we have to check whether the successor nodes are redundant. That is, we have to compare the `NodeIds` of their successors and so on. This results in the complete evaluation of the OBDD data structure if it is evaluated to head normal form. This is not surprising because the `NodeIds` determine the structure of the OBDD and we compare the `NodeIds` of the successors of the root node. That is, in fact we compare the structure of the successors of the root node.

Every check for equality of two OBDDs will cause the evaluation of at least the outermost constructors of the two OBDDs. That is, if we make any kind of redundancy check for every node the whole OBDD structure is evaluated if we evaluate it to head normal form. To gain any laziness in the construction of an ROBDD at all we relax the *no-redundancy* property. That is, we check whether a node is redundant for some nodes of an ROBDD but not for all.

4.4.2   Relaxed No-Redundancy

Even without *no-redundancy* property, i.e., if we do not perform any redundancy check the construction is completely strict. We have to check whether a node already exists by a look-up in the *reverse map*. This causes the evaluation of the NodeIds of both successors of a node. Therefore if all nodes are looked up in the *reverse map* the whole structure is evaluated just like it is the case with *no-redundancy* property.

As we have stated before a node can only be a reference if both its successors are references. We use this insight to save look-ups in the *reverse map* and gain laziness in the construction. We replace the old rOBDD implementation by a new one given below.

We only look up nodes whose successors are both references. The look-up of a node in the *reverse map* causes the evaluation of the NodeIds of the two successors. Thus we check whether a node is redundant for nodes that are looked up in the *reverse map*. The NodeIds of the successors of these nodes are evaluated by the look-up anyway.

```
rOBDD :: OBDD → Var → OBDD → RevMap → ROBDD
rOBDD Zero _ Zero revmap = ROBDD Zero revmap

rOBDD One _ One revmap = ROBDD One revmap

rOBDD low var high revmap
  | isRef low && isRef high =
    if getId low==getId high
       then ROBDD low revmap
       else
         case lookupRevMap low var high revmap of
           Just obdd → ROBDD obdd revmap
           Nothing   → rOBDD2 low var high revmap
  | otherwise = rOBDD2 low var high revmap
```

We keep the *no-redundancy* property for leaves. That is, there are no redundant nodes whose successor is a leaf. Therefore all tautologies are still represented by the single *one* leaf and all unsatisfiable expressions by the single *zero* leaf. That way the complexity of the satisfiability and the tautology check are still in $O(1)$.

In the following we will use the term relaxed OBDD (rOBDD) for an ROBDD with relaxed *no-redundancy* property. The term ROBDD will henceforth denote an ROBDD with full *no-redundancy* property as before.

We construct an rOBDD for the expression $(x_1 \wedge x_2) \vee (x_1 \wedge x_3) \vee (x_2 \wedge x_3)$ and check whether there is a satisfying binding for this rOBDD. We observe the OBDD data structure when applying `anySat` to the rOBDD. This results in the same observation as is shown on the right-hand side of figure 4.5. The left part shows the observation of an ROBDD.

The whole high successor of the root node is evaluated in the ROBDD while it is not in the rOBDD. In the example with relaxed *no-redundancy* no evaluated node is looked up in the *reverse map*. All evaluated nodes are known not to be reference nodes because their low successors are original nodes. The application of `anySat` to an rOBDD causes the evaluation of the same parts as an application to an OBDD.

An rOBDD might have more nodes than the corresponding ROBDD. Besides the additional memory that is used by the additional nodes this worsens the runtimes of some operations on an rOBDD in comparison to the same operations on an ROBDD. Furthermore an rOBDD is not canonical anymore. That is, there is more than one rOBDD that represents the same boolean function. By adding a redundant node to an rOBDD we change its structure but it still represents the same boolean function. The equality check for ROBDDs can be implemented by a check for isomorphy. For rOBDDs this is more difficult. Section 4.6 takes a closer look at the implementation of the equality check and measures its performance.

4.5   EXPERIMENTAL RESULTS

Figure 4.6 shows measurements of the construction of rOBDDs and ROBDDs for some boolean expressions and the application of the functions `anySat` and `eval`. The function `eval` is a structural equality check for OBDDs. This function is used to cause the evaluation of the whole OBDD data structure. It is linear in the number of nodes of the ROBDD and uses no additional memory. The measurements that are provided by applications of `eval` are used to check the worst-case performance of the rOBDD implementation in case it cannot benefit from laziness.

We measure the time that is consumed by an application, the allocated heap memory and the number of constructors that are evaluated in the OBDD data structure. For our performance test we use common boolean functions. `Integer 16` is the expression $(x_1 \wedge x_{17}) \vee (x_2 \wedge x_{18}) \vee \cdots \vee (x_{16} \wedge x_{32})$. This expression has a exponentially large ROBDD representation in the case of the canonical variable order. The boolean expression `Integer2` is the same boolean expression with another variable order. In this case the number of nodes of the ROBDD is linear in the number of variables.

The expression `Queens 8` models the eight queens problem. We use a simple coding that uses one boolean variable to indicate whether a square of the chessboard is occupied by a queen or not. The expressions whose names end with the string ".cnf" belong to a library of expressions that is used for measuring SAT solvers called SATLIB [10]. The expression `hole8.cnf` is a formulation of the pigeon hole problem with eight pigeons and nine holes. This expression is unsatisfiable.

For satisfiable boolean expressions, the quotient of evaluated constructors in the ROBDD and the rOBDD ranges between 1531.26 for `Integer 16` and 1.17

Expression	Operation	No-Red.	Time	Memory	Eval. Constr.
Integer 16	anySat	relaxed	0.00	202,064	214
		full	4.36	508,343,316	327689
	eval	relaxed	4.34	512,543,932	327689
		full	4.50	515,689,380	327689
Integer2 1000	anySat	relaxed	1.70	294,052,836	505498
		full	12.78	1,838,362,908	1504498
	eval	relaxed	18.00	1,825,750,612	1504498
		full	12.98	1,837,786,380	1504498
Queens 8	anySat	relaxed	25.28	2,918,337,044	1874446
		full	32.00	3,656,326,616	2214256
	eval	relaxed	32.06	3,630,827,808	2200765
		full	32.06	3,656,438,228	2214256
uf20-02.cnf	anySat	relaxed	0.04	5,287,788	4689
		full	0.54	70,327,860	49518
	eval	relaxed	0.54	71,705,676	50930
		full	0.52	70,337,040	49518
hole8.cnf	anySat	relaxed	20.32	2,628,758,076	1632847
		full	20.14	2,656,013,124	1635756
	eval	relaxed	20.10	2,628,775,708	1632847
		full	20.44	2,656,030,756	1635756

FIGURE 4.6.   Measurements for the construction of rOBDDs and ROBDDs

for Queens 8. The number of evaluated constructors is less for rOBDDs than for the ROBDD for all satisfiable expressions we have measured. The same holds for the time and memory consumption of the construction together with an application of anySat.

Because our implementation is purely functional we get an additional logarithmic term in the complexities of all operations of the BDD Package. This is caused by look-ups and inserts in the *reverse* and the *memo map*. The *memo map* is used by the operation to memoize partial results.

The number of evaluated constructors highly depends on the structure of the ROBDD. For an unsatisfiable expression the number of evaluated constructors is naturally the same for an ROBDD as for an rOBDD except for the additional redundant nodes.

All measurements show that the number of redundant nodes of rOBDDs is small. In the measurements in figure 4.6 only the example uf20-02.cnf causes the evaluation of more constructors in the rOBDD than of the ROBDD. In the examples Queens 8 and hole8.cnf the number of evaluated constructors of the rOBDD is even smaller than for the ROBDD. This is due to a feature called *don't cares*. If the boolean operator ∧ is applied to the *zero* leaf and an arbitrary ROBDD the result is a *zero* leaf independent of the second argument. Therefore we do not have to traverse the second argument. In a lazy language like Haskell we even do not have to evaluate the second argument. The implementation with

Fst Argument	Snd Argument	Check	Time	Memory
Queens 7	uf20/uf20-02.cnf	Eq1	8.76	1,072,678,276
		Eq2	6.52	805,236,876
		Eq3	8.36	1,074,401,436
Integer 16	Integer2 1000	Eq1	23.52	2,960,983,720
		Eq2	1.38	348,603,336
		Eq3	17.86	2,528,539,232
uf20-02.cnf	uf20-02.cnf	Eq1	1.14	155,922,460
		Eq2	1.12	155,722,408
		Eq3	1.02	152,363,716
Queens 7	Queens 7	Eq1	16.24	1,989,433,408
		Eq2	16.22	1,986,515,412
		Eq3	15.56	1,996,502,316

FIGURE 4.7.   Measurements of the Equality Check

full *no-redundancy* causes even the evaluation of these ROBDDs because of the redundancy checks.

4.6   EQUALITY CHECK

The equality check of rOBDDs can be implemented by a reduction with the full *no-redundancy* property and the standard equality check for ROBDDs on the results. The runtime of this implementation will be worse than the runtime of the equality check for ROBDDs. Furthermore this implementation is completely strict. That is, even if the compared rOBDDs are not equal both rOBDDs are completely evaluated by the equality check.

We implement the equality check of rOBDDs by an application of the boolean operator $\Leftrightarrow$ and a check whether the result is the *one* leaf. This implementation has a quadratic worst case complexity in a strict language. If the compared rOB-DDs are equal the complexity of this equality check is linear in the size of the rOBDD. In all other cases the operation benefits from laziness. To check whether the result of the application of $\Leftrightarrow$ is the *one* leaf it is evaluated to head normal form. This causes the evaluation of only parts of the rOBDD.

Figure 4.7 shows some measurements of equality checks. The first two columns state the arguments of the equality check. The third column states which equality check is used. $Eq1$ and $Eq2$ are equality checks of rOBDDs while $Eq3$ are checks of ROBDDs. $Eq1$ uses a reduction with full *no-redundancy* and an iso-morphy check while $Eq2$ uses `apply`.

The equality check that uses the isomorphy check of rOBDDs is always worse than the one of ROBDDs. This is caused by the additional reduction. The measurements for the lazy implementation that uses `apply` ($Eq2$) are almost as good as the equality check of the ROBDDs which is linear in its size ($Eq3$). If two unequal rOBDDs are checked this equality check performs even better than the equality check of ROBDDs, because of the laziness of this implementation.

4.7   RELATED WORK

There is only one available ROBDD implementation in Haskell [3]. This was
done by Jeremy Bradley in 1997. It uses a BDD table structure described in
[2]. This structure is intended for a simple imperative implementation. The table
structure is implemented by a list of tuples where one entry is the NodeId of a
node and the other one is the triple consisting of the NodeIds of the low and high
successor and the variable number. Furthermore the implementation does not try
to take advantage of laziness. Like stated on their page this implementation is an
alpha version and not very efficient. We compare the purely functional rOBDD
implementation with this implementation. Figure 4.8 shows the results.

Expression	Operation	Implementation	Time	Memory
Queens 4	anySat	rOBDD	0.04	6,397,652
		Bradley	4.04	816,380,772
	eval	rOBDD	0.06	7,957,572
		Bradley	4.02	816,382,228
Integer 11	anySat	rOBDD	0.00	138,392
		Bradley	33.72	4,784,688,228
	eval	rOBDD	0.08	13,717,360
		Bradley	34.04	4,789,579,276
uf20-02.cnf	anySat	rOBDD	0.04	5,100,168
		Bradley	93.12	17,784,793,116
	eval	rOBDD	0.52	69,648,632
		Bradley	93.10	17,784,817,912

FIGURE 4.8.   Comparison with the Bradley implementation

The Bradley implementation cannot compete with the implementation presented here. This implementation is far better no matter if we use relaxed or full
no-redundancy. The differences in runtime and memory usage are due to the implementations of the ROBDD data structure. We use maps that support look-up
and insert operations that are logarithmic with respect to time. The Bradley implementation uses a list whose operations are linear in the number of elements.
    There are two implementations of interfaces to BDD packages using the for-
eign function interface of the GHC. The first was presented in 1999 by Day,
Launchbury and Lewis [6]. We use an interface for the construction of boolean
expressions which is very similar to the one presented in that work. They use this
interface to bind the CMU Long BDD Package [12] to Haskell. This is a state of
the art BDD Package that is written in C. Their interface is referentially transparent which allows the user to ignore the details of the imperative implementation.
    The other binding of a BDD Package is HBDD [8]. This is a Haskell interface
that can be used with the CMU Long BDD Package, too. HBDD is used in MCK
[7] a model checker for the logic of knowledge written in Haskell. We compare
our implementation with the HBDD binding. This binding is more up to date.

This way we compare our implementation with the most efficient ROBDD manipulation that can be done in Haskell. Now we use an optimizing compiler flag in this measurement. Therefore the performance of the rOBDD implementation is better than in previous measurements.

Expression	Operation	Implementation	Time	Memory
Queens 8	anySat	rOBDD	8.14	1,413,390,596
		HBDD	1,04	1,476,988
	eval	rOBDD	10.36	1,754,746,240
		HBDD	1,04	1,377,600
Integer 19	anySat	rOBDD	0.00	166,972
		HBDD	0,00	69,916
	eval	rOBDD	10.54	2,223,653,380
		HBDD	0,00	58,256
Integer2 1800	anySat	rOBDD	2.92	587,783,116
		HBDD	0,04	6,103,648
	eval	rOBDD	21.82	3,138,158,752
		HBDD	0,04	4,080,732

FIGURE 4.9.   Comparison with the HBDD implementation

It is not completely clear at this moment whether the memory that is allocated by the C program is reflected in the values of the profiling. The HBDD implementation consumes less time and memory than the implementation presented here in all measurements. On the one hand this is due to the C implementation using lots of refinements. A major one is the variable reordering. The best example for the use of variable reordering is the `Integer` expression. This expression is of exponential size with the canonical variable order that is used by the rOBDD implementation. The best order causes `Integer` to be linear in the number of variables like `Integer2` which uses this optimal variable order. On the other hand C is more efficient than Haskell and uses hash tables for constant access which is not possible in a pure functional implementation.

To the best of our knowledge there is only one implementation in a strict functional language available. This implementation is in OCaml and it is extracted from an implementation in Coq [13]. Because of the extraction it is very difficult to compare it on the level of implementation. A performance comparison with this implementation is planed for future work.

4.8   CONCLUSION

This paper demonstrates that even a complex data structure like ROBDDs can benefit from laziness. We improve the performance of the operations on ROBDDs with respect to time and memory consumption. The *no-redundancy* property of ROBDDs causes the evaluation of the whole ROBDD when we apply an operation to it. Relaxing the *no-redundancy* property is an adequate answer to this problem. Experiments show that the disadvantages of relaxing are small or even non-existent. The number of redundant nodes is very small for all examples we have measured. More or less all operations benefit from laziness. Relaxing the *no-redundancy* property is an elementary modification of the ROBDD data structure. This is in fact a variation of the data structure and not an implementation detail.

One disadvantage of the implementation presented here is that it does not use one *reverse map* for all ROBDDs. This is an extension that was proposed shortly after the publication of the ROBDD data structure. We use a new *reverse map* every time a new ROBDD is constructed, i.e., for every application of `apply`. If we use one *reverse map* the number of nodes is reduced because sub-ROBDDs are shared across ROBDDs. Additionally the performance of the construction is improved. The `apply` operation memoizes the application of a boolean operator to a pair of sub-ROBDDs. With one *reverse map* all applications of `apply` with a specific boolean operator can share one memoization map. This increases the chance that an application of `apply` can be performed by a look-up.

The use of one *reverse map* requires passing the *reverse map* from one application of `apply` to another. Every application would perform look-ups in the *reverse map*. First tests showed that this extension does not cooperate with laziness. That is, we lose laziness in the construction if we use it. One look-up in the *reverse map* would cause the evaluation of all `NodeId`s of the nodes that were constructed so far.

Apart from the advantages in the semantics it is very hard to benefit from laziness if this should exceed the standard examples like infinite data structures. We have experienced that it is very easy to destroy the laziness of an algorithm. Furthermore it is very difficult to locate the origin of strictness because of the complexity of lazy evaluation. It's unlikely that an algorithm is implemented without bothering about laziness and benefits from it as a side effect. There are no tools that explicitly support the design of lazy algorithms.

We hope that this paper is the starting point for further research on the benefits and disadvantages of lazy evaluation for the efficiency of algorithms. Still today eight years after the definition of the Haskell 98 Standard this issue is highly up to date. Most data structures are not analysed with respect to the use of laziness to improve their performance.

REFERENCES

[1] S.B. Akers. Binary Decision Diagrams. *IEEE Transactions on Computers*, C-27(6):509–516, June 1978.

[2] Henrik Reif Andersen. An introduction to binary decision diagrams. http://www.itu.dk/people/hra/bdd97-abstract.html, 1997.

[3] Jeremy Bradley. Binary decision diagrams - A functional implementation. http://www.cs.bris.ac.uk/~bradley/publish/bdd/, 1997.

[4] Randal E. Bryant. Graph-based algorithms for boolean function manipulation. *IEEE Trans. Comput.*, 35(8):677–691, 1986.

[5] Randal E. Bryant. Symbolic boolean manipulation with ordered binary-decision diagrams. *ACM Comput. Surv.*, 24(3):293–318, 1992.

[6] Nancy A. Day, John Launchbury, and Jeff Lewis. Logical abstractions in Haskell. In *Proceedings of the 1999 Haskell Workshop*. Utrecht University Department of Computer Science, Technical Report UU-CS-1999-28, October 1999.

[7] P. Gammie and R. van der Meyden. MCK: Model checking the logic of knowledge. In *Proceedings of the 16th International conference on Computer Aided Verification, CAV*, pages 479–483, 2004.

[8] Peter Gammie. A Haskell binding to Long's BDD library. http://www.cse.unsw.edu.au/~mck/.

[9] A. Gill. Debugging Haskell by Observing Intermediate Data Structures. In *Proceedings of the 2000 Haskell Workshop*, 2000.

[10] Holger H. Hoos and Thomas Stützle. SATLIB: An online resource for research on SAT. In *SAT 2000*, pages 283–292. IOS Press, 2000. http://www.satlib.org.

[11] C.Y. Lee. Representation of switching circuits by binary decision diagrams. *Bell System Technical Journal*, 38:985–999, July 1959.

[12] Long. CMU BDD library. http://www.cs.cmu.edu/~modelcheck/bdd.html, 1993.

[13] K. Verma, J. Goubault-Larrecq, S. Prasad, and S. Arun-Kumar. Reflecting BDDs in Coq. *Lecture Notes in Computer Science*, 1961, Jan 2000.

Chapter 5

Efficient Interpretation by Transforming Data Types and Patterns to Functions

Jan Martin Jansen[1], Pieter Koopman[2], Rinus Plasmeijer[2]

Abstract: This paper describes an efficient interpreter for lazy functional languages like Haskell and Clean. The interpreter is based on the elimination of algebraic data types and pattern-based function definitions by mapping them to functions using a new efficient variant of the Church encoding. The transformation is simple and yields concise code. We illustrate the concepts by showing how to map Haskell and Clean programs to the intermediate language **SAPL** (**S**imple **A**pplication **P**rogramming **L**anguage) consisting of pure functions only.

    An interpreter is described for SAPL, based on straightforward graph reduction techniques. This interpreter can be kept small and elegant because function application is the only operation in SAPL. The application of a few easy to realize optimisations turns this interpreter into an efficient one. The resulting performance turns out to be competitive in a comparison with other interpreters like Hugs, Helium, GHCi and Amanda for a large number of benchmarks.

5.1 INTRODUCTION

In this paper we present an implementation technique for lazy functional languages like Haskell [1] and Clean [16] based on the representation of data types by functions. Although it is well known that it is possible to represent algebraic data types as functions by using the Church encoding or variants of it (Berarducci and Bohm ([6] and [7]) and Barendregt [5]), these representations have never

---

[1]Netherlands Defence Academy, Faculty of Military Sciences, Den Helder, the Netherlands; E-mail: `j.m.jansen@forcevision.nl`

[2]Institute for Computing and Information Sciences (ICIS), Radboud University Nijmegen, the Netherlands; E-mail: `{pieter,rinus}@cs.ru.nl`

been used in implementations for efficiency reasons. Therefore, intermediate languages always contain special constructs for data types and pattern matching (see e.g. Peyton Jones [12] and Kluge [10]). In this paper we present a new variant of the Church encoding for algebraic data types. This variant uses named functions and explicit recursion instead of lambda expressions for the conversion. We show how to convert a pattern-based function definition to a single function without patterns using this encoding. The encoding results in a program in the intermediate language SAPL consisting of pure functions only. The encoding we use has important advantages over the Church encoding because it allows for destructor functions with complexity $O(1)$, instead of proportional to the size of the data structure (list, tree, etc.).

In the second half of this paper an interpreter is described that can handle the functions that are the result of this transformation. The interpreter is based on straightforward graph reduction techniques. To optimise the performance of the interpreter two types of function annotations are introduced. The first annotation enables an optimal instantiation of function bodies that are the result of translating pattern-based function definitions, and the second annotation enables the inline execution of certain local function definitions. The annotations can easily be added during the translation of a Haskell or Clean program to SAPL. It is also possible to add them during a static analysis of the translated programs without knowledge of the original data types and pattern definitions.

Summarizing, the contributions of this paper are:

- We introduce a new encoding scheme that transforms algebraic data types to simple function definitions in the intermediate language SAPL. The encoding uses named functions and explicit recursion which simplify the encoding considerably in comparison with known encodings.

- We show how to transform a pattern-based function definition to a single function without patterns using this encoding.

- We describe how an efficient interpreter can be realized for lazy functional programming languages using minimal and elementary effort. The interpreter takes as input the result of the transformation mentioned above. The implementation of the interpreter is considerably shorter than that of byte code based interpreters like Helium, Hugs and GHCi with a better performance. The better performance of the interpreter can be attributed to the simplicity of the intermediate formalism enabling a high-level abstract machine having large atomic actions with minimal interpretation overhead.

The structure of this paper is as follows. In section 5.2 we introduce a new encoding of algebraic data types by functions and we compare this encoding with two existing encodings. In section 5.3 we introduce the intermediate functional programming language **SAPL**. SAPL has, besides integers and their operations, no data types. SAPL is similar to the pure functional kernel of languages like Haskell and Clean. We show how to transform complex pattern-based function definitions to SAPL based on the representation of data types from section 5.2.

In section 5.4 we define an interpreter for this language based on straightforward graph-rewriting techniques. We show how the interpreter can be optimised by using two simple annotations that can be added to SAPL programs. The performance of the optimised interpreter is compared with other implementations in section 5.5. In section 5.6 we give some conclusions and discuss further research possibilities.

5.2   REPRESENTATION OF DATA TYPES BY FUNCTIONS

In the lambda calculus several representations of algebraic data types by functions (or lambda expressions) exist. In this section we introduce a new representation and compare it with the two most important existing representations. We use two examples to demonstrate the differences: the Peano representation of natural numbers with the addition and predecessor operations and lists with the length and tail operations. We use Haskell syntax for all definitions, although some functions cannot be typed.

5.2.1   A New Representation of Data Types by Functions

Consider the following algebraic data type definition in Haskell or Clean:

$$\textit{typename } t_1 \ .. \ t_k \ ::= \ C_1 \ t_{1,1} \ .. \ t_{1,n_1} \ | \ .. \ | \ C_m \ t_{m,1} \ .. \ t_{m,n_m}$$

We map this type definition with m constructors to m functions:

$$C_1 \ v_{1,1} \ .. \ v_{1,n_1} \ = \lambda f_1 \ .. f_m \ \to \ f_1 \ v_{1,1} \ .. \ v_{1,n_1}$$
$$..$$
$$C_m \ v_{m,1} \ .. \ v_{m,n_m} = \lambda f_1 \ .. f_m \ \to \ f_m \ v_{m,1} \ .. \ v_{m,n_m}$$

Each constructor is represented by a function with the same name. Now consider the Haskell (multi-case) function f with as argument an element of this data type:

$$f \ (C_1 \ v_{1,1} \ .. \ v_{1,n_1}) \ \ = body_1$$
$$..$$
$$f \ (C_m \ v_{m,1} \ .. \ v_{m,n_m}) = body_m$$

This function is converted to the following function without patterns:

$$f \ el \ = \ el$$
$$(\lambda \ v_{1,1} \ .. \ v_{1,n_1} \ \to \ body_1)$$
$$..$$
$$(\lambda \ v_{m,1} \ .. \ v_{m,n_m} \ \to \ body_m)$$

The body of each case is turned into a lambda expression that is placed as an argument of the data type element. The actual data type argument will select the correct lambda expression and apply it to the arguments of the constructor. Therefore we call a function corresponding to a constructor a *selector* function. The result of the transformation of recursive functions on recursive data types cannot be typed by Hindley-Milner type inference (see examples in the next section). This is not a problem because the functions can be typed before the transformation.

5.2.2 Examples

The Haskell definitions for the examples are (note that we defined *tail Nil* as *Nil* and *pred Zero* as *Zero* in order to have total functions):

$$
\begin{aligned}
data\ Nat &= Zero \mid Suc\ Nat \\
add\ n\ Zero &= n \\
add\ n\ (Suc\ m) &= Suc\ (add\ n\ m) \\
pred\ Zero &= Zero \\
pred\ (Suc\ n) &= n
\end{aligned}
$$

$$
\begin{aligned}
data\ List\ t &= Nil \mid Cons\ t\ (List\ t) \\
length\ Nil &= 0 \\
length\ (Cons\ x\ xs) &= 1 + length\ xs \\
tail\ Nil &= Nil \\
tail\ (Cons\ x\ xs) &= xs
\end{aligned}
$$

Using the transformation to functions this becomes:

$$
\begin{aligned}
Zero &= \lambda f\ g \rightarrow f \\
Suc\ n &= \lambda f\ g \rightarrow g\ n \\
add\ n\ m &= m\ n\ (\lambda pm \rightarrow Suc\ (add\ n\ pm)) \\
pred\ n &= n\ Zero\ (\lambda pn \rightarrow n)
\end{aligned}
$$

$$
\begin{aligned}
Nil &= \lambda f\ g \rightarrow f \\
Cons\ x\ xs &= \lambda f\ g \rightarrow g\ x\ xs \\
length\ ys &= ys\ 0\ (\lambda x\ xs \rightarrow 1 + length\ xs) \\
tail\ ys &= ys\ Nil\ (\lambda x\ xs \rightarrow xs)
\end{aligned}
$$

pred and *tail* both have complexity $O(1)$. The functions *Zero, Suc, Nil, Cons, pred* and *tail* can be typed, but *add* and *length* cannot be typed using Hindley-Milner type inference. In general, the encoding of recursive functions on recursive data types cannot be typed. The definitions of *add* and *length* are explicitly recursive. In general, to encode recursive functions over recursive data structures, we need explicit recursion. This is not a problem since we use named functions instead of lambda expressions in our encoding. The notation is easy to read and close to the original Haskell data type and function definitions.

5.2.3 Church Encoding

For this encoding we need pairs with the selection functions *fst* and *snd*. They can be represented by functions as follows:

$$
\begin{aligned}
pair\ x\ y &= \lambda f \rightarrow f\ x\ y \\
fst\ p &= p\ (\lambda x\ y \rightarrow x) \\
snd\ p &= p\ (\lambda x\ y \rightarrow y)
\end{aligned}
$$

The Church encoding is a generalization of the Church numerals. The representation described here is based on Berarducci and Bohm [6] and Barendregt [5]. For comparison reasons we use a slightly different notation than is generally used for describing Church numerals:

$$
\begin{aligned}
Zero &= \lambda f\, g\, \to\, f \\
Suc\, n &= \lambda f\, g\, \to\, g\,(nf\, g) \\
add\, n\, m &= m\, n\,(\lambda\, rpm\, \to\, Suc\, rpm) \\
pred\, n &= snd\,(n\,(pair\, Zero\, Zero)\,(\lambda\, p\, \to\, pair\,(Suc\,(fst\, p))\,(fst\, p)))
\end{aligned}
$$

$$
\begin{aligned}
Nil &= \lambda f\, g\, \to\, f \\
Cons\, x\, xs &= \lambda f\, g\, \to\, g\, x\,(xs\, f\, g) \\
length\, ys &= ys\, 0\,(\lambda\, x\, rxs\, \to\, 1 + rxs) \\
tail\, xs &= snd\,(xs\,(pair\, Nil\, Nil) \\
&\qquad (\lambda\, x\, pxs\, \to\, pair\,(Cons\, x\,(fst\, pxs))\,(fst\, pxs)))
\end{aligned}
$$

In the *add* definition *add n (Suc m)* can be defined using the result of *add n m* (represented by *rpm*). The same holds for *length*. But in predecessor *pred (Suc n)* cannot be expressed in terms of *pred n*. Instead we need access to *n* in *Suc n* (we need to destruct *Suc n*). Kleene ([4]) found a way to overcome this by the use of pairs. In such a pair *n* is combined with the result of the recursive call, so access to *n* is also possible. For *tail* we also need this pair construction. Through this construction *pred n* has complexity $O(n)$ and *tail xs* has complexity $O(length\ xs)$. In this encoding the recursion is put into the data structures. Therefore, functions on data structures do not have to be recursive themselves. A disadvantage is that this encoding only works fine for iterative and primitive recursive functions (see [7]). For destructor functions we need the pair construction. In the Church encoding data types and functions acting on them can be typed using Hindley-Milner type inference.

5.2.4   Representation according to Berarducci and Bohm

Another representation is described in Berarducci and Bohm [7] and Barendregt [5]. Again we adapted the notation to make a comparison with the other representations possible.

$$
\begin{aligned}
Zero &= \lambda f\, g\, \to\, f\, f\, g \\
Suc\, n &= \lambda f\, g\, \to\, g\, n\, f\, g \\
add\, n\, m &= m\,(\lambda fz\, fs\, \to\, n)\,(\lambda\, pm\, fz\, fs\, \to\, Suc\,(pm\, fz\, fs)) \\
pred\, n &= n\,(\lambda fz\, fs\, \to\, Zero)\,(\lambda\, pn\, fz\, fs\, \to\, pn)
\end{aligned}
$$

$$
\begin{aligned}
Nil &= \lambda f\, g\, \to\, f\, f\, g \\
Cons\, x\, xs &= \lambda f\, g\, \to\, g\, x\, xs\, f\, g \\
length\, ys &= ys\,(\lambda fn\, fc\, \to\, 0)\,(\lambda\, x\, xs\, fn\, fc\, \to\, 1 + xs\, fn\, fc) \\
tail\, ys &= ys\,(\lambda fn\, fc\, \to\, Nil)\,(\lambda\, x\, xs\, fn\, fc\, \to\, xs)
\end{aligned}
$$

The basic idea in this representation is that the functions handling the different cases are propagated by the functions representing the data structures. Therefore, functions on data structures do not have to be recursive themselves. Here *pred n* and *tail xs* have complexity $O(1)$. In general, destructor functions have complexity $O(1)$, making this representation more powerful than the Church encoding. In this representation *Zero, Suc, Nil*, and *Cons*, as well as the functions acting on them, cannot be typed by Hindley-Milner type inference.

5.2.5   Conclusions

Our representation is more efficient than the Church encoding, because it realizes destructor functions with $O(1)$. Although this also holds for the representation of Berarducci and Bohm, the use of named functions and explicit recursion in our representation result in a simpler representation, which is suitable for an efficient implementation (see section 5.4).

5.3   SAPL: AN INTERMEDIATE FUNCTIONAL LANGUAGE

SAPL is an intermediate language that can be used for the compilation and interpretation of functional programming languages like Haskell and Clean. The main difference between SAPL and the intermediate formalisms normally used is the absence of algebraic data types and constructs for pattern matching in SAPL. This makes SAPL a compact and simple language. In section 5.4 we show that it is possible to make an efficient implementation for SAPL. SAPL is described by the following syntax:

function   ::= *identifier* {*identifier*} * '=' *expr*
expr   ::= *application* | 'λ' {*identifier*} + '→' *expr*
application ::= *factor* {*factor*}*
factor   ::= *identifier* | *integer* | '(' *expr* ')'

A function has a name followed by zero or more variable names. An expression is either an application or a lambda expression. In an expression only variable names, integers and other function names may occur. SAPL function definitions start in the first column and can extend over several lines (as long as these are indented). SAPL is un-typed. The language has the usual lazy rewrite semantics (see section 5.4). For efficiency we added integers and their basic operations to the language. In SAPL it is common that a curried application of a function is the result of a computation. This result will be presented as the application of the function name to the evaluated arguments.

SAPL's main difference with the lambda calculus is the use of explicitly named functions (enabling explicit recursion) which makes SAPL usable as a basic functional programming language and suitable for an efficient implementation.

For the use of SAPL as an intermediate language for implementing lazy functional languages like Haskell and Clean we must translate constructs from these languages to SAPL functions. Constructions like list-comprehensions, *where*-clauses, and *let(rec)*-expressions can be converted to functions with standard techniques as described in [12] and [14]. Algebraic data types and simple pattern-based functions are treated specially using the translation scheme from section 5.2. In the next subsection the transformation of complex pattern-based functions is sketched.

5.3.1   Compiling Complex Pattern Definitions to Functions

In the implementations of Haskell and Clean pattern-based definitions are traditionally compiled to dedicated structures in a special pattern formalism that can be used to generate pattern-matching code (Augustsson [3] and Peyton Jones [12]). Here we transform a pattern-based function definition from Clean or Haskell to a single SAPL function without patterns. This function is capable of handling an actual call for the original pattern-based function. The conversion to a single function can be obtained using techniques similar to those used for the generation of pattern-matching code (see [3] and [12]). We use three examples to illustrate this conversion: *mappair* (*zipWith*), *samelength* and *complex*. Note that the pattern compiler introduces a name for every constructor (e.g. *as* in *mappair*) and uses existing names whenever possible (e.g. *ps* and *qs* in *samelength*).

$$
\begin{aligned}
&mappair\ f\ Nil && zs && = Nil \\
&mappair\ f\ (Cons\ x\ xs)\ Nil && && = Nil \\
&mappair\ f\ (Cons\ x\ xs)\ (Cons\ y\ ys) && && = Cons\ (f\ x\ y)\ (mappair\ f\ xs\ ys)
\end{aligned}
$$

$$
\begin{aligned}
&samelength\ Nil && Nil && = True \\
&samelength\ (Cons\ x\ xs)\ (Cons\ y\ ys) && && = samelength\ xs\ ys \\
&samelength\ ps && qs && = False
\end{aligned}
$$

$$
\begin{aligned}
&complex\ (Cons\ a\ (Cons\ b\ (Cons\ c\ Nil))) && = a + b + c \\
&complex\ (Cons\ a\ (Cons\ b\ Nil)) && = 2 * a + b \\
&complex\ (Cons\ a\ Nil) && = 3 * a \\
&complex\ xs && = 0
\end{aligned}
$$

The translation to SAPL results in:

$$
\begin{aligned}
mappair\ f\ as\ zs\ =\ &as\ Nil\ (\lambda\,x\ xs\ \rightarrow\ zs\ Nil\ (\lambda\,y\ ys\ \rightarrow \\
&\qquad Cons\ (f\ x\ y)\ (mappair\ f\ xs\ ys)))
\end{aligned}
$$

$$
\begin{aligned}
samelength\ ps\ qs\ =\ &ps\ (qs\ True\ (\lambda\,y\ ys\ \rightarrow\ False)) \\
&(\lambda\,x\ xs\ \rightarrow\ qs\ False\ (\lambda\,y\ ys\ \rightarrow samelength\ xs\ ys))
\end{aligned}
$$

$$
\begin{aligned}
complex\ xs\ =\ &xs\ 0\ (\lambda\,a\ p1\ \rightarrow\ p1\ (mult\ 3\ a)\ (\lambda\,b\ p2\ \rightarrow \\
&p2\ \ (add\ (mult\ 2\ a)\ b) \\
&\qquad (\lambda\,c\ p3\ \rightarrow\ p3\ (add\ (add\ a\ b)\ c)\ (\lambda\,p4\ p5\ \rightarrow 0))))
\end{aligned}
$$

5.4   AN INTERPRETER FOR SAPL

The only operations in SAPL programs are function application and a number
of (built-in) integer operations. Therefore an interpreter can be kept small and
elegant. The interpreter is implemented in C and is based on straightforward
graph reduction techniques as described in Peyton Jones [12], Plasmeijer and van
Eekelen [14] and Kluge [10]. We assume that a pre-compiler has eliminated all
algebraic data types and pattern definitions (as described earlier), as well as all
let(rec)-expressions and *where*-clauses, and lifted all lambda expressions to the
global level. The interpreter is only capable of executing function rewriting and
the basic operations on integers. The most important features of the interpreter
are:

- It uses 4 types of memory Cells. A Cell corresponds to a node in the syntax
  tree and is either an: Integer, (Binary) Application, Variable or Function Call.
  To keep memory management simple, all Cells have the same size. A type
  byte in the Cell distinguishes between the different types. Each Cell uses 12
  bytes of memory.

- The memory heap consists only of Cells. The heap has a fixed size, definable
  at start-up. We use a mark and (implicit) sweep garbage collection. Cells are
  not recollected, but the dirty bit is inverted after every mark.

- It uses a single argument stack containing only references to Cells. The C
  (function) stack is used as the dump for keeping intermediate results when
  evaluating strict functions (numeric operations only) and for administration
  overhead during the marking phase of garbage collection.

- The state of the interpreter consists of the stack, the heap, the dump, an array
  of function definitions and a reference to the node to be evaluated next. In
  each state the next step to be taken depends on the type of the current node:
  either an application node or a function node.

- It reduces an expression to head-normal-form. The printing routine causes
  further reduction. This is only necessary for arguments of curried functions.

The interpreter is based on the following 'executable specification' (without integers and their operations):

$$data\ Expr\ =\ App\ Expr\ Expr\ |\ Func\ Int\ Int\ |\ Var\ Int$$

The first *Int* in *Func Int Int* denotes the number of arguments of the function, the
second *Int* the position of the function definition in the list of definitions. The *Int*
in *Var Int* indicates the position on the stack where the argument can be found.

  The interpreter consists of three functions:

$$instantiate\ (App\ l\ r)\ es = App\quad (instantiate\ l\ es)\ (instantiate\ r\ es)$$
$$instantiate\ (Var\ n)\ es\ \ = es\ !!\ n$$

$$instantiate\ x\ es \qquad\quad = x$$

$$rebuild\ e\ [] \qquad\qquad = e$$
$$rebuild\ e\ (x\ :\ xs) \qquad = rebuild(App\ e\ x)\ xs$$

$$eval :: \quad Expr\ \rightarrow\ [Expr]\ \rightarrow\ [Expr]\ \rightarrow\ Expr$$
$$eval \qquad (App\ l\ r)\ es\ fs\ = eval\ l\ (r\ :\ es)\ fs$$
$$eval \qquad (Func\ na\ fn)\ es\ fs$$
$$= \textbf{if} \quad length\ es\ \geq\ na$$
$$\qquad \textbf{then}\ eval\ (instantiate\ (fs\ !!\ fn)\ es)\ (drop\ na\ es)\ fs$$
$$\qquad \textbf{else}\ rebuild\ (Func\ na\ fn)\ es$$

Here *es* represents the stack and *fs* the list of function body definitions. One of the benchmarks in section 5.5 is a SAPL version of the interpreter (including integers and their operations), which is the translation to SAPL of the Haskell version of the interpreter (a meta-circular implementation for SAPL). The C versions (including integers and operations on them) of *eval* and *instantiate* are straightforward implementations of this specification and fit on less than one page.

5.4.1   Optimising the SAPL Interpreter

For data-type-free programs the interpreter from the previous subsection has a performance comparable to Helium, GHCi and Amanda. But for programs involving algebraic data types the performance is worse. The difference depends on the number of alternatives and the complexity of the data type definition and varies from 30% slower for programs involving only if-then-else constructs, to several hundreds of times slower for programs involving complex data types and pattern matching (see section 5.5). This is not surprising because a pattern definition is converted to one large function containing all different cases. Instantiation of such a function is therefore relatively expensive, particularly because only a small part of the body will actually be used in a call for the function.

For optimising the SAPL interpreter we used both general optimisation techniques, commonly used for implementing functional languages, as well as techniques that are more specific for the way SAPL handles data types and pattern definitions.

General Optimisations

We use a more efficient memory representation for function calls with one or two arguments. For these function applications *APP* nodes are removed. This reduces the size of the bodies of functions and consequently copying overhead.

In the interpreter curried function calls are rebuilt. This can be prevented by keeping a reference to the top node of the application. If the number of arguments for a function call can be computed at compile time, the top node of a curried call can be marked. In this way an attempt to reduce a curried call can even be prevented.

Applying these two optimisations results in an average speed-up of 60% (see section 5.5). This speed-up is high since many functions have only 1 or 2 arguments and because SAPL programs contain many curried functions (due to the representation of data types by functions).

Specific Optimisations

We applied two specific optimisations. The first one addresses the instantiation problem for functions that are the result of the translation of pattern-based function definitions. The second one optimises the use of lambda expressions in these functions. Although the speed-up realized by these optimisations is significant, the implementation of them requires only small changes in the interpreter.

Selective Instantiation of Function Bodies   The body of a transformed pattern-based definition consists of the application of a so-called selector function (see section 5.3) to a number of arguments consisting of anonymous local function definitions. The selector function will select one of these local function definitions and apply it to the arguments of the corresponding constructor. All other arguments of the selector function will be ignored. In the *mappair* example below we have tagged the applications of selector functions with the keyword *select*.

$$mappair\ f\ as\ zs\ =$$
$$select\ as\ Nil\ (\lambda\ x\ xs\ =$$
$$select\ zs\ Nil\ (\lambda\ y\ ys\ =\ Cons\ (f\ x\ y)\ (mappair\ f\ xs\ ys)))$$

The interpreter uses the *select* (semantically equivalent to the identity function) tag to optimise the instantiation of the body of *mappair*. Instead of copying the entire body, at first only the selector function part is instantiated (*as*) and depending on the result (*Nil* or *Cons x xs*), the correct remainder is instantiated. This is similar to evaluating the condition of an *if* expression before we decide to build the *then* part or the *else* part (but not both). In fact, in SAPL *True* and *False* are also implemented as selector functions. The optimisation is applied recursively to the bodies of all local definitions.

The optimisation realised in this way is significant. Varying from 30% faster for programs involving only if-then-else constructs, to up to 500 times faster for programs involving complex data type definitions like interpreters etc.

We can add the *select* tag during the transformation of the pattern-based function definition to SAPL, but it is also possible to infer the application of selector functions by a compile time analysis of a SAPL program. Selector functions must be recognized and the propagation of arguments and results of functions that are selector functions must be inferred. In this way this optimisation is a generic one and can even be used for the efficient reduction of lambda expressions.

Inlining of Local Definitions   As a last optimisation we again consider the bodies of transformed pattern-based definitions. They contain local function definitions corresponding to the different cases. Normally these definitions are lambda lifted to the global level. During this lifting extra arguments are added to the function, causing extra stack operations at run-time. These local functions can also be reduced in the context of the reduction of the surrounding function call. This means that the local function is called (reduced) while the arguments of the main function are still on the stack and that at the end all arguments together are cleared from the stack. This can only be done because the reduction to head-normal-form of the local function call is necessary for the reduction to head-normal-form of the original function call, which is indeed the case for these transformed pattern-based functions. This optimisation results in an extra speed-up of about 10 to 25% for programs involving transformed pattern-based functions (see section 5.5). The optimisation is implemented by replacing $\rightarrow$ by $=$ in the local definition as a signal for the interpreter not to lambda lift this local function (see example in 5.4.1).

Again this optimisation can be applied not only for local definitions in translated pattern-based functions, but for all local function calls that must be reduced to head-normal-form while reducing the surrounding function call. But the gain for SAPL programs will be higher than for applying this optimisation for other functional languages, because SAPL programs, due to the translation scheme for pattern-based functions, contain more local function definitions.

5.5   BENCHMARKS

In this section we present the results of several benchmark tests for SAPL and a comparison of SAPL with other implementations. We ran the benchmarks on a 2.66 Ghz Pentium 4 computer with 512Mb of memory under Windows XP. SAPL was implemented using the Microsoft Visual C++ compiler using the -O2 option. The benchmark programs we used for the comparison are:

1. **Prime Sieve** The prime number sieve program, calculating the 5000th prime number.

2. **Symbolic Primes** Symbolic prime number sieve using Peano numbers, calculating the 280th prime number.

3. **Interpreter** An interpreter for SAPL, as described in section 5.4 (including integers). As an example we coded the prime number sieve for this interpreter and calculated the 100th prime number.

4. **Fibonacci** The (naive) Fibonacci function, calculating *fib 35*.

5. **Match** Nested pattern matching (5 levels deep) like the *complex* function from section 5.3.1, repeated 2000000 times.

6. **Hamming** The generation of the list of Hamming numbers (a cyclic definition) and taking the 1000th Hamming number, repeated 4000 times.

7. **Twice** A higher order function (*twice twice twice twice (add 1) 0*), repeated 400 times.

8. **Sorting** Tree Sort (6000 elements), Quick Sort (6000 elements), Merge Sort (40000 elements, merge sort is much faster) and Insertion Sort (6000 elements).

TABLE 5.1. SAPL with/without Selective Instantiation (Time in seconds)

	Pri	Sym	Inter	Fib	Match	Twi	Sort	Qns	Kns	Parse	Plog
With	11.4	6.0	2.2	11.6	14.7	11.0	1.0	10.5	4.0	8.0	0.2
Without	21.5	107.0	53.0	19.2	23.0	10.9	17.8	16.0	6.1	16.0	106.0

9. **Queens** Number of placements of 11 Queens on a 11 * 11 chess board.

10. **Knights** Finding a Knights tour on a 5 * 5 chess board.

11. **Parser Combinators** A parser for Prolog programs based on Parser Combinators parsing a 17000 lines Prolog program.

12. **Prolog** A small Prolog interpreter based on unification only (no arithmetic operations), calculating ancestors in a four-generation family tree, repeated 500 times.

For sorting a list of size n we used a source list consisting of numbers 1 to n. The elements that are 0 modulo 10 are put before those that are 1 modulo 10, etc.

Three of the benchmarks (*Interpreter*, *Prolog* and *Parser Combinators*) are realistic programs, the others are typical benchmark programs that are often used for comparing implementations. They cover a wide range of aspects of functional programming (lists, laziness, deep recursion, higher order functions, cyclic definitions, pattern matching, heavy calculations, heavy memory usage). All times are machine measured. The programs where chosen in such a way that they ran for at least several seconds (interpreters only). Therefore start-up times can be neglected. The output was always converted to a single number (e.g. by summing the elements of a list) to eliminate the influence of slow output routines.

The input for the SAPL interpreter is code generated by an experimental data type and pattern compiler from sources equivalent to the Haskell and Clean programs (only minor syntactic differences). This compiler also generates the annotations needed for the optimisations. The *inline* optimisation is only applied for the lambda expressions that are the result of encoding a pattern- based definition. The benchmarks programs can be found in [17].

5.5.1 Optimisations for SAPL

In table 5.1 we first compare SAPL with and without the selective instantiation optimisation. In this comparison the other optimisation are not applied. *Hamming* is missing because the version of the interpreter without selective instantiation does not support cyclic definitions. We conclude that the selective instantiation optimisation is essential. Because SAPL also uses selective instantiation to optimise the if- then-else construct there is a speed-up for all benchmarks except *twice* (the only benchmarks without if-then-else and data structures). In the other examples the speed-up varies from around 1.5 times (*Primes, Fibonacci, Match, Queens, Knights*), around 20 times (*Symbolic Primes, Interpreter, Sorting*) to more than 500 times for *Prolog* (due to the complicated *unification* function).

Table 5.2 shows the results of applying the other optimisations.

TABLE 5.2.   Comparison Versions of SAPL (Time in seconds)

	Pri	Sym	Inter	Fib	Match	Ham	Twi	Sort	Qns	Kns	Parse	Plog
Full	6.1	17.6	7.8	7.3	8.5	6.4	7.9	5.9	6.5	2.0	4.4	4.7
Select	11.4	37.6	14.3	11.6	14.7	11.3	11.0	9.4	10.6	4.0	8.0	10.4
Mem	6.2	28.0	9.3	7.5	9.0	8.0	7.9	6.4	7.0	2.7	4.9	6.7
Inline	11.4	24.4	12.9	11.5	14.4	9.2	11.0	8.7	10.0	3.3	7.5	7.8

TABLE 5.3.   Different Memory Configurations (Time sec, Heap/Stack kB)

	Pri	Sym	Inter	Fib	Match	Ham	Twi	Sort	Qns	Kns	Parse	Plog
Heap	223	47	2350	12	101	105	785	2350	43	18	9700	150
Stack	270	35	1100	1	1	1	1	200	1	1	200	4
10.8 Mb												
Time	6.7	17.1	13.0	8.0	9.2	6.9	9.1	6.7	7.0	2.1	17.0	5.2
% GC	15	12	46	13	18	14	18	21	17	14	76	17
nr GC	87	204	150	117	157	100	120	83	114	32	190	83
24 Mb												
Time	6.4	17.5	8.8	7.8	9.1	6.7	8.8	6.5	7.0	2.1	6.0	5.1
% GC	13	10	24	13	18	15	15	15	14	14	38	16
nr GC	38	91	61	53	70	45	52	37	51	15	40	37
60 Mb												
Time	6.4	18.6	8.3	7.6	9.1	6.6	8.5	6.5	6.9	2.1	5.0	5.1
% GC	13	10	18	13	16	15	13	16	14	14	24	16
nr GC	15	36	24	28	28	18	21	15	21	6	14	15

- **Full** The fully optimised interpreter (Select, Mem and Inline).

- **Select** The interpreter using only the selective instantiation optimisation.

- **Mem** The interpreter using selective instantiation and the efficient representation of functions with 1 or 2 arguments.

- **Inline** The interpreter using selective instantiation and inlining of lambda expressions in encoded pattern-based functions.

From this comparison we learn that the fully optimised version is about 1.8 times faster than the version using only selective instantiation, 1.2 times faster than the version with selective instantiation and memory optimisation and 1.6 times faster than the version with selective instantiation and inlining. The benefit from the inline optimisation is modest, but the implementation of it in the run-time system consists of only moving a stack pop operation to another line. The more efficient memory representation gives a significant speed-up.

In table 5.3 we compare the behaviour of SAPL for a number of memory configurations: 10.8 Mb (90000 Cells), 24 Mb (2000000 Cells) and 60 Mb (5000000 Cells). 900000 Cells is the minimal heap size needed to run all benchmarks. We also give peak heap and stack usage in Kb and percentage of time spent in GC and number of GC. Because heap and stack usage are only measured at GC the actual maximum values can be (slightly) higher than those measured.   For these

TABLE 5.4.   Run-Times (in seconds) for different Implementations

	Pri	Sym	Inter	Fib	Match	Ham	Twi	Sort	Qns	Kns	Parse	Plog
SAPL	6.1	17.6	7.8	7.3	8.5	6.4	7.9	5.9	6.5	2.0	4.4	4.7
Helium	13,6	17,6	16,3	12,2	17.4	12.8	23.2	10,4	9,7	3.4	8.4	7.1
Amanda	18.0	33.0	-	8.8	17.2	14.0	-	12.5	7.7	2.4	10.9	8.5
GHCi	18.0	19.5	25.0	38.6	35.3	23.5	19.3	13.8	24.0	7.0	8.7	11.9
Hugs	44.0	26.0	-	120.0	66.0	36.0	-	54.0	42.0	13.0	10.4	16.2
GHC	1.8	1.5	8.2	4.0	4,1	3.8	6.6	1.6	3.7	0.9	2.3	1.3
GHC -O	0.9	1.5	1.8	0.2	1.0	1.4	0.1	1.1	0.4	0.2	1.6	0.4
Clean	0.9	0.8	0.6	0.2	0.9	1.4	2.4	0.7	0.4	0.2	4.9	0.6

tests we used a garbage collector with an explicit sweep phase instead of the implicit sweep (during memory allocation). This is done to make it possible to give meaningful figures about time spent in garbage collection. The price to be paid is a small performance penalty ($< 10\%$) and the use of an administration array for the collected free cells.

We conclude that if the peak heap memory stays under 30% of the total heap size execution times do not differ too much. If peak heap usage rises above 50% of total memory, performance drops radically and the amount of time spent in garbage collection grows rapidly. Because SAPL has a fixed heap, the memory management overhead is lower than in implementations with a flexible heap. SAPL uses relatively few GC cycles, because SAPL has a fixed heap and only starts garbage collection if there are less than 1000 free cells left.

The stack usage of SAPL is modest. Note, however, that SAPL also uses the C stack. The maximum amount of C stack for SAPL is 8Mb.

5.5.2   Comparison with other Implementations

In this subsection we compare SAPL with several other interpreters: Amanda V2.03 [9], Helium 1.5 [15], Hugs 20050113 [2] and GHCi V6.4 [1] and with the GHC V6.4 and Clean V2.1 compilers. We used the same amount of (fixed or maximal) heap space (64 Mb) and stack space (8 Mb) for all examples whenever this was possible (for Amanda the stack size cannot be set). For *Interpreter* and *Twice* the Amanda results are missing because of a stack overflow. Hugs also could not run these examples (C stack overflow).

Run-Time Comparison

The run-time results can be found in table 5.4. The results show us that the SAPL interpreter is almost 2 times faster than Amanda and Helium, about 3 times faster than GHCi and between 1.5 and 15 times faster than Hugs.

For the compilers there is more variation in the results due to the different optimisations applied by them. Comparing SAPL with GHC, the average speed-up of GHC is less than 3 times. The speed-ups of GHC -O and Clean vary between 1.1 (*Parser Combinators* in Clean) and 80 (*Twice* in GHC -O).

TABLE 5.5.   Comparison Max Heap (kB) usage (upper) and GC time (%) (lower)

	Pri	Sym	Inter	Fib	Mch	Ham	Twi	Sort	Qns	Kns	Parse	Plog
SAPL	223	47	2344	12	101	107	762	2344	43	17	9700	150
Helium	774	16000	3000	258	774	516	1800	9000	258	256	10700	500
GHC	140	21	1800	6	46	50	800	1600	7	6	7000	50
SAPL	13	10	24	13	18	15	15	15	14	14	38	16
Helium	47	7	45	5	25	25	59	7	12	46	47	17
GHC def	18	1	87	1	22	16	67	5	1	45	70	25
GHC 24M	1	1	23	1	1	1	4	1	1	5	59	1

Comparison of Heap Usage

In table 5.5 we compare the memory usage and the time spent in garbage collection of SAPL (24 Mb heap) with that of Helium (standard heap) and the GHC compiler (standard and 24 Mb initial heap). For Hugs, GHCi and Amanda no meaningful figures about memory usage can be given. We do not include a stack size comparison because SAPL also uses an unknown part of the C stack.

We conclude that GHC and SAPL use roughly the same amount of heap but that Helium uses more heap. The difference between SAPL and GHC can be explained by the fixed Cell size of 12 bytes used by SAPL. The unexpected high value of Helium for *Symbolic Primes* is probably a memory leak.

The amount of time spent in garbage collection of SAPL is mostly slightly lower than that of Helium and lower than that of GHC (default heap) for memory intensive programs like *Interpreter* and *Parser*. Variations of the (initial) heap size have only a small effect on the SAPL and Helium performance, but have a big impact on the performance of GHC. Setting the initial heap to 24Mb gives an almost 3-time speed-up for *Interpreter* and *Twice*, but halves the speed of almost all other benchmarks.

5.5.3   Discussion about Interpreter Comparison

What is the source of the good performance of SAPL compared with GHCi, Helium, Hugs and Amanda? The simplified memory management contributes to this better performance, but cannot be the only source (see table 5.5). Helium performs an overflow check on integer operations, which slows down integer intensive programs. If we compare SAPL with Amanda we see that for (almost) data type free programs there is not much difference in performance (*Fibonacci*, *Queens* and *Knights*). The difference in performance appears for programs using data types and pattern matching. Amanda uses a similar implementation of graph reduction as SAPL, but has a less sophisticated implementation of pattern matching using case-by-case matching [8]. If we compare the performance of SAPL with that of GHCi, Helium and Hugs we see that SAPL already has a better performance for data type free programs (*Twice*, *Fibonacci*). This increase in speed remains about the same for programs using data types and pattern matching. Helium uses techniques based on the STG machine to generate LVM byte code [11].

This byte code is interpreted. GHCi also compiles to byte code and is based on the GHC compiler that also uses the STG machine [13]. The Hugs implementation is based on byte code interpretation too. The SAPL interpreter is based on graph rewriting only and has no special constructs for data types and pattern matching. This enables a simple, high-level abstract machine with few, relatively large, atomic operations. There is no need for a more low level intermediate (byte code) formalism. The main difference between an interpreter and a compiler is that an interpreter has to check what to do next at every step. Keeping this overhead as small as possible is important for the construction of efficient interpreters. The easiest way to keep this overhead small is to use large atomic steps in the interpreter. Byte code instructions are mostly quite small. SAPL has a simple structure and uses large atomic steps. As a result the interpretation overhead for SAPL is lower than that for byte code based interpreters. The atomic operations in the SAPL interpreter are:

- Push a reference on the stack.
- Instantiate a function body, clear its arguments from the stack and place the result at the top application node.
- Call a built-in function, clear arguments from stack and place result at top application node.
- For a function call with as body a selector function application: Partly instantiate the body, recursively call *eval* for this instantiation and use the result to select and instantiate the appropriate other part of the body.

Except for the *push* operation these are all relatively large operations. The only benchmark for which the SAPL interpreter is not significant faster than Helium and GHCi, is *Symbolic Primes*. For this example the bodies of the (local) functions are mostly very small. Therefore the interpretation overhead will be much higher and comparable to the overhead of GHCi, Helium and Hugs.

Benefits of the Functional Encoding for the Interpreter Performance

First of all, we already concluded that the selective instantiation optimisation is essential for an efficient implementation of pattern-based function definitions using this encoding. It is therefore useless to try to run a SAPL program using another interpreter or compiler that doesn't uses the selective instantiation optimisation. Furthermore, in the previous subsection we concluded that the extra efficiency of the SAPL interpreter is not a result of the functional encoding and its implementation, but is a result of the simpler structure of the interpreter using a high level abstract machine with minimal interpretation overhead. The functional encoding enables this simple structure. It is possible to implement a traditional pattern matcher along the same lines as the functional pattern matcher with comparable performance, because both are based on the same techniques for encoding the pattern-based definition (see section 5.3.1).

We conclude that the most important benefit of the functional encoding is that it enables an elegant implementation of algebraic data types and pattern matching entirely within a pure functional domain and that this implementation can be made efficient by applying generic optimisations to a basic graph- rewriting interpreter.

5.6   CONCLUSIONS AND FURTHER RESEARCH POSSIBILITIES

In this paper we have defined the minimal (intermediate) functional programming language SAPL and an interpreter for it, based on a new variant of the Church encoding for algebraic data types. SAPL consists of pure functions only and has, besides integers, no other data types. For SAPL we have achieved the following results:

- The representation of data structures as functions in SAPL is more efficient than the Church encoding and the encoding of Berarducci and Bohm. The use of explicitly named functions (enabling explicit recursion) instead of lambda expressions enables an efficient implementation of this representation. We also showed how to translate pattern-based function definitions to SAPL. This makes SAPL usable as an intermediate language for interpretation of programs written in languages like Clean or Haskell.

- We described an efficient interpreter for SAPL based on straightforward graph rewriting techniques. The basic version of the interpreter is an ideal subject for educational purposes and for experimenting with implementation issues for functional languages. After applying two optimisations to speed up the execution of functions that are the result of the translation of pattern-based function definitions, the interpreter turns out to be competitive in a comparison with other interpreters. The results show us that for interpretation a high-level abstract machine with large atomic operations yields better results than low-level byte code interpreters based on techniques used for compilers.

5.6.1   Future Work

We plan to investigate the following issues for SAPL:

- We want to investigate whether the techniques used for implementing SAPL are also usable for realizing a compiler. We did some small experiments for this. We hand compiled the internal SAPL data structures to C code for a few benchmarks. This eliminates interpretation overhead and makes it possible to hard code the instantiation of functions (instead of a recursive copy). Speed-ups of 2 to 3 times seem possible, but more experiments are needed.

- We want to extend SAPL with IO features for creating interactive programs. Because SAPL is an interpreter it is also possible to use SAPL only as a calculation engine for another environment that does the IO.

- We want to investigate applications of SAPL. For example, SAPL can be used at the client side of Internet browsers as a plug-in, or inside a spreadsheet application.

REFERENCES

[1] *The Haskell Home Page*. www.Haskell.org.

[2] *Hugs Online*. www.Haskell.org/hugs.

[3] L. Augustsson. Compiling pattern matching. In Jouannaud, editor, *Conference on Functional Programming Languages and Computer Architectures, Nancy*, volume 201 of *Lecture Notes in Computer Science*, pages 368–381. Springer Verlag, 1985.

[4] H.P. Barendregt. *The Lambda Calculus, Its Syntax and Semantics*. Studies in Logic and the Foundations of Mathematics. North-Holland, 1981.

[5] H.P. Barendregt. The impact of the lambda calculus in logic and computer science. *The Bulletin of Symbolic Logic*, 3(2):181–215, 1997.

[6] A. Berarducci and C. Bohm. *A self-interpreter of lambda calculus having a normal form*, volume 702 of *Lecture Notes in Computer Science*, pages 85–99. Springer Verlag, 1993.

[7] C. Bohm and A. Berarducci. Automatic synthesis of typed λ–programs on term algebras. *Theoretical Computer Science*, 39:135–154, 1985.

[8] D. Bruin. Personal communication.

[9] D. Bruin. The amanda interpreter. www.engineering.tech.nhl.nl/engineering/personeel/bruin/data/amanda203.zip.

[10] W. Kluge. *Abstract Computing Machines*. Texts in Theoretical Computer Science. Springer-Verlag, 2004.

[11] D. Leijen. *The λ Abroad – A Functional Approach to Software Components*. PhD thesis, Department of Computer Science, Universiteit Utrecht, The Netherlands, 2003.

[12] S.L. Peyton Jones. *The Implementation of Functional Programming Languages*. International Series in Computer Science. Prentice-Hall, 1987.

[13] S.L. Peyton Jones. Implementing lazy functional languages on stock hardware: the spineless tagless g-machine. *Journal of Functional Programming*, 2(2):127–202, 1992.

[14] R. Plasmeijer and M. van Eekelen. *Functional Programming and Parallel Graph Rewriting*. International Computer Science Series. Addison-Wesley, 1993.

[15] Software Technology Group, the Institute of Information and Computing Sciences, Utrecht University, the Netherlands. *The Helium Project*. www.cs.uu.nl/helium.

[16] Software Technology Research Group, Radboud University Nijmegen. *The Clean Home Page*. www.cs.ru.nl/˜clean.

[17] Software Technology Research Group, Radboud University Nijmegen. *The SAPL Home Page*. www.cs.ru.nl/˜jmjansen/sapl.

Chapter 6

Object-Oriented Programming in Dependent Type Theory

Anton Setzer[1]

Abstract: We introduce basic concepts from object-oriented programming into dependent type theory based on the idea of modelling objects as interactive programs. We consider methods, interfaces, and the interaction between a fixed number of objects, including self-referential method calls. We introduce a monad-like syntax for developing objects in dependent type theory.

6.1 INTRODUCTION

In the conference TYPES 2003, the author gave a talk on how to represent lambda-terms in Java ([Set03]). At the end of this talk, Martin-Löf asked the question: What you have done is to represent functional programming in object-oriented programming. Can we do it the other way around as well? What he meant was: Can we represent object-oriented programming in dependent type theory?

The author has developed with P. Hancock the notion of interactive programs in dependent type theory. Objects can be considered as interactive programs: they receive requests (method calls) from the outside, and return answers to these requests to the outside. It seems to be interesting to explore the use of interactive programs in order to model objects and classes in dependent type theory.

There are two reasons why we think it is useful to model concepts from object-oriented programming in dependent type theory. On one hand this would allow

[1]Department of Computer Science, University Of Wales Swansea, Singleton Park, Swansea SA1 4PZ, UK. Email: `a.g.setzer@swan.ac.uk`. This research was supported by EPSRC grant GR/S30450/01. Part of this work was done while the author was an invited research follow at the Graduate School of Science and Technology, Kobe University, Japan.

91

to reason about object-oriented programs in a theorem prover based on dependent types. For instance, one can write a verified compiler for an object-oriented language. On the other hand we belief that it is interesting to develop an object-oriented programming language based on dependent types. In such a language, two different powerful programming paradigms – object-orientation and dependent types – would merge. This would give rise to powerful new types – note that one of the main contributions of both concepts is that they substantially increase the types available. By using dependent types one could write more generic object-oriented programs. One could as well write object-oriented programs with a higher degree of correctness. For instance, pre-conditions of methods could be enforced by having extra arguments, which require a proof of that pre-condition; post-conditions could be treated similarly. In general we would obtain one uniform framework in which both computing and reasoning takes place. So there is no need to introduce separate axioms for reasoning about programs, since correctness proofs are carried out in the same framework as the program, and have therefore direct access to it.

Along that route one would have to add of course at some point new language constructs to dependent type theory rather than implementing all concepts from object-oriented programming directly in it. The current paper, in which we model some object-oriented concepts in dependent type theory, serves as a first step in determining which additional language constructs are needed in order to facilitate writing object-oriented programs in dependent type theory.

In this paper we will make first steps in exploring the idea of modelling objects as interactive programs. We will cover objects, interfaces, methods and interaction between a fixed number of objects. We will see that the modelling of self-referential method calls in dependent type theory results in rather complex interactive programs.

We will as well see that with dependent type theory we obtain a higher degree of expressibility. For instance classes can have dependently typed methods, which means that the result type of a method might depend on the arguments. Because of the use of dependent types, all methods can be merged into a single method. In type theory, the body of a method is an element of a data type, and we can write generic functions, which transform this data type, and which can be used to generate method bodies.

Content of this article. In section 6.2 we introduce the basic concepts of dependent type theory. This will introduce as well our notations used for working in dependent type theory. In that section we will as well introduce coalgebraic types (codata). In section 6.3 we introduce interactive programs. In section 6.4 we explore the idea of an object as an interactive program. In section 6.5 we show how to deal with combining objects without self-referential calls. In section 6.6 we will extend this by allowing objects which directly or indirectly call themselves. We will as well introduce in this section a monad like syntax for representing object code, as it occurs in standard object-oriented languages like Java. This code will then be translated into objects in dependent type theory.

Related work. There is a rich literature on using object-calculi related to the λ-calculus and on using impredicative type theories in order to assign types to type theory. A lot of material can be found in [AC96]. Pierce and Turner [PT94] use impredicative existential types of $\mathcal{F}_{\leq}^{\omega}$ in order model objects. Jacobs [Jac95, Jac98] and Reichel [Rei95] have used coalgebras in order to model objects, but they do not deal with self-referential method calls in full, which, as we will see, results in rather complex structures. Meseguer [Mes93] has indicated how to formulate concurrent objects in a rewrite system. Kiselyov and Lämmel [KL05] have modelled object-oriented concepts in Haskell. We have not found any treatment of object-oriented programming in the context of predicative dependent type theory, which makes use of the expressive power of dependent types, and we belief that the use of interactive programs in this context is new.

6.2 BASIC CONCEPTS OF DEPENDENT TYPE THEORY

The basic type constructions used from standard dependent type theory are as follows:

- Dependent function types, written as $(x : A) \to B$ for the type of functions, mapping an element $a : A$ to an element of $B[x := a]$. We use standard abbreviations, such as $A \to B$ for $(x : A) \to B$ for a variable x which does not occur in B, $(x : A, y : B) \to C$ for $(x : A) \to (y : B) \to C$, etc. Elements of $(x : A) \to B$ are created by λ-abstraction $\lambda x.t$, and eliminated by application to elements of A, where application is written in functional style $(f\, a)$.

- Dependent products. For convenience, we use record notation in this article. The product of types $A_1, \ldots, A_n$ is thus written as

$$\Sigma(\mathsf{l}_1 : A_1, \ldots, \mathsf{l}_n : A_n)$$

Here A_i might depend on $\mathsf{l}_j : A_j$ for $j < i$, and l_i are the record selectors (sometimes called labels). Projection is written as record selection, i.e. for an element c of the type A just introduced the ith projection is written as $c.\mathsf{l}_i : A_i$. Our notation for introducing elements of type A is

$$\mathsf{record}(\mathsf{l}_1 = t_1, \ldots, \mathsf{l}_n = t_n)\ ,$$

where $t_i : A_i$. This is record notation for the n-tuple $\langle t_1, \ldots, t_n \rangle$.

Occasionally, we will use as well product notation, namely $(x : A) \times B$ for the product of A and B, where B might depend on $x : A$. Elements of this type are written as pairs $\langle a, b \rangle$. We use case distinction in order to unpack such pairs.

- Algebraic types are written as follows:

$$A = \mathsf{data}\ \mathsf{C}_1(a_1^1 : A_1^1, \ldots, a_{n_1}^1 : A_{n_1}^1)\ |\ \cdots\ |\ \mathsf{C}_m(a_1^m : A_1^m, \ldots, a_{n_m}^m : A_{n_m}^m)$$

Algebraic types correspond to the least set closed under those constructors. We have the usual condition that the types of the constructor are strictly positive in the type to be introduced. (This means that in the above definition A_j^i

either do not make use of A, or are of the form $B_1 \to \cdots \to B_l \to A$, where B_i do not make use of A). Furthermore, we will sometimes omit a variable a^i_j, if A^i_k for $k > j$ do not depend on it.

Elimination is defined by case distinction: Assume $a : A$, $D : A \to \mathsf{Set}$ [2] and

$$a^i_1 : A^i_1, \ldots, a^i_{n_i} : A^i_{n_i} \Rightarrow t_i[a^i_1, \ldots, a^i_{n_i}] : D \,(\mathsf{C}_i \, a^i_1 \cdots a^i_{n_i})$$

Then

$$\mathsf{case}\,(a)\,\mathsf{of}\,\{\ \begin{array}{lll} (\mathsf{C}_1 \, a^1_1 \cdots a^1_{n_1}) & \longrightarrow & t_1[a^1_1, \ldots, a^1_{n_1}];\ \cdots; \\ (\mathsf{C}_m \, a^m_1 \cdots a^m_{n_m}) & \longrightarrow & t_m[a^m_1, \ldots, a^m_{n_m}]\} \end{array}$$

is of type $(D\,a)$. Note that $t_i[\cdots]$ has a type corresponding to the branch of the case distinction. Functions defined using case-distinction can be recursive, as long as recursive function calls are made to structurally smaller elements.

- We introduce a convenient notation for the disjoint union:

$$C_1(x^1_1 : A^1_1, \ldots, x^1_{n_1} : A^1_{n_1}) + \cdots + C_n(x^m_1 : A^m_1, \ldots, x^m_{n_m} : A^m_{n_m})$$
$$:= \mathsf{data}\ C_1(x^1_1 : A^1_1, \ldots, x^1_{n_1} : A^1_{n_1}) \mid \cdots \mid C_n(x^m_1 : A^m_1, \ldots, x^m_{n_m} : A^m_{n_m})$$
$$A + B := \mathsf{inl}(a : A) + \mathsf{inr}(b : B) \qquad 1 + A := \mathsf{inl}() + \mathsf{inr}(x : A)$$

Here A^i_j should not refer to the new set being introduced. We will as well omit brackets in case one of C_i does not have any arguments.

- Furthermore, we will add coalgebraic types. A discussion on coalgebraic types in dependent type theory can be found in [HS04] (see as well [BC04]). Coalgebraic types are written as

$$A = \mathsf{codata}\ \mathsf{C}_1(a^1_1 : A^1_1, \ldots, a^1_{n_1} : A^1_{n_1}) \mid \cdots \mid \mathsf{C}_m(a_1 : A^m_1, \ldots, a^m_{n_m} : A^m_{n_m})$$

with the same condition on strict positivity as for algebraic types.

- The elimination principle is case distinction. However, after applying case distinction, one does not obtain a structural smaller term which can be used in order to write terminating recursive functions.

- Introduction is formally written as guarded recursion. However, guarded recursion is a syntactic notation, and, as pointed out in [HS04], guarded recursion is not supposed to be evaluated in full. Instead definitions by guarded recursion represent syntactic expressions introduced by the introduction rule for coalgebraic types. Essentially, guarded recursion is only evaluated, if the case-distinction construct is applied to a term introduced by guarded recursion. In this case, one step of the guarded recursion is evaluated, and then, depending on the case distinction, the term is reduced further. More details can be found in [HS04].

---

[2]See the remarks on the logical framework at the end of this section on what is meant by Set.

We will in this article make use of the *logical framework*. There we have two levels of types, called, as usual in dependent type theory, Set and Type. We have Set : Type and if A : Set, then A : Type. But we do not have Set : Set, otherwise the resulting type theory would be inconsistent (Girard's paradox). Both Set and Type are closed under dependent function types and dependent products. Set is as well closed under the formation of strictly positive algebraic and coalgebraic types. Especially, Set will contain the well-behaved simple types, as they occur in non-dependent functional programming, and dependent versions of these. Set is what would outside dependent type theory be denoted as "type". With the logical framework we have one layer on top of it. This allows to assign, for instance, the type Set $\rightarrow$ Set : Type to operations mapping elements of Set to Set, i.e. to type-manipulating operations.

6.3   INTERACTIVE PROGRAMS IN DEPENDENT TYPE THEORY

The main idea for representing object-oriented programming in dependent type theory is that objects are to be considered as interactive programs. Let us first review how interactive programs can be represented in dependent type theory.

In [HS99, HS00b, HS00a, HS04] the author has developed together with Peter Hancock a theory of interactive programs in dependent type theory (see as well [Han00, HH06] for some related work by Hancock and Hyvernat). An interface for a stateless (or non-state-dependent) interactive program[3] is given by a set of commands C : Set and a set of responses depending on a command c : C, i.e. we have

$$\mathsf{Interface} = \Sigma(\mathsf{C} : \mathsf{Set}, \mathsf{R} : \mathsf{C} \rightarrow \mathsf{Set}) : \mathsf{Type}$$

There are two kinds of interactive programs to be associated with an element $I := \mathsf{record}(\mathsf{C} = C, \mathsf{R} = R)$ of Interface:

- The set of client-side programs. These are programs which make a call $c : C$ to the real world, such as to output a string to the console, or requesting a string input from the keyboard. They then receive a response $r : R\ c$ from the real world (e.g. a success message in case of the writing of a string to console, or the string typed in by the user in case of the request for a string), and depending on it, execute the next command. This loop is then repeated until the program determines that it has terminated.

  If IO is the set of client-side programs, then this loop can be represented in type theory by a function $f : \mathsf{IO} \rightarrow ((c : C) \times ((R\ c) \rightarrow \mathsf{IO}))$. Executing this loop is necessarily an external procedure, which is outside type theory. If we execute this loop for $p : \mathsf{IO}$, this procedure will compute the command $c := \pi_0(f\ p)$ to be issued. It will then execute c in the real world, and receive a response r. Then it will compute $p' := \pi_1(f\ p)\ r$ and continue executing p'.

---

[3]Stateless refers to externally observable states – interactive programs for stateless interfaces can have internal states.

- The set of server-side programs. These programs receive a command $c : C$ from the real world, and respond to it with a response $r : R\,c$. Then the program is ready to get the next command, etc.

There exist as well programs like proxy servers with a combination of a server-side and client-side behaviour. Such combinations will occur on the object level later in this article.

In a monadic version (see below for the monad operations), we obtain two sets. Both will depend on an answer set A and a fixed interface I as above:

- The set of client-side programs, which possibly terminate, and if they terminate terminate by returning an element of type A.

- The set of server-side programs, which possibly terminate as well by returning an element of type A.

However, we have not specified when a program terminates. There are two choices, and depending on these choices we end up with 4 different sets. All of them depend on the answer set A.

- $(\mathsf{IO}^*_{\text{client}}\,A)$, $(\mathsf{IO}^*_{\text{server}}\,A)$, the set of client- and server-side programs which are guaranteed to terminate eventually and to return an element of type A. These types are defined as algebraic types.

- $(\mathsf{IO}^\infty_{\text{client}}\,A)$, $(\mathsf{IO}^\infty_{\text{server}}\,A)$, the set of client- and server-side programs which might run for ever or might terminate and return an element of type A. These types are defined as coalgebraic types.

All these data types might terminate immediately without having any interaction. The types are defined as follows:

$$
\begin{array}{lll}
\mathsf{IO}^*_{\text{client}}\,A & = & \text{data}\quad \text{return}(a : A) \quad | \quad \mathsf{do}(c : C, f : R\,c \to \mathsf{IO}^*_{\text{client}}\,A) \\
\mathsf{IO}^*_{\text{server}}\,A & = & \text{data}\quad \text{return}(a : A) \quad | \quad \mathsf{do}(f : (c : C) \to R\,c \times \mathsf{IO}^*_{\text{server}}\,A) \\
\mathsf{IO}^\infty_{\text{client}}\,A & = & \text{codata}\, \text{return}(a : A) \quad | \quad \mathsf{do}(c : C, f : R\,c \to \mathsf{IO}^\infty_{\text{client}}\,A) \\
\mathsf{IO}^\infty_{\text{server}}\,A & = & \text{codata}\, \text{return}(a : A) \quad | \quad \mathsf{do}(f : (c : C) \to R\,c \times \mathsf{IO}^\infty_{\text{server}}\,A)
\end{array}
$$

If we want to make the dependency on the interface explicit, we write the interface I as an additional subscript.

We can define the operations of a monad for all four of these types. For instance, in case of $\mathsf{IO}^*_{\text{client}}$, return is given by the constructor return. For $p : \mathsf{IO}^*_{\text{client}}(A)$, $q : A \to \mathsf{IO}^*_{\text{client}}(B)$, the monadic bind $p * q : \mathsf{IO}^*_{\text{client}}(B)$[4] can be defined as follows: $(\text{return}\,a) * q := q\,a$, $\quad (\mathsf{do}\,c\,f) * q := \mathsf{do}\,c\,(\lambda r.f\,r * q)$.

We introduce some simple operations:

- If I, I' are two interfaces, we introduce their disjoint union as

$$
I \oplus I' := \mathsf{record}\{\mathsf{C} = I.\mathsf{C} + I'.\mathsf{C}, \mathsf{R} = [I.\mathsf{R}, I'.\mathsf{R}]\} : \mathsf{Interface}
$$

---

[4]In Haskell this is written as $p >>= q$.

where

$$[I.R + I'.R] : I.C + I'.C \to \mathsf{Set}$$
$$[I.R + I'.R]\,(\mathsf{inl}\ c) \quad := \quad I.R\ c \qquad [I.R + I'.R]\,(\mathsf{inr}\ c) \quad := \quad I'.R\ c$$

- If I, I' are interfaces, $f : I'.C \to I.C$, $g : (c : I'.C, I.R\ (f\ c)) \to I'.R\ c$, then we can define rename $: \mathsf{IO}^{\infty}_{I,\mathsf{server}}\ A \to \mathsf{IO}^{\infty}_{I',\mathsf{server}}\ A$ by

$$\text{rename}\ p = \mathsf{case}\ p\ \mathsf{of}\{(\mathsf{return}\ a) \to \mathsf{return}\ a;$$
$$(\mathsf{do}\ b) \quad \to \mathsf{do}\ (\lambda c.\mathsf{case}\ (b\ (f\ c))\ \mathsf{of}$$
$$\{\langle r, p'\rangle \to \langle g\ c\ r, \text{rename}\ p'\rangle\})\}$$

So (rename p) operates as p, but translates the commands it receives into commands for p and responses from p back into its own responses. This operation allows hiding and renaming of an interface.

State-dependent interfaces. The notation of interface can be extended to state-dependent interfaces. A state-dependent interface is given by

- a set of externally observable states,

- a set of commands depending on the states,

- a set of responses depending on states and commands,

- and a next function, which determines the observable state one obtains after an interaction consisting of a command and a response to it has been carried out.

So we get

$$\mathsf{Interface}_{\mathsf{statedep}} = \Sigma(\mathsf{S} : \mathsf{Set},$$
$$\mathsf{C} : \mathsf{S} \to \mathsf{Set},$$
$$\mathsf{R} : (s : \mathsf{S}, \mathsf{C}\ s) \to \mathsf{Set},$$
$$\mathsf{n} : (s : \mathsf{S}, c : \mathsf{C}\ c, \mathsf{R}\ s\ c) \to \mathsf{S})\ : \mathsf{Type}$$

Let the following be fixed:

$$I := \mathsf{record}(\mathsf{S} = S, \mathsf{C} = C, \mathsf{R} = R, \mathsf{n} = n) : \mathsf{Interface}_{\mathsf{statedep}}$$

Assuming $A : S \to \mathsf{Set}$ and $s : S$ we introduce the set of client/server side interactive programs starting in state s and possibly terminating in a state s' with result $(A\ s')$ as follows:

$$\mathsf{IO}^*_{\text{statedep,client}}\ A\ s$$
$$= \mathsf{data} \quad \mathsf{return}(a : A\ s)$$
$$\quad\quad\quad\quad |\quad \mathsf{do}(c : C\ s, f : R\ s\ c \to \mathsf{IO}^*_{\text{statedep,client}}\ A\ (n\ s\ c\ r))$$
$$\mathsf{IO}^*_{\text{statedep,server}}\ A\ s$$
$$= \mathsf{data} \quad \mathsf{return}(a : A\ s)$$
$$\quad\quad\quad\quad |\quad \mathsf{do}(f : (c : C\ s) \to R\ s\ c \times \mathsf{IO}^*_{\text{statedep,server}}\ A\ (n\ s\ c\ r))$$
$$\mathsf{IO}^\infty_{\text{statedep,client}}\ A\ s$$
$$= \mathsf{codata} \quad \mathsf{return}(a : A\ s)$$
$$\quad\quad\quad\quad |\quad \mathsf{do}(c : C\ s, f : R\ s\ c \to \mathsf{IO}^\infty_{\text{statedep,client}}\ A\ (n\ s\ c\ r))$$
$$\mathsf{IO}^\infty_{\text{statedep,server}}\ A\ s$$
$$= \mathsf{codata} \quad \mathsf{return}(a : A\ s)$$
$$\quad\quad\quad\quad |\quad \mathsf{do}(f : (c : C\ s) \to R\ s\ c \times \mathsf{IO}^\infty_{\text{statedep,server}}\ A\ (n\ s\ c\ r))$$

Execution of interactive programs is an external operation. For this we assume an interface corresponding to the real world (stateless or state-dependent).

- In case of a client-side program, commands correspond to interactive commands the program can demand from the real world like writing a string to console, demanding some user input from the keyboard, or manipulating a GUI. Responses correspond to responses the real world makes to such a command. For instance, in case of the writing a string this would be a simple success element $x : \{*\}$, in case of reading a string, it would be the string typed in. Running a program means that case distinction is applied to the program. If one obtains $(\mathsf{return}\ a)$, the program stops and returns a. If one obtains $(\mathsf{do}\ c\ f)$, then command c is carried out in the real world. Once one has obtained a real world response r, the program continues by executing $(f\ r)$.

- In case of server-side programs, commands are requests the real world can make to the program. Responses are answers the program can give in response to such a request. The execution of such a program is carried out as follows: First case distinction is applied to the program. If one obtains $(\mathsf{return}\ a)$, the program stops and returns a. Otherwise, it is of the form $(\mathsf{do}\ f)$. Then the program waits for a request by the real world. If it receives a request c, $(f\ c)$ is evaluated to a pair $\langle r, p \rangle$ consisting of a response r and a next program p. This response r is sent back as answer to the real world and the program continues by carrying out the execution loop with program p.

6.4 SIMPLE OBJECTS

The basic idea of our approach to object-oriented programming in dependent type theory is that an object is considered as an interactive program, and that classes are functions which generate objects. Let us restrict ourselves first to a simple class, which has methods which take input from one set and return in response to this input an answer which is an element of another set. These methods might change the internal state of an object, but do not receive or return elements from other classes or interact with other objects. Later we will indicate how to deal with the situation in which a method might call methods of other objects, including the object itself. In the current simple situation we have methods $(i = 1, \ldots, m)$

$$\mathsf{method}_i : (x^i_1 : A^i_1, \ldots, x^i_{n_i} : A^i_{n_i}) \to R_i[x^i_1, \ldots, x^i_{n_i}]$$

Note that these are not functions, but each method call depends on the internal state of an object, and changes the state of the object. In dependent type theory we can allow the set $R_i[x^i_1, \ldots, x^i_{n_i}]$ to depend on $x^i_1, \ldots, x^i_{n_i}$. Public instance variables $x : A$ can be modelled by having methods $\mathsf{setx} : A \to \{*\}$ for setting the variable to the value, and $\mathsf{getx} : \{*\} \to A$ for obtaining the value of this variable.

The interface definition of methods as introduced above corresponds in dependent type theory to the stateless interface

$$I = \mathsf{record}\{\mathsf{C} = C, \mathsf{R} = R\}$$

where

$$C = \mathsf{data}\ \mathsf{method}_1\,(x^1_1 : A^1_1, \ldots, x^1_{n_1} : A^1_n)\ |\ \cdots\ |\ \ \mathsf{method}_m(x^m_1 : A^m_1, \ldots, x^m_{n_m} : A^m_{n_m})$$
$$R\,(\mathsf{method}_i\ x^i_1\ \cdots\ x^i_{n_i})\ \ =\ \ R_i[x^i_1, \ldots, x^i_{n_i}]$$

An object of this interface is an element of

$$\mathsf{Object}\ I := \mathsf{IO}^{\infty}_{\mathsf{server},I}\ \emptyset$$

It is a server-side program, which receives requests (message-calls) $c : C$, and depending on them, computes a response $r : R\ c$ and changes its internal state. Note that by using dependent type theory we have encoded several methods method_1, $\ldots$, method_m into one of type $(c : I.\mathsf{C}) \to I.\mathsf{R}\ c$.

C as given above models the notion of an interface as it occurs, for instance, in Java.[5] In addition to interfaces, classes have constructors, each of which constructs an object of this class. This means that a constructor Constr with arguments $(x_1 : A_1, \ldots, x_n : A_n)$ is a function

$$\mathsf{Constr} : (x : A_1, \ldots, x_n : A_n) \to \mathsf{Object}\ I$$

As an example we represent a very simple example in dependent type theory, namely that of a memory cell holding one element $x : A$. Such a class has methods

$$\mathsf{setx}\ \ :\ \ A \to \{*\}\qquad \mathsf{getx}\ \ :\ \ \{*\} \to A$$

This means that the interface $I_A = \mathsf{record}\{\mathsf{C} = C_A, \mathsf{R} = R_A\}$ is of the form

$$\begin{aligned}C_A\ &=\ \mathsf{data}\ \mathsf{setx}\,(a : A)\ |\ \mathsf{getx}\\ R_A\,(\mathsf{setx}\,a)\ &=\ \{*\}\qquad\ \ R_A\ \mathsf{getx}\ =\ A\end{aligned}$$

---

[5] More precisely one should say: interfaces without static constants; because of such constants Java interfaces are a hybrid between pure interfaces and abstract classes.

The standard implementation of a memory cell has constructor $f : A \to \text{Object } I_A$ which is defined by guarded recursion as

$$f\ a = \text{do } (\lambda c.\text{case } (c) \text{ of } \{ \quad (\text{setx } a') \quad \longrightarrow \quad \langle *, f\ a' \rangle;$$
$$(\text{getx}) \quad \longrightarrow \quad \langle a, f\ a \rangle \})$$

Manipulation of objects. The operation "rename" introduced in section 6.3 allows to take an interface and hide and rename its methods. One can introduce as well operations which extend an object in order to deal with an extended interface.

6.5 COMBINING OBJECTS WITHOUT SELF-REFERENTIAL CALLS

We will now consider how to deal with objects, which might call methods of other objects. Let us take as an example 3 objects o_1, o_2, o_3, which can be called from the outside world using interfaces I_1, I_2, I_3. The method calls are $I_i.\text{C}$, and the response to a method call $c : I_i.\text{C}$ is $(I_i.\text{R } c)$. We call I_i the *receiving interface* of object o_i. In a first step we will exclude self-referential calls. Then o_1 might call o_2, o_3. The outside world as presented to this object is therefore given by the interface $O := I_2 \oplus I_3$ (one might extend O by an additional external interface corresponding to communication with the real world, e.g. communications with GUIs or the console). We call O the *outside interface* of the object.

The object o_1 would in this situation receive a command $c : I_1.\text{C}$. It can then carry out a possibly unbounded sequence of communications with its outside world, which possibly terminates, and if it terminates, returns an element $r : I_1.\text{R } c$ and a program o_1' (i.e. a call-back) for interfaces I_1 and O. Then it continues with executing o_1'. So o_1 is an element of

$$\text{Object}_{\text{simple}}\ I_1\ O = \text{codata do}(f : (c : I_1.\text{C}) \to \text{IO}^\infty_{\text{client},O}\ (I_1.\text{R } c \times \text{Object}_{\text{simple}}\ I_1\ O))$$

The interpretation loop for this object would be as follows: Assume the object is $o = \text{do } f$. Then o waits for a command $c : I_1.\text{C}$ from interface I_1. When it has received c, it computes $p := f\ c$. It executes p as a client-side program, which issues commands to O and receives responses from it until it terminates with an element $\langle r, o' \rangle$. Then the object returns the answer r on interface I_1, and the interpretation loop is iterated starting with object o' (the call-back).

In order to exclude indirect self-referential calls (that, for instance, o_1 calls o_2 which in turn calls o_1), o_2 would only be allowed to communicate with o_3 (i.e. have outside interface I_3) and o_3 would not be allowed to communicate with any other object at all. We can combine o_1, o_2, o_3 into one interactive program with interface $I := I_1 \oplus I_2 \oplus I_3$, and define from the resulting program an interactive program which has the following behaviour: it receives a call c from $I.\text{C}$, passes it on to one of o_1, o_2, o_3, and simulates the communication between o_1, o_2, o_3. If this communication terminates it will return an answer $r : I.\text{R } c$, and wait for the next method call. We will not go into details and instead move to a more complex situation, in which self-referential method calls are allowed. There we will introduce the resulting combined program in more detail.

6.6 COMBINING OBJECTS WITH SELF-REFERENTIAL CALLS

Complications arise if we want to extend the above in order to include self-referential calls.[6] For instance, we might replace $O = I_2 \oplus I_3$ as the outside world for o_1 by $O' := I_1 \oplus I_2 \oplus I_3$ and interpret a method call to the I_1 component of O' as a method call to o_1 itself. Or one might allow indirect self-referential calls, i.e. that o_1 calls o_2 and o_2 in turn calls o_1. The consequence of allowing such self-referential calls is that when an object has issued a command to the outside world, a method call to it might be made, before it has received the answer.

An element of $\mathsf{Object}_{\mathsf{simple}}$ has two phases: a phase in which it receives a command from the outside, and a phase where it issues commands to the outside. We need to extend this in such a way that we have objects, which always can receive a command from the outside, even if a method call made by them has not been answered yet. Note that these self-referential calls might affect the state of the object. Consider, for instance, a class with methods `method1` and `method2`, where `method1` is defined using Java-like code as follows (`y`, `u` are instance variables of the class):

```
A method1(B x){u = 0;
                y = method2(x);
                return y + u;}};
```

The self-referential call to `method2` will interrupt the execution of `method1`, but will refer to the state of the class which has been changed by the line `u=0`. `method2` might change `u`, so the result returned by `method1` need not be `y+0`.

The consequence of the above considerations is that an object o with receiving interface I, external interface O, and the possibility of self-referential calls refers to a list[7] icl of elements of $I.\mathsf{C}$, namely the method calls to o, which it has not answered yet, and a list ocl of elements of $O.\mathsf{C}$, the set of external commands, for which o has made a request without having received an answer yet.

Let us fix some notations for dealing with lists: $(l)_i$ is the ith element of the list l, $(\mathsf{delete}_i\, l)$ is the result of deleting the ith element from the list l; $(\mathsf{insert}_i\, l\, x)$ is the result of inserting into list l at position i element x. Using these notations, we obtain the following definition, where $icl : \mathsf{List}\, I.\mathsf{C}$ and $ocl : \mathsf{List}\, O.\mathsf{C}$:

$$
\begin{aligned}
\mathsf{Object}_{\mathsf{server}}\, & I\, O\, icl\, ocl = \\
& \Sigma(\mathsf{receive\_request:}\, (ic : I.\mathsf{C}, i \leq \mathsf{length}\, icl) \\
& \qquad\qquad\qquad \to \mathsf{Object}_{\mathsf{client}}\, I\, O\, (\mathsf{insert}_i\, icl\, ic)\, ocl, \\
& \quad\; \mathsf{receive\_answer:}\, (i < \mathsf{length}\, ocl, r : O.\mathsf{R}\, (ocl)_i) \\
& \qquad\qquad\qquad \to \mathsf{Object}_{\mathsf{client}}\, I\, O\, icl\, (\mathsf{delete}_i\, ocl)) \\
\mathsf{Object}_{\mathsf{client}}\, & I\, O\, icl\, ocl = \\
& \mathsf{codata}\; \mathsf{send\_answer}(i < \mathsf{length}(icl), r : I.\mathsf{R}\, (icl)_i, \\
& \qquad\qquad\qquad\quad o : \mathsf{Object}_{\mathsf{server}}\, I\, O\, (\mathsf{delete}_i\, icl)\, ocl) \\
& \quad |\; \mathsf{send\_request}(oc : O.\mathsf{C}, i \leq \mathsf{length}\, ocl, \\
& \qquad\qquad\qquad\quad o : \mathsf{Object}_{\mathsf{server}}\, I\, O\, icl\, (\mathsf{insert}_i\, ocl\, oc))
\end{aligned}
$$

---

[6] Note that this paper does not treat the dynamic creation of objects.

[7] As it is the default in functional programming, lists are 0-based.

An element of $(\text{Object}_{\text{server}} \; I \; O \; icl \; ocl)$ can receive method calls (elements of $I.C$) and receive an answer for any of its pending requests to the outside world (elements of ocl).[8] It then switches to client mode. In that mode it either sends an answer to one of the requests made to it (elements of icl) or it sends requests $oc : O.C$ to the outside using its external interface O. It then switches back to server mode.

Note that we have made our definition in such a way that an object can receive answers for any of its open requests in ocl and can answer any of its requests in icl, not only the last one. Otherwise, for instance, the definition of $o_0 \oplus o_1$ below would become rather complicated. Furthermore, we are allowed to insert new elements to icl and ocl at arbitrary positions, not only in a stack-like way at front. This makes programming much easier, since it allows to keep icl and ocl synchronised.

Constructing an interactive program from several objects with internal communications.   We will show how to construct an interactive program from the combination of several objects, which possibly call each other. In a first step we combine two objects o_1 and o_2 with receiving interfaces I_1, I_2 and the same outside interface O into one object $o_1 \oplus o_2$ with interfaces $I_1 \oplus I_2$ and O. If we consider our main example, namely having objects o_1, o_2, o_3 with receiving interface I_1, I_2, I_3, respectively and the same outside interface $O = I_1 \oplus I_2 \oplus I_3$, we see that $o_1 \oplus o_2 \oplus o_3$ is an object, for which the receiving and the outside interface are the same, namely O. In a second step we will then show how to simulate a program for which the receiving and outside interface coincides – let it be I – by an interactive program which has no outside interface and I as receiving interface.

Step 1: Definition of $o_0 \oplus o_1$.   Let o_i have receiving interface I_i and the same outside interface O. Let $I := I_0 \oplus I_1$, and $O' := O \oplus O$. For $icl : \text{List } I.C$ we define $(\text{proj}_0 \; icl)$ to be the list of elements $ic : I_0.C$ s.t. $(\text{inl } ic)$ occurs in icl (taken in the same order as they occur in icl). Similarly, we define $\text{proj}_1 \; icl : \text{List } I_1.C$ and $\text{proj}_i \; ocl : \text{List } O.C$, where $ocl : \text{List } O'.C$. Furthermore, if $ocl : \text{List } O'.C$ then let unify $ocl : \text{List } O.C$ be the result of replacing $(\text{inl } oc)$ and $(\text{inr } oc)$ occurring in ocl by oc. One can define from elements $icl : \text{List } I.C$, $ocl : \text{List } O'.C$, $o_i :$ $\text{Object}_{\text{server}} \; I_i \; O \; (\text{proj}_i \; icl) \; (\text{proj}_i \; ocl)$ an element

$$o := o_0 \oplus o_1 : \text{Object}_{\text{server}} \; (I_0 \oplus I_1) \; O \; icl \; (\text{unify } ocl) \; .$$

---

[8]Two referees commented that in most object-oriented languages, an object is only able to receive an answer to its most recent open request. Similarly it only sends an answer to the most recent open request it has received. One could modify the behaviour of the objects defined in this section so as to have this behaviour. However, we think that our current version is more flexible, since it allows to deal with concurrency. In a concurrent situation, an object may send several request and receive answers to it in a different order. If we want that an object in our setting only is able to deal with the most recent open request, we can implement such an object as follows: If it receives an answer which is not due yet, it stores this answer internally. It then delays dealing with this answer until it has become an answer to the most recent open request.

We compute the component $o' := o.$receive_request (inl ic) i and leave the other cases to the reader. Let $icl' := $insert$_i$ icl (inl ic), $o'_0 := (o_0.$receive_request ic i') for the index i' corresponding to i in (proj$_0$ icl). If $o'_0 = ($send_answer j r o''_0), then $o' = ($send_answer j' r $(o''_0 \oplus o_1)$), and if $o'_0 = ($send_request oc j o''_0), then $o' = ($send_request oc j' $(o''_0 \oplus o_1)$). Here j' is the index corresponding to j in icl' and ocl, respectively.

Step 2: Simulating the internal communications. The second step is to consider one object for which both receiving interface and outside interface coincide, let it be I. We want to obtain from such an object an interactive program which has only a receiving interface I. This program receives calls via I and passes them to its corresponding object o. If o makes calls to its outside interface I, these are then passed back to o itself as a request from its receiving interface I. Any answers o returns via its receiving interface in response to such requests are passed back to o itself as an answer from its outside interface in response to its original request.

A more general situation, which we do not consider here because of lack of space, would be to have an object with receiving interface $I \oplus X$ and outside interface $O \oplus X$, which can receive requests from the outside via I, send requests to the outside via O, and for which any calls via X to the outside are bounced back to the object in question via its receiving interface part X.

There is one complication, namely that the internal communications between the objects might not terminate. The way of dealing with it is to simulate this program by a state-dependent interactive program. That program receives a request via I. Then its command set changes to {continue}. Whenever it receives continue it will carry out one more step of its internal communication, until an answer to the original request is obtained. Then the answer is given back, the program switches back to its original state where it can receive requests via $I.$C.

Therefore we define a function

$$\text{simulate} : \text{Object}_{\text{server}} \; I \; I \; \text{nil} \; \text{nil} \to \text{IO}^{\infty}_{\text{statedep,server}} \; I' \; s_0$$

for a suitable state-dependent interface I' and $s_0 : I'.$S.

$I'.$S has one state in which it can receive commands from $I.$C, and a second state in which its set of commands is {continue}. In the latter case we need to store the command $c : I.$C it has received but not answered. So the set of states is $1 + I.$C. Let $s_0 := $inl. In state inl, the program can receive commands $c : I.$C. It either replies with response $r : I.$R c, or answers with delay and switches into state (inr c). In state (inr c), it can only receive request continue. It replies with an answer to the original request, or with delay and continues in state (inl c). We obtain the interface $I' := $Interface$_{\text{statedep}}(S = S, C = C, R = R, n = n)$, where

S	$=$	$1 + I.$C			
C inl	$=$	$I.$C	C (inr c)	$=$	{continue}
R inl c	$=$	R (inr c) continue	$-$		delay + reply($r : I.$R c)
n inl c delay	$=$	n (inr c) continue delay	$=$		inr c
n inl c (reply r)	$=$	n (inl c) continue (reply r)	$=$		inl

We consider one case of the definition of $p := \text{simulate } o$. Assume p receives a request $c : C \text{ inl} = I.C$. Then we make case distinction on $o' := o.\text{receive\_request } c \, 0$. If we obtain $(\text{send\_answer } 0 \, r \, o'')$, then the response is $(\text{reply } r)$ and we continue with $(\text{simulate } o'')$. If we obtain $(\text{send\_request } c' \, 0 \, o'')$ then p returns delay. We bounce back c' as a request to o'' by computing $o''' := o''.\text{receive\_request } c' \, 0$, from which we compute the next execution steps of p. The full details will be given in a follow-up paper.

Translation of standard object-oriented code into objects of dependent type theory. We show how to translate object-oriented code, e.g. written in Java, into elements of $(\text{Object}_{\text{server}} \mid O \, icl \, ocl)$. We are able to deal with objects which communicate with a fixed number of other objects and do not create new objects dynamically on the heap. So, when constructed, the object receives references to a fixed number of other objects and is then allowed to communicate with them without modifying them. The code can be represented by the following data:

- We have a global state $G : \text{Set}$ of the system which determines the state of those global instance variables, which are not objects. Instance variables which are objects will be treated as defining an outside interface O.

- We have methods with their arguments and result types, which can be given as a stateless interface I.

- We have an outside interface O, which is obtained as the union of receiving interfaces of all the objects, to which the object can send method calls.

- The body of method $ic : I.C$ is an interactive program which operates as follows: Depending on the global state $g : G$, it computes a new global state, and computes either an answer $r : I.R \, ic$, or it makes a call to its outside interface, i.e. sends $oc : O.C$. Depending on the response $r : O.R \, oc$ it returns a new program of the same form. The updating of G is best dealt with by making use of the state monad $M_G \, X = G \to G \times X$. Then the method body is an element of

$$\begin{aligned} \text{MethodBody } ic &= \text{codata do } (f : M_G \, (\text{Action } ic)) \;, \quad \text{where} \\ \text{Action } ic &= \text{return}(r : I.R \, ic) \\ &\quad + \text{call}(oc : O.C, f' : O.R \, oc \to \text{MethodBody } ic) \end{aligned}$$

The methods are then given as an element

$$\text{methodBody} : (ic : I.C) \to \text{MethodBody } ic \;.$$

The complete code is given as a tuple

$$\langle G, I, O, \text{methodBody} \rangle$$

which we call a *class code*.

Example: We consider as an example a class which computes the Fibonacci numbers efficiently by memorising values it already has computed. We use a Java-like syntax with some functional additions:

```
class Fib{Map mem;
        nat fib_aux(nat n){
          if (n <= 1) {return 1;}
          else {nat k = fib (n-1);
                nat l = fib (n-2); return k+l;}};

        nat fib (nat n){case (lookup(mem,n)){
                          (just(k)) -> {return k;};
                          (nothing) -> {nat k = fib_aux(n);
                                        put(mem,n,k);
                                        return k;}}}};
```

Map is the data type of finite maps from nat to nat, where nat stands for the type of natural numbers. lookup(mem, n) : Maybe(nat) returns just(k) if n is in the domain of mem and $mem(n) = k$, and nothing otherwise. put(mem, n, k) updates mem so that it returns on argument n value k. We have not defined Map as an object with method calls but as a value parameter, in order to obtain a non-trivial global state.

Then the class code for `Fib` is $\langle G, I, O, \text{MethodBody} \rangle$. Here G, I, O are defined as follows:

$$
\begin{array}{lcl}
G & := & \text{Map} \\
I.C & := & \text{fib\_aux}(n : \text{nat}) + \text{fib}(n : \text{nat}), \\
I.R\,c & := & \text{nat} \\
O & := & I
\end{array}
$$

$O = I$, since all method calls to the outside are to the object itself. If we had defined mem to be an object with receiving interface O', then we would have $G = 1$ and $O = I \oplus O'$ instead.

Before defining methodBody we introduce some convenient syntax for dealing with $(M_G\,X)$: Let $\text{return}_G := \lambda x.\lambda g.\langle g, x \rangle : X \to M_G\,X$, and do_G : Action $ic \to \text{MethodBody}\,ic$, $\text{do}_G\,x := \text{do}\,(\text{return}_G\,x)$. Then we define

$$
\begin{aligned}
& \text{methodBody}\,(\text{fib\_aux}\,n) \\
& = \text{if }(n \le 1)\text{ then}(\text{do}_G(\text{return }1)) \\
& \qquad\qquad \text{else }(\text{do}_G\,(\text{call }(\text{fib }(n-1)) \\
& \qquad\qquad\qquad (\lambda k.\text{do}_G\,(\text{call }(\text{fib }(n-2)) \\
& \qquad\qquad\qquad\qquad (\lambda l.\text{do}_G\,(\text{return }(k+l)))))))
\end{aligned}
$$

We leave the definition of methodBody (fib n) to the reader.

Translation of a class code into an object of dependent type theory. The intermediate state of an object determined by a class code

$$\langle G, I, O, \text{methodBody} \rangle$$

is given by $g : G$ and an element $lmc :$ List OpenMethodCall, where

$$\text{OpenMethodCall} := (ic : \text{I.C}) \times (oc : \text{O.C}) \times (f : \text{O.R } oc \to \text{MethodBody } ic)$$

An element $\langle ic, oc, f \rangle :$ OpenMethodCall consists of the original method call ic, the last outside request oc done by the method, and a function f, which determines, depending on a response r to oc the next step in the evaluation of the method. We define a function

$$\text{translate} : (g : \text{G}, lmc : \text{List OpenMethodCall}) \to \text{Object}_{\text{server}} \text{ I O (icl } lmc) \text{ (ocl } lmc)$$

which depends on a suppressed class code and computes from an intermediate state of that program given by g and lmc an object of dependent type theory. Here, (icl lmc) and (ocl lmc) are the results of projecting the elements of lmc to I.C and O.C, respectively. Then the constructor for the object, which depends on the initial internal state $g : G$ is the function

$$\lambda g.\text{translate } g \langle \rangle : G \to \text{Object}_{\text{server}} \text{ I O } \langle \rangle \langle \rangle \ .$$

The definition of $o := \text{translate } g \ lmc$ is by guarded recursion, and we compute only $o' := (o.\text{receive\_request } ic \ i)$, i.e. the case when o receives a method call ic: Let methodBody $ic = \text{do } f$, $f \ g = \langle g', m \rangle$. We make case distinction on m. If we obtain (call $oc \ f'$), $o' := \text{send\_request } oc \ i$ (translate $g' \ lmc'$) where $lmc' = \text{insert}_i \ lmc \ \langle ic, oc, f' \rangle$. If we obtain (return r), $o' := \text{send\_answer } i \ r$ (translate $g' \ lmc$).

6.7 CONCLUSION

We have reviewed the basics of interactive programs in dependent type theory. Then we have introduced a notion of an object which is isolated (no interaction with other objects). We have seen how to combine objects with and without self-referential calls. Finally we have shown how to translate standard object-oriented class code into dependently typed objects.

The above deals only with some aspects of object-oriented programming. We have touched hiding and renaming, but we have not dealt yet in full with inheritance. Already subtyping is known to be quite complicated in the context of dependent type theory, and inheritance is even more sophisticated. However, it seems not to be too complicated to translate an object from one interface to a restricted one, which gives some notion of subtyping.

The most difficult problem seems to be to deal with a heap and pointers, in order to be able to construct, for instance, linked lists. We have some ideas based on the IORef monad in Haskell, but we do not have space to discuss these in this article.

What is, of course, missing is to translate typical object-oriented programs into this language and see how they execute. For this it is necessary to introduce an improved syntax for representing object-oriented programs in dependent type theory. The class code introduced in section 6.6 seems to be pretty close to a satisfactory solution.

ACKNOWLEDGMENTS

We would like to thank the referees for valuable comments.

REFERENCES

[AC96]   Martín Abadi and Luca Cardelli, editors. *A Theory of Objects*. Springer, 1996.

[Alt01] Thorsten Altenkirch. Representations of first order function types as terminal coalgebras. In *Typed Lambda Calculi and Applications, TLCA 2001*, number 2044 in LNCS, pages 8 – 21, 2001.

[BC04]   Yves Bertot and Pierre Castéran. *Interactive Theorem Proving and Program Development*. Springer, 2004.

[Bru02] Kim B. Bruce. *Foundations of object-oriented languages: types and semantics*. MIT Press, Cambridge, MA, USA, 2002.

[Coq94] Thierry Coquand. Infinite objects in type theory. In Henk Barendregt and Tobias Nipkow, editors, *Types for Proofs and Programs*, volume 806 of *LNCS*, pages 62–78, 1994.

[Geu92] Herman Geuvers. Inductive and coinductive types with iteration and recursion. In B. Nordström, K. Petersson, and G. Plotkin, editors, *Informal proceedings of the 1992 workshop on Types for Proofs and Programs, Bastad 1992, Sweden*, pages 183 – 207, 1992.

[Gim94] E. Gimenéz. Codifying guarded definitions with recursive schemes. In *Proceedings of the 1994 Workshop on Types for Proofs and Programs*, pages 39–59. LNCS No. 996, 1994.

[Gor94] A.D. Gordon. *Functional programming and Input/Output*. Distinguished Dissertations in Computer Science. Cambridge University Press, 1994.

[Han00] Peter Hancock. *Ordinals and interactive programs*. PhD thesis, LFCS, University of Edinburgh, 2000.

[HH06]   Peter Hancock and Pierre Hyvernat. Programming interfaces and basic topology. *Ann. Pure Appl. Logic*, 137(1-3):189–239, 2006.

[HS99]   Peter Hancock and Anton Setzer. The IO monad in dependent type theory. In *Electronic proceedings of the workshop on dependent types in programming, Göteborg, 27-28 March 1999*, 1999. Available via http://www.md.chalmers.se/Cs/Research/Semantics/APPSEM/dtp99.html.

[HS00a] Peter Hancock and Anton Setzer. Interactive programs in dependent type theory. In P. Clote and H. Schwichtenberg, editors, *Proceedings of CSL 2000*, volume 1862 of *LNCS*, pages 317–331, 2000.

[HS00b] Peter Hancock and Anton Setzer. Specifying interactions with dependent types. In *Workshop on subtyping and dependent types in programming, Portugal, 7 July 2000*, 2000. Electronic proceedings, http://www-sop.inria.fr/oasis/DTP00/Proceedings/proceedings.html.

[HS04]   Peter Hancock and Anton Setzer. Interactive programs and weakly final coalgebras (extended version). In T. Altenkirch, M. Hofmann, and J. Hughes, editors, *Dependently typed programming*, number 04381 in Dagstuhl Seminar Proceedings, 2004. Available via http://drops.dagstuhl.de/opus/.

[Jac95]   Bart Jacobs. Objects and classes, co-algebraically. In Burkhard Freitag, Cliff B.
          Jones, Christian Lengauer, and Hans-Jörg Schek, editors, *Object Orientation
          with Parallelism and Persistence*, pages 83–103. Kluwer, 1995.

[Jac98]   Bart Jacobs. Coalgebraic reasoning about classes in object-oriented languages.
          Electronical Notes in Computer Science, 11:231 – 242, 1998. Special issue on
          the workshop Coalgebraic Methods in Computer Science (CMCS 1998).

[KL05]   Oleg Kiselyov and Ralf Lämmel. Haskell's overlooked object system. Submit-
          ted, 2005.

[Mes93]   José Meseguer. A logical theory of concurrent objects and its realization in the
          Maude language. In *Research directions in concurrent object-oriented program-
          ming*, pages 314–390, Cambridge, MA, USA, 1993. MIT Press.

[Mog89]   E. Moggi. Computational lambda-calculus and monads. In *Proceedings of the
          Logic in Computer Science Conference*, 1989.

[MS05]   Markus Michelbrink and Anton Setzer. State dependent IO-monads in type the-
          ory. *Electronic Notes in Theoretical Computer Science, Elsevier*, 122:127 – 146,
          2005.

[NPS90]   Bengt Nordström, Kent Petersson, and Jan M. Smith. *Programming in Martin-
          Löf's Type Theory: An Introduction*. Clarendon Press, 1990.

[Pie92]   Benjamin C. Pierce. Bounded quantification is undecidable. In *POPL '92:
          Proceedings of the 19th ACM SIGPLAN-SIGACT symposium on Principles of
          programming languages*, pages 305–315, New York, NY, USA, 1992. ACM
          Press.

[PT94]   Benjamin C. Pierce and David N. Turner. Simple type-theoretic foundations for
          object-oriented programming. *Journal of Functional Programming*, 4(2):207–
          247, 1994.

[PW93]   S. L. Peyton Jones and Philip Wadler. Imperative functional programming. In
          20'th ACM Symposium on Principles of Programming Languages, Charlotte,
          North Carolina, January 1993.

[Rei95]   H. Reichel. An approach to object semantics based on terminal co-algebras.
          Mathematical Structures in Computer Science, 5:129–152, 1995.

[Set03]   Anton Setzer. Java as a functional programming language. In Herman Geuvers
          and Freek Wiedijk, editors, *Types for Proofs and Programs*, pages 279 – 298.
          LNCS 2646, 2003.

[Wad97]   Philip Wadler. How to declare an imperative. *ACM Comput. Surv.*, 29(3):240–
          263, 1997.

Chapter 7

A Sharing Analysis for SAFE

Ricardo Peña[1], Clara Segura[1], Manuel Montenegro[1]

Abstract: We present a sharing analysis for the functional language *Safe*. This is a first-order eager language with facilities for programmer-controlled destruction and copying of data structures. It provides also *regions*, i.e. disjoint parts of the heap where the programmer may allocate data structures. The analysis gives upper approximations to the sets of variables respectively sharing a recursive substructure, or any substructure, of a given variable. Its results will be used to guarantee that destruction facilities and region management are done in a safe way. In order to have a modular and efficient analysis, we provide signatures for functions, which summarize their sharing behaviour. The paper ends up describing the implementation of the analysis and some examples.

7.1 INTRODUCTION

Many imperative languages offer low-level mechanisms to allocate and free heap memory, which the programmer may use in order to dynamically create and destroy pointer based data structures. These mechanisms give the programmer complete control over memory usage but are very error prone. Well-known problems that may arise when using a programmer-controlled memory management are dangling references, undesired sharing between data structures with complex side effects as a consequence, and polluting memory with garbage.

Functional languages usually consider memory management as a low-level issue. Allocation is done implicitly and usually a garbage collector takes care of the memory exhaustion situation.

In a previous paper [11] we proposed a semi-explicit approach to memory control by defining a functional language, called *Safe*, in which the programmer cooperates with the memory management system by providing some information

---

[1]Dpto. Sistemas Informáticos y Computación, Univ. Complutense de Madrid, Spain
`ricardo@sip.ucm.es`, `csegura@sip.ucm.es`, `manuelmont@gmail.com`
Work partially supported by the Spanish project TIN2004-07943-C04.

about the intended use of data structures. For instance, the programmer may indicate that some particular data structure will not be needed in the future and that, as a consequence, it may be safely destroyed by the run-time system and its memory recovered. The language uses regions to locate data structures. It also allows controlling the degree of sharing between different data structures. A garbage collector is not needed. Allocation and destruction of data structures are done as execution proceeds.

More interesting is the definition of a type system guaranteeing that destruction facilities and region management can be done in a safe way. This type system will be the main topic of an ongoing paper (a draft version can be found at [11]). In particular, it guarantees that dangling pointers are never created in the live heap. An ill-constructed program is rejected by the type system. It makes a heavy use of sharing information, given by two functions called *shareall* and *sharerec*. Given a subexpression e of a function body and a free variable x such that e is included in the lexical scope of x,

- *shareall*(x,e) returns the set of all the variables in scope in e which, at runtime, may share any substructure of the structure pointed to by x.

- *sharerec*(x,e) returns the set of all the variables in scope in e which, at runtime, may share any recursive substructure of the structure pointed to by x.

In this paper an upper approximation to these two functions is computed at compile time by an abstract interpretation-like analysis. Additionally we formally define the operational semantics of the language.

The structure of the paper is as follows: In section 7.2, we provide a summary of the syntax and the operational semantics of *Safe*. Then, section 7.3 presents in detail the sharing analysis. In sections 7.4 and 7.5, the implementation of the analysis is described and it is applied to some illustrative examples. Section 7.6 surveys some related work and concludes.

7.2 SUMMARY OF *SAFE*

7.2.1 Syntax

We start by reproducing some crucial definitions which underlie the language. In section 7.6 we compare our language design with other approaches using regions and memory management facilities.

Definition 7.1. *A **region** is a contiguous memory area in the heap where data structures can be constructed, read, or destroyed. It is allocated and freed as a whole, in constant time.*

Definition 7.2. *A **cell** is a small memory space, big enough to hold a data constructor. In implementation terms, a cell contains the mark (or code pointer) of the constructor, and a representation of the free variables to which the constructor is applied. These may consist either of basic values or of pointers to non-basic values.*

Definition 7.3. *A* **data structure**, *in the following a DS, is the set of cells obtained by starting at one cell considered as the root, and taking the transitive closure of the relation $C_1 \rightarrow C_2$, where C_1 and C_2 are cells of the same type T, and in C_1 there is a pointer to C_2.*

That means that, for instance, in a list of type `[[a]]`, we are considering as a DS the cons-nil spine of the *outermost* list, but not those belonging to the individual innermost lists. Each one of the latter constitutes a separate DS.

The following decisions were taken:

1. A DS completely resides in one region.

2. One DS can be part of another DS, or two DSs can share a third one.

3. The basic values —integers, booleans, etc.— do not allocate cells in regions. They live inside the cells of DSs, or in the stack.

4. A function of n parameters can access:

   - Its n parameters, each one residing in a possibly different region.

   - Its **output region**, whenever it builds a DS as a result. There is at most one output region per function. Delivering this region identifier as a parameter is the responsibility of the call. We force functions to leave their result in an output region belonging to the calling context in order to safely delete the intermediate results computed by the function.

   - Its (optional) **working region**, referred to through the reserved identifier *self*, where it may create intermediate DSs. The working region has the same lifetime as the function call: It is allocated at each invocation and freed at function termination.

5. If a parameter of a function is a DS, it can be destroyed by the function. We will say that the parameter is **condemned** because this capability depends on the function definition, not on its use.

6. The capabilities a function has on its accessible DSs and regions are: a function may only read a DS which is a read-only parameter; a function may read (before destroying it), and must destroy, a DS which is a condemned parameter; a function may construct, read, or destroy DSs, in either its output or its working region.

The syntax of *Safe* is shown in figure 7.1. This is a first-order eager functional language where sharing is expressed using variables in function and constructor applications. We intend *Safe* to be a core language resulting from the desugaring of a higher level language similar to Haskell or ML. The analysis defined in this paper is, however, done at core level. This is a usual approach in many compilers.

A program *prog* in *Safe* is a sequence of possibly recursive polymorphic function definitions[3] followed by a main expression *expr*, calling them, whose value

---

[3]The extension to mutual recursion would pose no special problems, but we restrict ourselves to non-mutual recursion in order to ease the presentation.

$$
\begin{array}{rll}
prog & \rightarrow & dec_1; \ldots; dec_n; expr \\
dec & \rightarrow & f\ \overline{x_i}^n\ r = expr \qquad\qquad \{\text{recursive, polymorphic function}\} \\
& & \mid f\ \overline{x_i}^n = expr \\
expr & \rightarrow & a \qquad\qquad\qquad\quad \{\text{atom: literal } c \text{ or variable } x\} \\
& & \mid x@r \qquad\qquad\qquad \{\text{copy}\} \\
& & \mid x! \qquad\qquad\qquad\quad \{\text{reuse}\} \\
& & \mid (f\ \overline{a_i}^n)@r \qquad\quad \{\text{function application}\} \\
& & \mid (f\ \overline{a_i}^n) \qquad\qquad \{\text{function application}\} \\
& & \mid (C\ \overline{a_i}^n)@r \qquad\quad \{\text{constructor application}\} \\
& & \mid \mathbf{let}\ x_1 = expr_1\ \mathbf{in}\ expr \quad \{\text{non-recursive, monomorphic}\} \\
& & \mid \mathbf{case}\ x\ \mathbf{of}\ \overline{alt_i}^n \qquad \{\text{read-only case}\} \\
& & \mid \mathbf{case!}\ x\ \mathbf{of}\ \overline{alt_i}^n \quad\; \{\text{destructive case}\} \\
alt & \rightarrow & C\ \overline{x_i}^n \rightarrow expr \\
\end{array}
$$

FIGURE 7.1.   First-order functional language *Safe*

is the program result. Function definitions building and returning a new DS will have an additional parameter r, which is the output region, where the resulting DS is to be constructed. In the right-hand side expression only r and its own working region *self* may be used. Polymorphic algebraic data types definitions are also allowed. We will assume they are defined separately through **data** declarations.

The program expressions include variables, literals, function and constructor applications, and also **let** and **case** expressions, but there are some additional expressions:

If x is a DS, the expression $x@r$ represents a copy in region r of the DS accessed from x. The DS x must live in a region $r' \neq r$. Both x and $x@r$ have the same recursive structure and they share their non-recursive substructures.

The expression $x!$ means the reusing of the destroyable DS to which x points. This is useful when we do not want to destroy completely a condemned parameter but instead to reuse part of it. In semantic terms, x and $x!$ point to the same physical structure but, in language terms, once $x!$ is used, the name x becomes unaccessible in the subsequent text.

In function application we have a special syntax $@r$ to express the inclusion of the additional output region parameter. Using the same syntax, we express that a constructor application is to be allocated in region r.

The **case!** expression indicates that the outer constructor of x is disposed after the pattern matching so that x is not accessible anymore. The recursive substructures may be explicitly destroyed in the subsequent code via another **case!** or reused via $x!$. A condemned variable may be read but, once its content has been destroyed or reused in another structure, it may not be accessed again. This is what the type system guarantees. It annotates the type of such variable with a !.

We show now with several examples how to use the language facilities. In some of them we will write $x!$ or $(C\ \overline{a_i}^n)@r$ as actual parameters of applications in order to abbreviate, when a **let** binding would in fact be needed. In these examples we show also the types that the functions have in the type system previously

$$revD :: \forall a, \rho_1, \rho_2.[a]!@\rho_1 \rightarrow \rho_2 \rightarrow [a]@\rho_2$$
$$revD\ xs\ r = (revauxD\ xs\ [\ ]@r)@r$$

$$revauxD :: \forall a, \rho_1, \rho_2.[a]!@\rho_1 \rightarrow [a]@\rho_2 \rightarrow \rho_2 \rightarrow [a]@\rho_2$$
$$revauxD\ xs\ ys\ r = \textbf{case}!\ xs\ \textbf{of}$$
$$[\ ] \rightarrow ys$$
$$x : xx \rightarrow (revauxD\ xx\ (x : ys)@r)@r$$

FIGURE 7.2.   Destructive list inversion

$$insertD :: \forall a, \rho.a \rightarrow Tree\ a!@\rho \rightarrow \rho \rightarrow Tree\ a@\rho$$
$$insertD\ x\ t\ r = \textbf{case}!\ t\ \textbf{of}$$
$$Empty \quad \rightarrow (Node\ Empty@r\ x\ Empty@r)@r$$
$$Node\ i\ y\ d \rightarrow \textbf{let}\ c = compare\ x\ y$$
$$\textbf{in case}\ c\ \textbf{of}$$
$$LT \rightarrow (Node\ (insertD\ x\ i)@r\ y\ d!)@r$$
$$EQ \rightarrow (Node\ i!\ y\ d!)@r$$
$$GT \rightarrow (Node\ i!\ y\ (insertD\ x\ d)@r)@r$$

FIGURE 7.3.   Destructive insertion with reuse in a binary search tree

mentioned. The first example is the function that reverses a list and, at the same time, destroys it. The code is shown in figure 7.2. We use the usual auxiliary function with an accumulator parameter. Notice that the differences with the usual functional version are, on the one hand, the use of the region parameter r and, on the other, that a **case**! is used over the original list. The recursive application of the function destroys it completely. Those who call *revD* should know that the argument is lost in the inversion process, and should not try to use it anymore. This is reflected in the type of the first argument with a ! annotation.

The next example illustrates the reuse of a condemned structure. It is the function, shown in figure 7.3, that inserts an element in a binary search tree in such a way that the original tree is partially destroyed. Everything but the path from the root to the inserted element is reused to build the new tree but these parts can no longer be accessed from the original tree.

Notice that when the inserted element is already in the tree (*EQ* branch) the tree t that has just been destroyed is rebuilt. The purely functional version is obtained by removing the ! annotations and returning t in the *EQ* branch.

7.2.2   Big-Step Operational Semantics

We have developed a big-step operational semantics for this language and a small-step operational semantics which have been proved equivalent. In figure 7.4 we show the big-step operational semantics for *Safe* expressions. A **judgment** of the

$$\Delta, k : c \Downarrow \Delta, k : c \quad [Lit]$$

$$\Delta, k : C\,\overline{a_i}^n @\,j \Downarrow \Delta, k : C\,\overline{a_i}^n @\,j \quad [Cons]$$

$$\Delta[p \mapsto w], k : p \Downarrow \Delta, k : w \quad [Var_1]$$

$$\frac{j \leq k \quad l \neq j \quad (\Theta, C\,\overline{a_i'}^n) = copy(\Delta, j, C\,\overline{a_i}^n)}{\Delta[p \mapsto (l, C\,\overline{a_i}^n)], k : p @\,j \Downarrow \Theta, k : C\,\overline{a_i'}^n @\,j} \quad [Var_2]$$

$$\Delta \cup [p \mapsto w], k : p! \Downarrow \Delta, k : w \quad [Var_3]$$

$$\frac{\Sigma \vdash f\,\overline{x_i}^n = e \quad \Delta, k+1 : e\overline{[a_i/x_i}^n, k+1/self] \Downarrow \Theta, k'+1 : v}{\Delta, k : f\,\overline{a_i}^n \Downarrow \Theta \mid_{k'}, k' : v} \quad [App_1]$$

$$\frac{\Sigma \vdash f\,\overline{x_i}^n\,r = e \quad \Delta, k+1 : e\overline{[a_i/x_i}^n, k+1/self, j/r] \Downarrow \Theta, k'+1 : v}{\Delta, k : f\,\overline{a_i}^n @\,j \Downarrow \Theta \mid_{k'}, k' : v} \quad [App_2]$$

$$\frac{\Delta, k : e_1 \Downarrow \Theta, k' : c \quad \Theta, k' : e[c/x_1] \Downarrow \Psi, k'' : v}{\Delta, k : \textbf{let}\ x_1 = e_1\ \textbf{in}\ e \Downarrow \Psi, k'' : v} \quad [Let_1]$$

$$\frac{\Delta, k : e_1 \Downarrow \Theta, k' : C\,\overline{a_i}^n @\,j \quad j \leq k' \quad fresh(p) \quad \Theta \cup [p \mapsto (j, C\,\overline{a_i}^n)], k' : e[p/x_1] \Downarrow \Psi, k'' : v}{\Delta, k : \textbf{let}\ x_1 = e_1\ \textbf{in}\ e \Downarrow \Psi, k'' : v} \quad [Let_2]$$

$$\frac{C = C_r \quad \Delta, k : e_r\overline{[a_j/x_{rj}}^{n_r}] \Downarrow \Theta, k' : v}{\Delta[p \mapsto (j, C\,\overline{a_i}^{n_r})], k : \textbf{case}\ p\ \textbf{of}\ \overline{C_i\,\overline{x_{ij}}^{n_i} \to e_i}^m \Downarrow \Theta, k' : v} \quad [Case]$$

$$\frac{C = C_r \quad \Delta, k : e_r\overline{[a_j/x_{rj}}^{n_r}] \Downarrow \Theta, k' : v}{\Delta \cup [p \mapsto (j, C\,\overline{a_i}^{n_r})], k : \textbf{case!}\ p\ \textbf{of}\ \overline{C_i\,\overline{x_{ij}}^{n_i} \to e_i}^m \Downarrow \Theta, k' : v} \quad [Case!]$$

FIGURE 7.4. *SAFE* **big-step operational semantics**

form $\Delta, k : e \Downarrow \Theta, k' : v$ means that expression e is successfully reduced to normal form v under heap Δ with $k + 1$ regions, ranging from 0 to k, and that a final heap Θ with $k' + 1$ regions is produced as a side effect.

A **heap** Δ is a function from fresh variables p (in fact, heap pointers) to closures w of the form $(j, C\,\overline{a_i}^n)$, meaning that the closure resides in region j. If $[p \mapsto w] \in \Delta$ and $w = (j, C\,\overline{a_i}^n)$, we will say that $region(w) = j$ and also that $region(p) = j$.

A **normal form** v is either a basic value c or a construction $C\,\overline{a_i}^n @\,j$ to be stored in region j. The actual parameters a_i are either basic values or pointers to other closures. Actual region identifiers j are just natural numbers. Formal regions appearing in a function body are either the formal parameter r or the constant *self*.

By $\Delta[p \mapsto w]$ we denote a heap Δ where the binding $[p \mapsto w]$ is highlighted. In contrast, by $\Delta \cup [p \mapsto w]$ we denote the disjoint union of heap Δ with the binding $[p \mapsto w]$.

The semantics of a complete *Safe* program $d_1; \ldots; d_n; e$ (not shown) is the semantics of the main expression e in an environment Σ containing the declarations

$d_1, \ldots, d_n$ of all the functions.

Rules *Lit* and *Cons* just say that basic values and constructions are normal forms. Rule *Cons* does not create a closure. Closures are actually created by rule *Let*$_2$ which is the only one allocating fresh memory.

Rule *Var*$_1$ brings a copy of a closure into the main expression. Rule *Var*$_2$ makes a complete copy of the DS pointed to by a variable p into a new region j. Function *copy* follows the pointers in recursive positions of the original structure residing in region l and creates in region j a copy of all recursive closures except for the root closure $C\,\overline{a_i}^n$. In our run-time system we foresee that some type information is available so that it is possible to implement this function.

Should *copy* find a dangling pointer during the traversal, the whole rule would fail and the derivation would be stuck at this rule. If there is no failure, then the main expression becomes a copy $C\,\overline{a_i'}^n$ of this root closure where the pointers a_i in recursive positions pointing to closures in region l have been replaced by pointers a_i' to the corresponding closures in region j. The pointers in non-recursive positions of all the copied closures are kept identical in the new closures. This implies that both DSs, the old and the new, may share some sub-structures. For instance, if the original DS is a list of lists, the structure created by *copy* is a copy of the outermost list, while the innermost lists become shared between the old and the new list.

Rule *Var*$_3$ is similar to rule *Var*$_1$ except for the fact that the binding $[p \mapsto w]$ is deleted and p does not belong to the domain of the resulting heap. This action may create dangling pointers in the living heap as some closures may have free occurrences of p.

Rules *App*$_1$ and *App*$_2$ show when a new region is created. Notice that the body of the function is executed in a heap with $k+2$ regions. That is, the formal identifier *self* is bound to the new region $k+1$ so that the function body may create DSs in this region or pass this region as a parameter to function calls. By $\Theta\,|_{k'}$ we denote the heap Θ restricted to closures belonging at most to region k'. In other words, before returning from the function, all closures created in region $k'+1$ are deleted. This action is another source of possible dangling pointers.

Rules *Let*$_1$ and *Let*$_2$ show the eagerness of the language: first, the auxiliary expression e_1 is reduced to normal form and then the main expression is evaluated. The occurrences of the program variable x_1 are replaced either by the normal form if it is a basic value, or by a pointer to it if it is a construction. Notice also that a construction is converted into a closure only if it is bound to a variable in a **let**.

Finally, rule *Case* is the usual one while rule *Case*! expresses what happens in a destructive pattern matching: the binding of the discriminant variable p disappears from the heap. This action is the last source of possible dangling pointers.

Proposition 7.4. *If* $\Delta, k : e \Downarrow \Theta, k' : v$ *is derivable, then* $k = k'$.
Proof: Straightforward, by induction on the depth of the derivation.

In the following, we will feel free to write the derivable judgments as $\Delta, k : e \Downarrow \Theta, k : v$.

By $fv(e)$ we denote the set of free variables of expression e, excluding function names and region variables, and by $frv(e)$, the set of free region variables of e. By *Fresh*, we denote the set of names from which the function *fresh* in rule Let_2 selects fresh names, and by $\mathbb{N}$ the set of natural numbers. Also, by $dom(\Delta)$ and $range(\Delta)$ we denote the following sets:

$$dom(\Delta) \quad \overset{def}{=} \quad \{p \mid [p \mapsto w] \in \Delta\}$$
$$range(\Delta) \quad \overset{def}{=} \quad \bigcup\{fv(w) \mid [p \mapsto w] \in \Delta\}$$

Proposition 7.5. *If e is an expression satisfying $fv(e) \subseteq Fresh$ and $frv(e) \subseteq \mathbb{N}$, and $\Delta, k : e \Downarrow \Theta, k : v$ is derivable, and $range(\Delta) \subseteq Fresh$, then all judgments $\Delta_i, k_i : e_i \Downarrow \Theta_i, k_i : v_i$ of the derivation satisfy:*

1. $fv(e_i) \cup fv(v_i) \subseteq Fresh$.

2. $frv(e_i) \cup frv(v_i) \subseteq \mathbb{N}$.

Proof: By induction on the depth of the derivation.

For this reason, in the rules of figure 7.4 we have systematically used letter p —intended to mean a pointer— when referring to free variables, and letter j — intended to mean a natural number— when referring to free region variables.

7.3   SHARING ANALYSIS

In this section we define an analysis that approximates the sharing relations between the variables of a program. At this point, Hindley-Milner types have already been inferred (see implementation details in section 7.4), so the analysis can ask for the type of a variable through a function called *type*.

7.3.1   Sharing relations

In order to capture sharing, we define four different binary relations between variables:

Definition 7.6. *Given two variables x and y, in scope in an expression,*

1. $x \lhd\!\!\sim y$ denotes that x is a recursive descendant of y.

2. $x \triangle\!\!\sim y$ denotes that x shares a recursive descendant of y.

3. $x \lhd y$ denotes that x is any substructure of y.

4. $x \triangle y$ denotes that x shares any substructure of y.

In figure 7.5 we illustrate these relations using trees to represent data structures in the heap. A black subtree represents a recursive substructure while a white subtree represents any substructure (recursive or not).

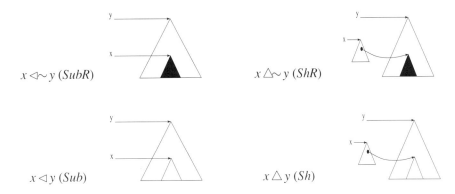

FIGURE 7.5.   Sharing relations

We note that all the four relations are reflexive, $\triangle$ is also symmetric, and $\triangleleft\!\!\sim$ and $\triangleleft$ are transitive. Moreover, the following implications hold:

$$x \triangleleft\!\!\sim y \Rightarrow x \triangleleft y \Rightarrow x \triangle y$$
$$x \triangleleft\!\!\sim y \Rightarrow x \triangle\!\!\sim y \Rightarrow x \triangle y$$

but $\triangleleft$ and $\triangle\!\!\sim$ do not necessarily imply each other.

The interpretation defined in figure 7.6 does a top-down traversal of a program, accumulating these relations as soon as bound variables become free variables.

Whenever convenient, non-symmetric relations can be read as functions $Var \rightarrow \{Var\}$, giving $R(x)$ the set of all y such that yRx (i.e. $(y,x) \in R$). Also we will write $R = [x \rightarrow S]$ to indicate that $S = R(x)$.

The symmetric relation $\triangle$ is kept in a set of sets of variables. If $S \in \triangle$ then $x \triangle y$ for all $x, y \in S$.

Based on the above considerations, we will define an abstract interpretation S (meaning *sharing*) which, given an expression e, delivers the following seven sets:

$$(SubRP, ShRP, SubP, SubR, ShR, Sub, Sh)$$

which contain respectively all the variables z such that $e \triangleleft\!\!\sim z$, $e \triangle\!\!\sim z$, $e \triangleleft z$, $z \triangleleft\!\!\sim e$, $z \triangle\!\!\sim e$, $z \triangleleft e$ and $z \triangle e$, where eRx and xRe means that the normal form of e, when evaluated at run-time, is related to x through R.

7.3.2   Function signatures

In order to achieve a modular analysis, we decide to reflect the result of the analysis of a function f in a *function signature*. We keep these signatures in a function environment ρ. A function signature $\rho(f)$ has the following type: $(\{Int\}, \{Int\}, \{Int\}, \{Int\}, \{Int\}, \{Int\}, \{Int\})$.

The meaning of the seven sets is as above, except for the fact that these contain only parameter indexes instead of all the (free and bound) variables of the body expression. This is reasonable as the effect of a function should be completely reflected in the relationship between the parameters and the result.

In figure 7.6 the interpretation S for expressions is defined. We explain it in detail later. When applied to a function definition $f\ x_1\ldots x_n = e$, it is straightforward to extract the signature of the function while computing the least fixpoint, in case it is recursive. The interpretation of a definition adds the signature of the new definition to the signatures environment:

$$S_d[\![f\ x_1\ldots x_n = e]\!]\ \rho = fix\ (\lambda\rho.\rho\ [f \to extract([x_1,\ldots,x_n],S[\![e]\!]\ R_0\ R_0\ R_0\ R_0\ \rho)])\ \rho_0$$
$$\textbf{where}\ \ \rho_0 = \rho\ [f \to (\emptyset,\emptyset,\emptyset,\emptyset,\emptyset,\emptyset,\emptyset)]$$
$$R_0 = \{(x_i,x_i)\ |\ i \in \{1..n\}\}$$
$$extract(xs,(S_1,\ldots,S_7)) = (\{i\ |\ x_i \in xs \cap S_1\},\ldots,\{i\ |\ x_i \in xs \cap S_7\})$$

where $\rho\ [f \to s]$ either adds signature s for f or replaces it in case there was already one for it. As function S and function $extract$ are monotone over a finite lattice, the least fixpoint exists and can be computed using Kleene's ascending chain.

Given a whole program $P = dec_1;\ldots dec_k;\ e$ the analysis first builds an increasing function environment and then analyses the main expression given initially empty relations (there are no free variables but function names):

$$S_p[\![P]\!] = S[\![e]\!]\ \emptyset\ \emptyset\ \emptyset\ \emptyset\ (S_d[\![dec_k]\!]\ (\ldots(S_d[\![dec_1]\!]\ [\ ])\ldots))$$

Notice that the right-hand sides of the definitions are analysed given relations where each parameter is only related to itself. This means that the signatures are computed assuming that all the parameters are disjoint. When they are not, the function application computes the additional sharing.

7.3.3   Interpretation of expressions

We explain now the details of the interpretation S for expressions. By abuse of notation, we will write $Sh(x)$ even though Sh is not a function, with the following convention:

$$Sh(x) \overset{\text{def}}{=} \bigcup\{S\ |\ x \in S \wedge S \in Sh\}$$

A basic value c neither has substructures nor is part of any structure, so its interpretation is just seven empty sets.

If x is returned as the result of a function, we use the information in the accumulator parameters of S to extract all the relevant information about its sharing. Notice that, from the operational semantics point of view, $x!$ is just the same structure as x, hence its interpretation. The semantics of $x@r$ is the creation of a copy of the recursive part of x in a new region r. As a consequence, the first, third, fourth and fifth sets of the interpretation are empty, and the third set excludes those variables with the same (recursive) type as x. The non-recursive part of $x@r$ is shared with x and potentially with any variable sharing substructures with x, hence the seventh set. However only the non-recursive children of x may be children of $x@r$, hence the sixth set.

$S \; [\![c]\!] \; SubR \; ShR \; Sub \; Sh \; \rho \qquad\qquad = \quad (\emptyset, \emptyset, \emptyset, \emptyset, \emptyset, \emptyset, \emptyset)$

$S \; [\![x]\!] \; SubR \; ShR \; Sub \; Sh \; \rho \qquad\qquad = \quad (\{z \mid x \in SubR(z)\},$
$\qquad\qquad\qquad\qquad\qquad\qquad\qquad\qquad \{z \mid x \in ShR(z)\},$
$\qquad\qquad\qquad\qquad\qquad\qquad\qquad\qquad \{z \mid x \in Sub(z)\},$
$\qquad\qquad\qquad\qquad\qquad\qquad\qquad\qquad SubR(x), ShR(x), Sub(x), Sh(x))$

$S \; [\![x!]\!] \; SubR \; ShR \; Sub \; Sh \; \rho \qquad\quad = \quad S \; [\![x]\!] \; SubR \; ShR \; Sub \; Sh \; \rho$

$S \; [\![x@r]\!] \; SubR \; ShR \; Sub \; Sh \; \rho \qquad = \quad (\emptyset,$
$\qquad\qquad\qquad\qquad\qquad\qquad\qquad\qquad \{z \mid x \in ShR(z) \wedge type(z) \neq type(x)\},$
$\qquad\qquad\qquad\qquad\qquad\qquad\qquad\qquad \emptyset, \emptyset, \emptyset,$
$\qquad\qquad\qquad\qquad\qquad\qquad\qquad\qquad Sub(x) - SubR(x), Sh(x))$

$S \; [\![g \; \overline{a_i}^m @r]\!] \; SubR \; ShR \; Sub \; Sh \; \rho \quad = \quad (\{z \mid \exists j \in SubRPg.a_j \in SubR(z)\},$
$\qquad\qquad\qquad\qquad\qquad\qquad\qquad\qquad \{z \mid \exists j \in ShRPg.a_j \in ShR(z)\},$
$\qquad\qquad\qquad\qquad\qquad\qquad\qquad\qquad \{z \mid \exists j \in SubPg.a_j \in Sub(z)\},$
$\qquad\qquad\qquad\qquad\qquad\qquad\qquad\qquad \bigcup_j \{SubR(a_j) \mid j \in SubRg\},$
$\qquad\qquad\qquad\qquad\qquad\qquad\qquad\qquad \bigcup_j \{ShR(a_j) \mid j \in ShRg\},$
$\qquad\qquad\qquad\qquad\qquad\qquad\qquad\qquad \bigcup_j \{Sub(a_j) \mid j \in Subg\},$
$\qquad\qquad\qquad\qquad\qquad\qquad\qquad\qquad \bigcup_j \{Sh(a_j) \mid j \in Shg\})$

where $(SubRPg, ShRPg, SubPg, SubRg, ShRg, Subg, Shg) = \rho(g)$

$S \; [\![C \; \overline{a_i}^m @r]\!] \; SubR \; ShR \; Sub \; Sh \; \rho \quad = \quad (\emptyset,$
$\qquad\qquad\qquad\qquad\qquad\qquad\qquad\qquad \{z \mid \exists a_j \in ShR(z)\},$
$\qquad\qquad\qquad\qquad\qquad\qquad\qquad\qquad \emptyset,$
$\qquad\qquad\qquad\qquad\qquad\qquad\qquad\qquad \bigcup_j \{SubR(a_j) \mid j \in RecPos(C)\},$
$\qquad\qquad\qquad\qquad\qquad\qquad\qquad\qquad \bigcup_j \{ShR(a_j) \mid j \in RecPos(C)\},$
$\qquad\qquad\qquad\qquad\qquad\qquad\qquad\qquad \bigcup_j \{Sub(a_j) \mid j \in \{1..m\}\},$
$\qquad\qquad\qquad\qquad\qquad\qquad\qquad\qquad \bigcup_j \{Sh(a_j) \mid j \in \{1..m\}\})$

$S \; [\![\textbf{let} \; x_1 = e_1 \; \textbf{in} \; e]\!] \; SubR \; ShR \; Sub \; Sh \; \rho \quad = \quad (S \; [\![e]\!] \; SubR_2 \; ShR_2 \; Sub_2 \; Sh_2 \; \rho) \backslash \{x_1\}$

where $(SubRP_1, ShRP_1, SubP_1, SubR_1, ShR_1, Sub_1, Sh_1) = S \; [\![e_1]\!] \; SubR \; ShR \; Sub \; Sh \; \rho$
$\qquad SubR_2 = (SubR \cup [x_1 \mapsto SubR_1] \cup \{[z \mapsto \{x_1\}] \mid z \in SubRP_1\})^*$
$\qquad ShR_2 = ShR \cup [x_1 \mapsto ShR_1] \cup \{[z \mapsto \{x_1\}] \mid z \in ShRP_1\} \cup SubR_2$
$\qquad Sub_2 = (Sub \cup [x_1 \mapsto Sub_1] \cup \{[z \mapsto \{x_1\}] \mid z \in SubP_1\})^*$
$\qquad Sh_2 = Sh \cup \{\{x_1\} \cup Sh_1\} \uplus (Sub_2 \cup ShR_2)$

$S \; [\![\textbf{case}\,x\,\textbf{of}\,\overline{C_i \, \overline{x_{ij}}^{n_i} \to e_i}]\!] \; SubR \; ShR \; Sub \; Sh \; \rho \quad = \quad \bigcup_i ((S \; [\![e_i]\!] \; SubR_i \; ShR_i \; Sub_i \; Sh_i \; \rho) \backslash \{\overline{x_{ij}}^{n_i}\})$

where $SubR_i = (SubR \cup [x \mapsto \{x_{ij} \mid j \in RecPos(C_i)\}]$
$\qquad\qquad\qquad \cup \{[x_{ij} \mapsto SubR(x) \backslash \{x\}] \mid j \in RecPos(C_i)\})^*$
$\qquad ShR_i = ShR \cup \{[x_{ij} \mapsto ShR(x)] \mid j \in RecPos(C_i)\} \cup SubR_i$
$\qquad Sub_i = (Sub \cup [x \mapsto \{x_{ij} \mid j \in \{1..n_i\}\}] \cup \{[x_{ij} \mapsto Sub(x) \backslash \{x\}] \mid j \in \{1..n_i\}\})^*$
$\qquad Sh_i = (Sh \cup \{\{y, x_{ij}\} \mid y \in Sh(x) \wedge j \in \{1..n_i\}\}) \uplus (Sub_i \cup ShR_i)$

FIGURE 7.6. Definition of the abstract interpretation S

The interpretation of a function application $g \, \overline{a_i}^m @ r$ returning a DS is rather involved. Regarding the first set, the recursive descendant relation is transitive. So, the result of g is a recursive descendant of a variable z if and only if an actual parameter a_j of g is a recursive descendant of z and the result of g is a recursive descendant of a_j. The same transitivity applies to the third set. Regarding the second set, the result of g shares a recursive descendant of a variable z if an actual parameter a_j of g shares a recursive descendant of z, and a_j is in sharing relation with the result of g. This probably will give us more variables than the ones actually sharing a recursive descendant of z, but it is a safe approximation. This is a place where signatures may lose information. The fourth and sixth sets are defined taking respectively into account the transitivity of the relations $\lhd\!\!\sim$ and $\lhd$. The fifth and seventh sets are safe, but may be imprecise, approximations to respectively the set of variables sharing a recursive substructure and sharing any substructure with the result of g. The interpretation of a function application $g \, \overline{a_i}^m$ of a function g not having an output region as a parameter is identical to the previous one.

In the interpretation of a data construction $C \, \overline{a_i}^m @ r$, the first and third sets are empty because a newly created DS cannot be a substructure of any other. However, it will share a recursive descendant of a variable z if any of its substructures a_j already shared it. Any variable being a recursive descendant of a recursive parameter a_j of C will also be a recursive descendant of the construction. The set $RecPos(C)$ contains the recursive positions of the constructor C. Similar reasoning can be applied to the fifth set containing the variables which share a recursive descendant of the construction. The next set definition exploits the transitivity of the $\lhd$ relation. The last set consists also of a union over all the parameters of C, because the construction inherits the sharing of all its substructures.

The **let** expression introduces a new bound variable x_1 which may appear free in the main expression e. First, the interpretation of the auxiliary expression e_1 is launched and the sharing created by it is accumulated in the parameters. Then, the main expression e is interpreted taking into account the new sharing. If R represents a reflexive, non-symmetric, transitive relation, by R^* we mean its reflexive, transitive closure. Operator $\uplus$ computes the union of a reflexive, symmetric and non-transitive relation and a reflexive, non-symmetric transitive one. Notice that the addition of $SubR_2$ to ShR_2, and the addition of this latter set and that of Sub_2 to Sh_2, just implements the inclusion of the underlying relations, as explained above. Finally, the information related to x_1 is deleted as the variable will not be in scope in the context.

As usual, the interpretation of a **case** is the least upper bound of the interpretation of its alternatives, and this involves a loss of information. Before each alternative is interpreted, we accumulate the sharing of the bound variables x_{ij} introduced by it. Part of this sharing is straightforward: all these variables are descendants of the parent structure x and some of them are recursive descendants of it. Additionally, if we have $y \in SubR(x) \land y \neq x$, that means $y \lhd\!\!\sim x$. As there is no more information available, it may be the case that $y \lhd\!\!\sim x_{ij}$ for some recursive child of x. The only safe way to cope with this possibility is to include in $SubR_i$

the pairs $y \lhd\!\!\sim x_{ij}$ for all the recursive children of x. Similar reasoning applies to the rest of the sets.

The interpretation of **case**! is the same as the previous one. Although the discriminant variable is being condemned we cannot eliminate its sharing information as we do not know whether the rest of variables are safely used. For example, we could write $z = $ **case**! x **of** $C\ y \rightarrow x$. The analysis says that variables x and z share a substructure, although such sharing is unsafe because x has been destroyed.

7.4 IMPLEMENTATION AND EXAMPLES

In this section we present the implementation of the analysis and give some examples of functions to which it has been applied. We have defined a concrete sugared syntax for *Safe* in which programs look very much like Haskell programs, i.e. functions are defined by means of equations and pattern matching, guards and **where** clauses are allowed, as well as data type declarations and infix operators and constructors.

A complete front-end has been developed from scratch by using standard tools such as lexical analyzer and parser generators. In figure 7.7 we show its (already implemented) phases. The renamer phase ensures that every identifier is well defined and that every bound variable is given a different name. A Hindley-Milner type inference is done at this level in order to reject ill-typed programs, and to provide report messages related to the sugared syntax. Also, the sharing analysis needs the underlying type of a variable and the recursive positions of data constructors (cf. figure 7.6). This phase decorates each expression in the abstract syntax tree with its Hindley-Milner type.

The desugarer transforms the high-level syntax into the *Safe* core syntax presented in section 7.2. During this transformation new bound variables may be introduced. They are given appropriate types and fresh names.

After these steps, the sharing analysis described in this paper is done. Its main function has the following type:

```
analyzePrg :: Prog TypeExp -> Prog (TypeExp, Maybe ShareInfo)
```

That is, given a program decorated with Hindley-Milner types, it returns a program additionally decorated with sharing information. This sharing information has different shapes depending on the entity being decorated:

- If it is a function definition, it consists of its signature.

- If it is a **let** or a **case**! expression, it consists of the sharing information accumulated from the beginning of the function body this expression belongs to, up to the root of the expression. These are the only expressions where we need to keep the sharing information, which consists of the seven sets corresponding to the variable either defined by the **let** expression, or inspected by the **case**! expression.

- Binding occurrences of variables are not decorated.

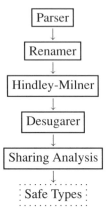

FIGURE 7.7.   Phases of the Safe compiler implementation

In this way, it is easy to extract the *shareall* and *sharerec* sets for any given variable x in any given context. Then, $ShR(x)$ and $Sh(x)$ give us the desired information. Such information is used in the following phase, whose result consists of Hindley-Milner types decorated with destruction (!) annotations, i.e. *Safe* types. This phase is also implemented but it is not part of this paper.

The front-end and the analysis have been implemented in Haskell using the GHC to compile it. In total, about 3,000 Haskell lines have been written. In order to improve efficiency, the analyzer stores the four relations in a single balanced tree, using the modules `Map` and `Set` of the GHC library [1]. Also, the inverses of the three first relations are kept in the tree. In this way, the symmetric and/or transitive closures, the union, and some other operations on relations needed by the analysis, are done in a more concise and efficient way. Let n be the number of bound variables of a function body, m the size of its abstract syntax tree, and p the number of function arguments. Then, the analysis cost is in $O(nmp)$ in the worst case. The analysis of a function can be done independently of each other.

When applied to the functions defined in section 7.2, the analysis computes the following signatures:

$$\rho(revauxD) = (\{2\}, \{2\}, \{2\}, \{2\}, \{2\}, \{2\}, \{1,2\})$$
$$\rho(revD) = (\emptyset, \emptyset, \emptyset, \emptyset, \emptyset, \emptyset, \{1\})$$
$$\rho(insertD) = (\emptyset, \{1,2\}, \emptyset, \emptyset, \{2\}, \{1\}, \{1,2\})$$

which are accurate descriptions of the input-output sharing relations of these functions.

Function *revauxD* appends the reverse of its first parameter to its second one. Since it does not reuse the recursive cells of its first parameter, the only remaining recursive sharing is related to its second parameter. Nevertheless the sharing with the non-recursive elements of the first list is reflected in the last set of the signature. Function *revD* consists of a simple call to *revauxD* passing it an empty list as the second actual parameter, so the only remaining sharing is that between the

$$splitD :: \forall a, \rho.Int \rightarrow [a]!@\rho \rightarrow \rho \rightarrow ([a]@\rho,[a]@\rho)@\rho$$
$$splitD \; 0 \; xs! \; r \quad = ([\,]@r,xs!)@r$$
$$splitD \; n \; [\,]! \; r \quad = ([\,]@r,[\,]@r)@r$$
$$splitD \; n \; (x:xs)! \; r = ((x:xs_1)@r,xs_2)@r$$
$$\textbf{where} \; (xs_1,xs_2) = splitD \; (n-1) \; xs \; r$$

$$mergeD :: \forall a, \rho.[a]!@\rho \rightarrow [a]!@\rho \rightarrow \rho \rightarrow [a]@\rho$$
$$mergeD \; [\,]! \; ys! \; r \qquad = ys!$$
$$mergeD \; (x:xs)! \; [\,]! \; r \qquad = (x:xs!)@r$$
$$mergeD \; (x:xs)! \; (y:ys)! \; r =$$
$$\quad | \; x \le y \quad = (x : mergeD \; xs \; (y:ys!)@r \; @r)@r$$
$$\quad | \; otherwise = (y : mergeD \; (x:xs!)@r \; ys \; @r)@r$$

$$msortD :: \forall a, \rho.[a]!@\rho \rightarrow \rho \rightarrow [a]@\rho$$
$$msortD \; xs \; r$$
$$\quad | \; n \le 1 \qquad = xs!$$
$$\quad | \; otherwise = mergeD \; (msortD \; xs_1 \; @r) \; (msortD \; xs_2 \; @r) \; @r$$
$$\quad \textbf{where} \; (xs_1,xs_2) = splitD \; (n \; `div` \; 2) \; xs \; @r$$
$$\qquad n = length \; xs$$

FIGURE 7.8.   Destructive mergesort

non-recursive structures of the input and output lists.

Function *insertD* builds a new tree which shares with the original tree everything but the path from the root to the inserted element. This means that the resulting tree and the original one share both recursive and non-recursive parts. This is the reason why 2 appears in the second, fifth and seventh sets of the signature. Also the resulting tree has x as a non-recursive descendant, so the 1 in the second, sixth and seventh sets.

7.5   A MORE INVOLVED EXAMPLE

In this section we show a more involved example, a *mergesort* algorithm. In order to give compact code, the functions shown in this section are sugared although the analysis is executed over their desugared versions.

First, we define auxiliary functions to split the input list and merge two ordered lists in a single ordered list. In figure 7.8 (top) we show a destructive version of the splitting function. As in the previous examples, there are small differences with a purely functional version. In the base case ($n = 0$) we reuse the list in the output; in the recursive case we use a **case**! (written as a destructive pattern) over the argument list. We also have to add $@r$ where necessary.

The sharing analysis produces the following signature for this function:

$$\rho(splitD) = (\emptyset, \{2\}, \emptyset, \emptyset, \emptyset, \{2\}, \{2\})$$

meaning that:

- The result of the function may share a recursive substructure of the argument list, which is obvious.

- The argument list may be a child of the result, which is true when n is 0.

- The argument list and the result share some substructure, which again is obvious.

Figure 7.8 (middle) shows the destructive version of the merging function. In the recursive calls to *mergeD* one of the parameters is one of the original lists. But the original list may not be referenced as its top cell has been destroyed by a **case!**, so the original list is rebuilt by reusing its components. This is the only detail to care about.

The sharing analysis produces the following signature for this function:

$$\rho(mergeD) = (\{2\}, \{1,2\}, \{2\}, \{2\}, \{1,2\}, \{2\}, \{1,2\})$$

meaning that the argument lists and the result may share recursive and non-recursive substructures one of the other. Notice that only the second argument list may be a recursive child of the result (and vice versa) because we build a new cell for each cell of the first argument while we reuse the second argument list when the first one is empty.

Finally, in figure 7.8 (bottom) we show the destructive mergesort *msortD*, that uses the previously defined functions. Both the input list *xs* and the intermediate results are either destroyed or reused into the result. This allows us to conclude that this function consumes a constant additional heap space. In [11] we proved this by induction on the length of the argument list. The sharing analysis produces the following signature for this function:

$$\rho(msortD) = (\{1\}, \{1\}, \{1\}, \{1\}, \{1\}, \{1\}, \{1\})$$

meaning that the argument list and the result may share recursive and non-recursive substructures one of the other.

Recall that this sharing analysis does not take into account the fact that some substructures are destroyed because it is not known yet whether the program is type-safe. In this sense the analysis is an upper approximation of the sharing.

7.6   RELATED WORK AND CONCLUSIONS

Several approaches have been taken to memory management, some of which have inspired our work. In [5] a comparison of some of them are presented by using a Game of Life example:

$$nextgen\ g = \{\text{create and return new generation}\}$$
$$life\ n\ g = \textbf{if}\ n = 0\ \textbf{then}\ g$$
$$\qquad\qquad \textbf{else}\ life\ (n-1)\ (nextgen\ g)$$

Assuming that a generation g is a big data structure allocated in the heap, a functional program like this would allocate n generations in the heap until a garbage collector would decide to dispose the intermediate ones. However, if the intended use of one intermediate generation is only the creation of the next one, it seems reasonable to dispose the intermediate data structure as soon as possible. In *Safe* we would modify the program as follows in order to get such behaviour:

$$nextgen \ g \ r = \textbf{case!} \ g \ \textbf{of} \rightarrow \ldots$$
$$\{\text{create new generation in region r}\}$$
$$life \ n \ g \ r = \textbf{if} \ n = 0 \ \textbf{then} \ g! \quad \{\text{reuse argument } g\}$$
$$\textbf{else} \ life \ (n-1) \ (nextgen \ g@r)@r$$

Tofte and Talpin [13] introduced the use of nested regions with a **letregion** ρ construct as an extension to Core ML. Like ours, regions are memory areas where DSs can be constructed, and they are allocated and deallocated as a whole. A difference is that, in our system, region allocation/deallocation are synchronized with function calls. Also, we have an additional mechanism that allows us to selectively destroy DSs in the working or in the output region. In their framework, in the previous example a single region is forced to contain all the intermediate data structures and no memory advantages are obtained.

An extension to their work [3, 12] allows to *reset* all the data structures in a region without deallocating the whole region. In the previous example the old generation region is resetted once the new generation is created. So, a new temporary region is created to allocate the new generation which must be copied into the output region after resetting it. The user is responsible for introducing the copy functions but not for annotating the program with resetting annotations.

$$nextgen \ g = \{\text{create and return new generation}\}$$
$$life \ n \ g = \textbf{if} \ n = 0 \ \textbf{then} \ g$$
$$\textbf{else} \ life \ (n-1) \ (\textbf{copy} \ (nextgen \ g))$$

The *copy* function allows to build the new generation in a separated region and makes possible to run *life* in constant heap space. However, this version may waste a lot of time just in copying, once for each recursive call. Additionally, inserting the *copy* function requires a deep knowledge of the resetting mechanism as this is not explicit in the program. In our opinion, the **case!** annotation is more intuitive: the user just says that the old generation may be liberated as it will not be used anymore. And it is only said for a particular data structure, not for the whole region.

The AFL system [2] inserts (as a result of an analysis) allocation and deallocation commands separated from the **letregion** construct which now only brings new regions into scope. In the example, this allows to free the old region as soon as the new generation is computed, without needing a copy in each recursive call. This is only required in the base case:

$$nextgen \ g - \{\text{create and return new generation}\}$$
$$life \ n \ g = \textbf{if} \ n = 0 \ \textbf{then} \ \textbf{copy} \ g$$
$$\textbf{else} \ life \ (n-1) \ (nextgen \ g)$$

Again, inserting the *copy* function in the appropriate place requires a deep knowledge of the annotations that will be inserted after the analysis.

Our region system is simpler than those of the above approaches and it does not require such complex inference algorithms. Although the version of the language presented here has explicit regions, we have designed a region inference algorithm which hides them from the programmer. It is a simple extension of the Hindley-Milner type inference one.

Hughes and Pareto [8] also incorporate in Embedded-ML the concept of region to their sized-types system so that heap and stack consumption can be type-checked. In this approach, region sizes are bounded. Our main differences to them are again the region-function association and the explicit disposal of structures. Their sized types system could be a good starting point for our future work, as we also intend to compute region sizes at compile time.

More recently, in a proof carrying code framework, Hofmann and Jost [6] have developed a type system to infer heap consumption. Theirs is also a first-order eager functional language with a construct *match'* which has inspired our **case**!. They associate to each function the space required by its execution and the remaining space after it. They also use a linear type system but they do not achieve a complete safety in using destructive facilities. Unlike us they do not use the concept of nested regions where DSs are allocated, so that sharing is not controlled in the same way.

There are many works devoted to sharing analysis in functional and logic languages, some of them rather old. In the functional field, the aim of most analyses has been performing part of the garbage collection at compile time, or detecting when destructive updating of data structures could be done safely.

In Hudak's approach [7] a reference count of shared data is done at compile time by using abstract interpretation on a first-order, eager functional language with updatable arrays. The abstract domains consist of just natural numbers. In order to have a terminating analysis the domains are restricted to finite intervals $\{1 \ldots n\}$, for an arbitrary n, and topped with ∞ meaning 'too much sharing'. An array-based quicksort algorithm using in-place updating is shown correct by the analysis.

Jones and Le Métayer [10] also use abstract interpretation on a first-order, eager functional language with non-homogeneous lists in order to avoid allocation of fresh cells and to reuse instead cells not needed by the rest of the computation. Their analysis is a combination of sharing and absence analyses and the abstract domains are nested tuples of booleans. Again, domains are forced to be finite by bounding the nesting depth of the tuples by an arbitrary number n. The analysis looks rather complex and not very efficient as it does several traversals of the same code. Also the authors do not show evidence of having implemented it.

Inoue et al. [9] use non-standard techniques, such as context-free languages and intersection between such languages, in order to perform garbage collection at compile time. The language analyzed is a first-order subset of LISP. The idea is to detect cells created by a function but not belonging to the result. Such cells are disposed of at the end of the function body. They show good results for some

LISP test programs. In the logic programming field, Gudjonsson et al. [4] provide a comprehensive survey of sharing analyses. Sharing is important here for much the same reasons than in the functional field but also to detect opportunities for parallel evaluation.

The main novelty of our approach is, on the one hand, the context — a functional language with explicit destruction — and on the other its modularity. In the previously described works, the analyses are done at the whole program level while ours is done function by function. Reflecting the result of a function analysis in a signature provides the connection between the different functions of the program. The subsequent safety analysis, based on a special type system, will also be done function by function, so the sharing signature can be seen as an annotation associated to the function type.

We find our sharing analysis to be precise enough for successfully analysing the examples we have tried so far, but its quality will be evaluated when both phases, the sharing and the safety analysis, work together. The safety type system, not described here, has some characteristics of linear types (see [14] as a basic reference and [6] as a nearer one) and, as it has already been said, it heavily uses the result of the sharing analysis.

As future work, we will prove the correctness of the analysis with respect to the small-step operational semantics (not shown in this paper) of the language. Also, as we have already said, the region annotations $@r$ will be inferred so that the programmer will forget about regions: each data structure not sharing any substructure with the function result will be considered local and, consequently, built in the working (self) region of the function. The rest of them will be built in the output region.

Our final aim is to develop a type-based analysis that automatically infers memory consumption. A sized-types system could automate induction reasoning like the one mentioned in section 7.5.

REFERENCES

[1] S. Adams. Efficient sets –a balancing act. *Journal of Functional Programming*, 3(4):553–561, 1993.

[2] A. Aiken, M. Fähndrich, and R. Levien. Better static memory management: improving region-based analysis of higher-order languages. In *Proceedings of the ACM SIGPLAN 1995 conference on Programming language design and implementation, PLDI'95*, pages 174–185. ACM Press, 1995.

[3] L. Birkedal, M. Tofte, and M. Vejlstrup. From region inference to von neumann machines via region representation inference. In *Conference Record of POPL '96: The* 23rd *ACM SIGPLAN-SIGACT*, pages 171–183, 1996.

[4] G. Gudjónsson and W. H. Winsborough. Compile-time memory reuse in logic programming languages through update in place. *ACM TOPLAS*, 21(3):430–501, 1999.

[5] F. Henglein, H. Makholm, and H. Niss. A direct approach to control-flow sensitive region-based memory management. In *Proceedings of the 3rd ACM SIGPLAN*

international conference on Principles and Practice of Declarative Programming, PPDP'01, pages 175–186. ACM Press, 2001.

[6] M. Hofmann and S. Jost. Static prediction of heap space usage for first-order functional programs. In *Proceedings of the 30th ACM SIGPLAN-SIGACT Symposium on Principles of Programming Languages*, pages 185–197. ACM Press, 2003.

[7] P. Hudak. A Semantic Model of Reference Counting and its Abstraction. In *Lisp and Functional Programming Conference*, pages 351–363. ACM Press, 1986.

[8] R. J. M. Hughes and L. Pareto. Recursion and Dynamic Data-Structures in Bounded Space; Towards Embedded ML Programming. In *Proceedings of the Fourth ACM SIGPLAN International Conference on Functional Programming, ICFP'99*, ACM Sigplan Notices, pages 70–81, Paris, France, September 1999. ACM Press.

[9] K. Inoue, H. Seki, and H. Yagi. Analysis of Functional Programs to Detect Run-Time Garbage Cells. *ACM TOPLAS*, 10(4):555–578, 1988.

[10] S. B. Jones and D. Le Metayer. Compile Time Garbage Collection by Sharing Analysis. In *Int. Conf. on Functional Programming and Computer Architecture*, pages 54–74. ACM Press, 1989.

[11] R. Peña and C. Segura. A First-Order Functional Language for Reasoning about Heap Consumption. In *16th International Workshop on Implementation and Application of Functional Languages, IFL'04. Technical Report 0408, Christian-Albrechts University of Kiel*, pages 64–80, 2004.

[12] M. Tofte, L. Birkedal, M. Elsman, N. Hallenberg, T. H. Olesen, and P. Sestoft. Programming with regions in the MLKit (revised for version 4.3.0). Technical report, IT University of Copenhagen, Denmark, 2006.

[13] M. Tofte and J.-P. Talpin. Region-based memory management. *Information and Computation*, 132(2):109–176, 1997.

[14] P. Wadler. Linear types can change the world! In *IFIP TC 2 Working Conference on Programming Concepts and Methods*. North Holland, 1990.

Chapter 8

Memory Usage Improvement Using Runtime Alias Detection

Ryo Hanai[1], Tomoharu Ugawa[2], Masashi Yoneda[2], Masahiro Yasugi[2], Taiichi Yuasa[2]

Abstract: Region-based memory management replaces runtime garbage collection and it enables each memory operation to be constant time operation. This is very important feature for real time applications. However, there are some kinds of programs which are not amenable to region inference. When executed on region-based systems, these programs can cause significant memory leakage and in the worst case, they cannot finish their execution because of memory shortage.

In this paper, we present a technique to improve memory usage of Tofte/-Talpin region-based system[8] . Our technique adds some changes to Storage Mode Analysis (SMA)[2], which is a succeeding phase of region inference, and delays some decisions till runtime as to whether or not it is possible to overwrite existing objects. Our method is especially useful for a program compiled separately, where we cannot see the contexts in which top-level functions are called. We implemented this technique to MLKit[7][3] and confirmed that the amount of memory used during execution is reduced for some programs.

---

[1]Graduate School of Information Science and Technology, The University of Tokyo; E-mail: `hanai@jsk.t.u-tokyo.ac.jp`

[2]Graduate School of Informatics, Kyoto University; E-mail: `foosen@kuis.kyoto-u.ac.jp`, `myoneda@kuis.kyoto-u.ac.jp`, `yasugi@kuis.kyoto-u.ac.jp`, `yuasa@kuis.kyoto-u.ac.jp`

8.1 INTRODUCTION

Tofte and Talpin proposed a novel method for memory management called region inference in typed, higher-order languages. In their method, memory is composed of blocks called regions, and when to allocate and deallocate regions are determined automatically by the compiler using a type system, and source programs are translated into target programs with region annotations. Their method realizes fairly economical use of memory for many programs. However, there are some kinds of programs which are not amenable to region inference. When executed on region-based systems, these programs can cause large amount of memory leak and in the worst case, they cannot finish their execution because of memory shortage. Therefore, some people proposed methods to improve memory usage of Tofte/Talpin system and others proposed different region inference systems.

In this paper, we propose another technique to improve memory usage of Tofte/Talpin system by checking alias relations between region variables at runtime, which depends on the dynamic context.

Figure 8.1 shows an example of ML-like program. This is translated into the

```
letrec f(x, y) =
      let a = if x < 0 then - x else x in
            let b = if y < 0 then - y else y in a + b
      end end
in
      let u = 1 and v = 2
      in f(u, u) + f(u, v) + f(v, u) end
end end
```

FIGURE 8.1. An example program

program shown in figure 8.2 by Tofte/Talpin system. Note that there are many other region annotation inserted. However, we show only the minimum of region annotations needed to explain our basic idea for simplicity. This program has letregion constructs and allocation directives (attop ρ and atbot ρ) in it. When a program is translated by region inference, all allocation directives in the translated program are at ρ, and then SMA turns these directives into extended allocation directives such as attop ρ or atbot ρ.

There are two kinds of annotations. letregion ρ in e allocates a new region and binds it to the region variable ρ. The scope of ρ is the expression e. Upon completion of the evaluation of e, the region bound to ρ is deallocated. At the same time, all values it contains are discarded. The expressions e attop ρ and

```
letrec f [ρ₁, ρ₂] (x, y) =
  let a = if x < 0 then - x attop ρ₁ else x
  in let b = if y < 0 then - y attop ρ₂ else y
     in a + b
  end end
in
  letregion ρ₃, ρ₄
  in let u = 1 atbot ρ₃ and v = 2 atbot ρ₄
     in f [ρ₃, ρ₃] (u , u) + f [ρ₃, ρ₄] (u , v) + f [ρ₄, ρ₃] (v , u)
end end end
```

FIGURE 8.2.   An example program with region annotations

e atbot ρ evaluate e and write the result in ρ. We assume all values including integers are each stored in some region.

The difference among these three directives is how to create an object. Each region can grow dynamically. When an object is created with attop ρ directive, the object is added to the top of the region. That is, the size of the region bound to ρ is increased by the size of the object. On the other hand, when an object is created with atbot ρ directive, first the region is reset, meaning that all objects in the region are deallocated, and then the new object is allocated. This enables memory used by objects in the region to be recycled before the region itself is deallocated.

Functions defined by letrec construct are region polymorphic. They can take extra region parameters, which are bound to actual regions by a region instantiation construct. This region polymorphism is very important from the viewpoint of memory usage because it allows expressions to perform operations on different regions depending on the context. However, it can cause region aliases, i.e., region variables bound to the same region at runtime.

8.1.1   Extending Tofte/Talpin system

Informally, SMA first makes a graph expressing the possibility of aliases by analyzing the whole program, and then generates one definition for each function. Therefore, even if a region in which an object will be stored is not actually aliased at runtime by any of region variables which may be accessed by the remaining computation, SMA gives up region-resetting.

In the translated program, values of -x and -y are both stored without resetting. This is because both of the region parameters ρ_1 and ρ_2 can be aliases of the same region bound to ρ_3 (or ρ_4).

This fact means that we can increase the region-resetting by comparing the regions bound to possible region aliases at runtime (ρ_1 and ρ_2 in the example). To realize this, we list up possible region aliases in compile time, and determine whether we reset the region or not at runtime. Our method is especially useful for a program compiled separately where we cannot see the contexts in which top-level functions are called.

In the next section, we pick up some features of Tofte/Talpin system, on which our method is based, and then present our method in section 8.3. Evaluation of our method is in section 8.4, and a discussion of related work is in section 8.5. Section 8.6 presents future work. Finally we conclude this paper in section 8.7.

8.2   OVERVIEW OF THE TOFTE/TALPIN SYSTEM

In this section, we give a short description of the Tofte/Talpin system especially of SMA, on which our proposal is based. Please refer to [2][6][8] for more details.

8.2.1   Region Inference

Since the source language of Tofte/Talpin system is an ML-like functional language[5], we present only the core language. The grammar is as follows. We use f and x to

$$
\begin{aligned}
e \quad ::= \quad & c \mid x \mid \lambda x.e \mid e_1 \, e_2 \\
\mid \quad & \texttt{let } x = e_1 \texttt{ in } e_2 \texttt{ end} \\
\mid \quad & \texttt{letrec } f(x) = e_1 \texttt{ in } e_2 \texttt{ end}
\end{aligned}
$$

FIGURE 8.3.   Source Language

range over variables and c to range over integer constants. The `letrec` construct defines recursive functions. The operational semantics of the source language is quite standard.

Tofte/Talpin region inference system translates source language into target language below. The target language is essentially conventional polymorphically typed lambda calculus [4], but it has several constructs to express region operations explained in section 8.1. The allocation directive a indicates the region where the value should be put. For example, the form $\lambda x.e$ at ρ puts the closure representing $\lambda x.e$ into the region bound to ρ. The output of region inference contains only at ρ allocation directive. The other three directives are used in the output of SMA as we explain in the next subsection. The `letrec` construct puts a region function closure into the region indicated by a, and the application form $f \, [a_1, \ldots, a_n] \, a_0$ extracts this region function closure, applies it to arguments and creates a function closure in the region indicated by a_0. The reason allocation

$$
\begin{array}{rcl}
e & ::= & c\,a \mid x \mid \lambda x.e\,a \mid e_1\,e_2 \\
  & \mid & \mathtt{let}\ x = e_1\ \mathtt{in}\ e_2\ \mathtt{end} \\
  & \mid & \mathtt{letrec}\ f[\rho](x)\,a = e_1\ \mathtt{in}\ e_2\ \mathtt{end} \\
  & \mid & \mathtt{letregion}\ \rho\ \mathtt{in}\ e\ \mathtt{end} \\
  & \mid & f\,[a]\,a \\
a & ::= & \mathtt{at}\ \rho \mid \mathtt{attop}\ \rho \mid \mathtt{atbot}\ \rho \mid \mathtt{sat}\ \rho
\end{array}
$$

FIGURE 8.4.   Target Language

directives are written as arguments instead of just region variables is explained in 8.2.2.

For each expression, Tofte/Talpin region inference system infers the place of the value and the regions accessed during the evaluation of the expression. These regions accessed during the evaluation is called the *effect* of the expression. For this purpose, the type of the target language describes an expression's use of regions, as well as the type of its value. The grammar is given below.

$$
\begin{array}{rcll}
\tau & ::= & \mathtt{int} \mid \alpha \mid \mu \xrightarrow{\varepsilon.\varphi} \mu & (type) \\
\mu & ::= & (\tau,\rho) & (type\ with\ place) \\
\eta & ::= & \mathtt{get}(\rho) \mid \mathtt{put}(\rho) \mid \varepsilon & (effect)
\end{array}
$$

The $\varepsilon.\varphi$ denotes an *arrow effect* which is the effect of applying a function. The ε is called *effect variable* and used to express the dependency between effects.

Type schemes are given as follows.

$$
\begin{array}{rcll}
\sigma & ::= & \forall \alpha_1 \cdots \alpha_n \varepsilon_1 \cdots \varepsilon_m.\underline{\tau} & (simple\ type\ scheme) \\
\pi & ::= & \forall \rho_1 \cdots \rho_k \alpha_1 \cdots \alpha_n \varepsilon_1 \cdots \varepsilon_m.\underline{\tau} & (compound\ type\ scheme)
\end{array}
$$

Simple type schemes quantify over both ordinary type variables and effect variables, and are introduced by `let`. Compound type schemes quantify over region variables as well and are introduced by `letrec`. For the region inference algorithm, there is a good overview in [1]. Please refer to it.

8.2.2   Storage Mode Analysis

SMA is a successive phase of region inference in Tofte/Talpin system. SMA takes a program with all allocation directives being `at` ρ as its input, and replaces those directives into extended allocation directives `attop` ρ, `atbot` ρ, `sat` ρ. Therefore, the source and target languages for SMA are both the language shown in figure 8.4.

Regions introduced by letregion construct cannot be deallocated until the control flow of the program exits its scope. As a result, objects created in a region during successive function calls cannot be deallocated until the program returns to its outermost call even if those objects become useless. This means that the size of some regions and/or the number of regions may keep growing until the program returns.

To alleviate this situation, Tofte et al. use an optimization after the region inference phase. They call this optimization storage mode analysis, which is abbreviated to SMA. SMA is a kind of flow analysis and changes some object creations into the ones with region-resetting. Here, region-resetting means that all values in the region are discarded but the region itself is not deallocated. For this purpose, they extend allocation directives at ρ to two different kinds of allocation directives, attop ρ and atbot ρ. The allocation directive attop ρ is the same as at ρ operationally, but atbot ρ means a value is created after the region is reset. They also add another allocation directive sat ρ, meaning "somewhere at" for letrec bound region variables to realize more efficient memory usage. Generally, letrec bound region variables are bound to regions passed by their callers. Therefore, when a function creates a new object in a region, it cannot tell if the region still has objects which will be used by the caller only from the function-local analysis. So sat ρ in a function decides whether it uses reset or not using the information passed by its caller. The allocation directive written in a position of arguments of the region application form indicates how to pass this information. When an argument is indicated by atbot, it means that the region is not used by the caller anymore. The sat directive is used for letrec-bound region variables, which indicates that the caller passes the information given by its caller as it is.

SMA first analyzes the whole program and make a directed graph G expressing the dependency of region and effect variables. This graph is called region flow graph. There is one node in G for every region variable and every effect variable which occurs in the program. Thus, we can identify variables with nodes. Whenever the program has a letrec bound program variable f with type scheme:

$$\pi \quad = \quad \forall \cdots \rho_i \cdots \alpha_j \cdots \varepsilon_k \cdots . \underline{\tau}$$

and whenever there is an applied occurrence of f instantiated by a substitution:

$$S = (\{\cdots \rho_i \mapsto \rho_i' \cdots\}, \{\cdots \tau_j \mapsto \tau_j' \cdots\}, \{\cdots \varepsilon_k \mapsto \varepsilon_k'.\varphi_k \cdots\})$$

there is an edge from ρ_i to ρ_i', and from ε_k to ε_k'. Similarly for let bound variables. Finally, for every effect $\varepsilon.\varphi$ occurring anywhere in the program, there is an edge from ε to every region and effect variable which occurs free in φ. Intuitively, region variables reachable from a region variable ρ can be aliases of ρ, and region variables reachable from an effect variable ε can be accessed by calling a function whose arrow effect is $\varepsilon.\varphi$ (for some φ).

Next, at each allocation point, SMA identifies live program variables, and then identifies region variables which may be accessed by the rest of the computation using types of the live variables and the graph G. First, three kinds of contexts are introduced to express the situation where there is no λ between the region variable we are to allocate a value and its binder (figure 8.5). These contexts are *local expression context L*, *local allocation context R*, and *global expression context E* respectively. Here, we assume the input program is in K-normal form.

$$
\begin{aligned}
L \quad ::= \quad & [\,] \\
| \quad & \texttt{let } x = L \texttt{ in } e_2 \\
| \quad & \texttt{let } x = e_1 \texttt{ in } L \\
| \quad & \texttt{letrec } f[\rho](x)\, a = e_1 \texttt{ in } L \texttt{ end} \\
| \quad & \texttt{letregion } \rho \texttt{ in } L \texttt{ end} \\
R \quad ::= \quad & L[v\,[\,]] \\
| \quad & L[f[a_1,\ldots,a_{i-1},[\,],a_{i+1},\ldots,a_k]\, a\, x] \\
| \quad & L[f[a]\,[\,]\, x] \\
| \quad & L[\texttt{letrec } f[\rho](x)\,[\,] = e_1 \texttt{ in } e_2 \texttt{ end}] \\
E \quad ::= \quad & L \\
| \quad & L[\texttt{let } x = (\lambda x.E)\, a \texttt{ in } e_2 \texttt{ end}] \\
| \quad & L[\texttt{letrec } f[\rho](x)\, a = E \texttt{ in } e_2 \texttt{ end}]
\end{aligned}
$$

FIGURE 8.5.   Contexts

Then, the set of live program variables at the hole of a local context L and a local allocation context R is defined as follows.

$$
\begin{aligned}
& LV([\,]) \\
& LV(\texttt{let } x = L \texttt{ in } e_2) = LV(L) \cup (FV(e_2)\setminus\{x\}) \\
& LV(\texttt{letrec } f[\rho](x)\, a = e_1 \texttt{ in } L \texttt{ end}) = LV(L) \\
& LV(\texttt{letregion } \rho \texttt{ in } L \texttt{ end}) = LV(L)
\end{aligned}
$$

$$
\begin{aligned}
& LV(L[v\,[\,]]) = FV(v) \cup LV(L) \\
& LV(L[f[a_1,\ldots,a_{i-1},[\,],a_{i+1},\ldots,a_k]\, a\, x]) = LV(L) \\
& LV(L[f[a]\,[\,]\, x]) = \{f,x\} \cup LV(L) \\
& LV(L[\texttt{letrec } f[\rho](x)\,[\,] = e_1 \texttt{ in } e_2 \texttt{ end}]) = \\
& \quad (FV(e_1)\setminus\{f,x\}) \cup (FV(e_2)\setminus\{f\}) \cup LV(L)
\end{aligned}
$$

Here, $FV(e)$ means the set of program variables that occur free in e.

Using these definitions, the translation rules of SMA is written in figure 8.6. For simplicity, we assume that every region-polymorphic function has at precisely one region parameter. Let $\text{frv}(A)$ be the set of free region variables for a semantic objects A such as expressions, types, and type schemes. Similarly, let $fev(A)$ be the set of free effect variables. For every node n in the region flow graph G, let $\langle n \rangle$ denote the set of variables that are reachable in G starting from n, including n itself. This definition is naturally extended to the set of nodes. Let $lrv(x)$ to be the set of the *live region variables*, $\{\langle \rho \rangle \mid \rho \in frv(T, \rho)\} \cup \{\langle \varepsilon \rangle \cap RegionVars \mid \varepsilon \in fev(T)\}$.

$$\frac{\rho \notin lrv(LV(R))}{\begin{array}{l} \texttt{letregion}\, \rho \,\texttt{in}\, R[\texttt{at}\, \rho]\, \texttt{end} \\ \Rightarrow \texttt{letregion}\, \rho \,\texttt{in}\, R[\texttt{atbot}\, \rho]\, \texttt{end} \end{array}} \qquad (8.1)$$

$$\frac{\rho \in lrv(LV(R))}{\begin{array}{l} \texttt{letregion}\, \rho \,\texttt{in}\, R[\texttt{at}\, \rho]\, \texttt{end} \\ \Rightarrow \texttt{letregion}\, \rho \,\texttt{in}\, R[\texttt{attop}\, \rho]\, \texttt{end} \end{array}} \qquad (8.2)$$

$$\frac{lrv(LV(R)) \cap \langle \rho \rangle = \emptyset}{\begin{array}{l} \texttt{letrec}\, f[\rho](x)\, a{=}R[\texttt{at}\, \rho]\, \texttt{in}\, e\, \texttt{end} \\ \Rightarrow \texttt{letrec}\, f[\rho](x)\, a{=}R[\texttt{sat}\, \rho]\, \texttt{in}\, e\, \texttt{end} \end{array}} \qquad (8.3)$$

$$\frac{lrv(LV(R)) \cap \langle \rho \rangle \neq \emptyset}{\begin{array}{l} \texttt{letrec}\, f[\rho](x)\, a{=}R[\texttt{at}\, \rho]\, \texttt{in}\, e\, \texttt{end} \\ \Rightarrow \texttt{letrec}\, f[\rho](x)\, a{=}R[\texttt{attop}\, \rho]\, \texttt{in}\, e\, \texttt{end} \end{array}} \qquad (8.4)$$

FIGURE 8.6.   **Translation rules of SMA**

8.3   RUN-TIME ALIAS DETECTION

This section describes our technique using runtime alias detection. The third storage mode sat(somewhere at) for letrec bound region variables accomplishes polymorphism in storage mode and enables regions to be reset in more allocation points. However, SMA sometimes translates an allocation directive too conservatively to attop. This is because it translates the directive to sat only if a region we are to allocate an object is never accessed through other region aliases in any instance of the corresponding region-polymorphic function in the whole program.

Then we use the fact that a region bound to each region variable is determined at runtime. For example, figure 8.7 shows a part of region flow graph of the example shown in figure 8.1. This graph shows that ρ_1 and ρ_2 may be bound to the same region ρ_3(or ρ_4). However, in the second instance of f, ρ_1 is bound to ρ_3 and ρ_2 is bound to ρ_4 (figure 8.8 (b)). In the third instance of f, ρ_1 is bound to ρ_4 and ρ_2 is bound to ρ_3 (figure 8.8 (c)). Therefore ρ_1 and ρ_2 are not aliases in these cases. On the other hand, both of ρ_1 and ρ_2 are bound to the region bound to ρ_1 in the first instance of f (figure 8.8 (a)). So, by checking the existence of the problematic aliases (in the example, ρ_1 and ρ_2) at runtime, we can improve

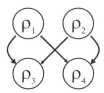

FIGURE 8.7. **A region flow graph for the example program**

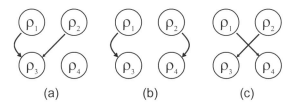

FIGURE 8.8. **Runtime alias relations**

memory usage of Tofte/Talpin system. In the example, resetting is possible in the third instance. Though ρ_1 and ρ_2 are not bound to the same region in the second instance, resetting is not possible since regions passed as parameter is used in the third instance. This is specified by runtime storage.

8.3.1   Extending `sat` allocation directive

We want to delay some of decisions till runtime as to whether or not it is possible to overwrite existing objects. Therefore, we first extend the allocation directive `sat`.

$$a ::= \ldots \mid \mathtt{sat}\ \rho\ \mathtt{unless}\ \{\rho_1, \ldots, \rho_n\}$$

This extended `sat` directive is a version of `sat` and takes a set of region variables after a keyword `unless`. It behaves as `attop` if the target region in which we store an object is aliased by some region variables in the following set. If not, it behaves as original `sat`. In other words, the region is reset if it is not used by the caller. Region variables in the following set are candidates of aliases at the program point.

8.3.2   New Translation Rules

Next, we present new translation rules to replace allocation directives in program. These are based on the rules of SMA.

We define $LR(R)$ to be the set of all region variables which appear free in the type with place of a live program variable in R, $\bigcup \{\mathrm{frv}(T, \rho) \mid x : (T, \rho) \in \mathrm{LV}(R)\}$. We also define $LE(R)$ to be a set $\bigcup \{\mathrm{fev}(T) \mid x : (T, \rho) \in LV(R)\}$. We define

$$\frac{\rho \ \in \ \langle LR(R)\rangle \cup \langle LE(R)\rangle}{E[\texttt{letregion}\, \rho \ \texttt{in}\, R[\texttt{at}\, \rho]\ \texttt{end}]}$$
$$\Rightarrow E[\texttt{letregion}\, \rho \ \texttt{in}\, R[\texttt{attop}\, \rho]\ \texttt{end}] \qquad (8.5)$$

$$\frac{\rho \ \notin \ \langle LR(R)\rangle \cup \langle LE(R)\rangle}{E[\texttt{letregion}\, \rho \ \texttt{in}\, R[\texttt{at}\, \rho]\ \texttt{end}]}$$
$$\Rightarrow E[\texttt{letregion}\, \rho \ \texttt{in}\, R[\texttt{atbot}\, \rho]\ \texttt{end}] \qquad (8.6)$$

$$\frac{\rho \in LR(R) \ \lor \ \langle \rho \rangle \cap \langle LE(R)\rangle \neq \emptyset}{E[\texttt{letrec}\, f[\rho](x)\, a_0{=}R[\texttt{at}\, \rho]\ \texttt{in}\, e\ \texttt{end}]}$$
$$\Rightarrow E[\texttt{letrec}\, f[\rho](x)\, a_0{=}R[\texttt{attop}\, \rho]\ \texttt{in}\, e\ \texttt{end}] \qquad (8.7)$$

$$\frac{\rho \notin LR(R) \quad \langle \rho \rangle \cap \langle LE(R)\rangle = \emptyset}{E[\texttt{letrec}\, f[\rho](x)\, a_0{=}R[\texttt{at}\, \rho]\ \texttt{in}\, e\ \texttt{end}]}$$
$$\Rightarrow E[\texttt{letrec}\, f[\rho](x)\, a_0{=}R[\texttt{sat}\, \rho\ \texttt{unless}\, CS(R,\rho)]\ \texttt{in}\, e\ \texttt{end}] \qquad (8.8)$$

$$\frac{\rho \text{ bound non-locally in } E[R]}{E[R[\texttt{at}\, \rho]] \Rightarrow E[R[\texttt{attop}\, \rho]]} \qquad (8.9)$$

FIGURE 8.9.   New translation rules

$CS(R,\rho)$ to be a set of alias candidates, $\{\rho' \mid \rho' \in \ LR(R), \langle \rho \rangle \cap \langle \rho' \rangle \neq \emptyset\}$. When an object is stored in the region bound to ρ in a local allocation context R, the elements of $CS(R,\rho)$ are free region variables of R, and by tracing the graph G, we can reach a node which is also reachable from ρ.

In our scheme, all at ρ allocation directives for `letrec` bound region variables can be translated to the extended sat ρ directives (rule 8.8). However, every live region cannot always be checked by using region variables within the current scope. Suppose that we are to store an object in a region bound to a region variable ρ, and we can reach a node starting from ρ and a live effect variable in the graph G defined in the previous section. In this case, there may be a live closure which might access the region bound to ρ, but we cannot generate an enough set to confirm that there is no problematic aliases because the current region environment and the region environment of the closure may bind same region variable (by name) to different regions. Therefore we translate these directives conservatively into `attop` (rule 8.7). The other rules are the same as original ones of SMA.

8.3.3   Translation of the Example

Here we consider the example program in figure 8.1 again. When the value of the expression - x is stored in the region bound to ρ_1, the program variable y is alive. Since the value bound to y is in ρ_2 and we can reach nodes ρ_3 (and ρ_4) starting from both ρ_1 and ρ_2 in the graph, we turn "- x at ρ_1" into "- x sat ρ_1 unless $\{\rho_2\}$". Similarly, we turn "- y at ρ_2" into "- y sat ρ_2 unless $\{\rho_1\}$". In this case, a live program variable is "a" and the value of "a" is in the region bound to ρ_1.

```
        mov [ρ₀], reg₁                    mov [ρ₀], reg₁
        bt $1, reg₁                       bt $1, reg₁
        jnc L1                            jnc L2
        foreach ρ in CS{                  foreach ρ in CS{
              mov [ρ], reg₂                     mov [ρ], reg₂
              cmp reg₁, reg₂                    cmp reg₁, reg₂
              je L1                             je L1
        }                                 }
        call resetregion                  jmp L2
  L1:   call allocate               L1:   btr $1, reg₁
                                     L2:   push reg₁
```

FIGURE 8.10.   Code for allocation

FIGURE 8.11.   Code for region parameter passing

8.3.4   Code Generation

Allocation directives are used for two purposes in the language given in figure 8.4. One is to specify how to create objects, and the other is to pass the information as to whether a region is used by the caller or not when region polymorphic functions are instantiated. Figure 8.10 and 8.11 show the code we generate in each case for the extended sat directive. Here, let $reg_i (i = 1, 2)$ to be registers, and $[ρ]$ to be a pointer to the region bound to $ρ$, and *foreach* statement means the body of the statement is generated for each element of the comparison set CS.

As you can see from the figures, both cases are the same until comparisons of regions. First, we load the pointer to the region where we are creating an object, and test its second least significant bit (bt $1, reg_1). MLKit encodes storage mode in the second least significant bit of the pointer to a region. If this bit is zero, the region might be used outside the local context of the current function.

In case of allocation (figure 8.10), if the bit is one, runtime alias checking is of no use. Therefore we just skip the process of comparing regions. Otherwise, we compare the region where we are to allocate an object with regions bound to the region variables in the comparison set, and if there is no region alias in the comparison set, we reset the region before creating the object.

In case of passing a region parameter (figure 8.11), if the storage mode bit is one, we just push the region parameter on the stack. Otherwise, we compare regions and if there is an alias for the region parameter, we set the storage mode bit of the region parameter to zero (btr $1, reg_1), because this region might be used in this local context through a region alias.

TABLE 8.1.   **The number of comparisons and increased percentage of resets**

	# of comparisons	# of resets (SMA)	# of resets (Our Method)	increased ratio of resets
FuhMishra	2,750	1,487	2,091	40.6%
Knuth-Bendix	345,492	2,916,586	2,918,986	0.1%
life	58,812	57,691	80,614	39.7%
Mandelbrot	0	6	6	0.0%
FFT	1,245,184	262,147	655,362	150%
dangle	3,000	3,006	6,006	99.8%

Note that there is no overhead for the object creation when the storage mode bit is zero because we check the bit before comparing regions and the Tofte/Talpin system also needs this check.

MLKit analyzes the size of each region after SMA, and by using size information we can see that some region variables in the comparison set never bind the same region as the region variables where an object is to be allocated. This means we can remove those region variables from the comparison set.

8.4   EVALUATION

We implemented our scheme in MLKit 4.1.4, which is an implementation of Tofte and Talpin system, and evaluated memory usage and some other features for several benchmark programs listed in table 8.1. These benchmarks are supplied with MLKit.

FuhMishra is a type checker for subtyping, *dangle* is a small program which generates garbage lists while making a closure to add up to 1000, and *life* simulates the Game of Life. There are several versions of *Knuth-Bendix* and *life* supplied with MLKit, and programs we used are revised for MLKit.

Table 8.1 shows the number of comparisons and resets of regions executed during the execution and an increased ratio of resets. There are extended sat directives inserted in every program other than *Mandel*, and actually the number of resets has increased. As a result, the maximum size of used memory is much reduced for *Knuth-Bendix* and *life*, and a little reduced for *FuhMishra* and *dangle* as is shown in figure 8.12.

Figure 8.12 also says that the performance degradation by using our technique is only a little (less than 5%). There are mainly two kinds of overhead. One is the increase of resetting regions. There is a trade-off between memory usage and the cost for resetting regions and we think memory usage to be more important. The other kind of overhead comes from comparing regions at runtime. However, this overhead is very small for next reasons.

- Resetting regions is much heavier than comparing regions
  We need only a few assembly instructions to compare regions, but to reset a region we call a function implemented by C-language and it needs com-

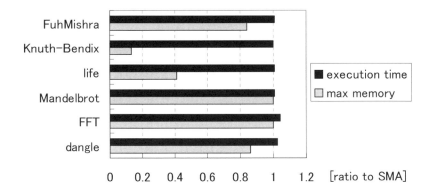

FIGURE 8.12.   Maximum memory size and execution time

TABLE 8.2.   The number of elements in the following set of sat

number of elements	0	1	2	3	>= 4
FuhMishra	23	23	2	5	0
Knuth-Bendix	15	15	1	0	0
life	1	1	0	0	0
Mandelbrot	0	0	0	0	0
FFT	15	11	1	0	0
dangle	0	1	0	0	0

paratively heavy work including management of pages of which regions are composed.

- We check storage mode before comparing regions
  As we explained in section 8.3.4, we check storage mode first, so when we can see that comparing regions is useless by checking storage mode, we don't make any wasteful comparisons.

- The number of elements in the comparison set is not so large
  Though the more elements are in the comparison set, the more time comparing region takes in the worst case, the number of elements in the comparison set is generally small as the table 8.2 shows.

Graphs in figure 8.13 show the memory usage over time. This measurement counts only heap memory usage, and we can see asymptotic improvement for *Knuth-Bendix* and *life* rather than just measurable improvement. These programs repeat the same computation three times. As the size of the problems becomes

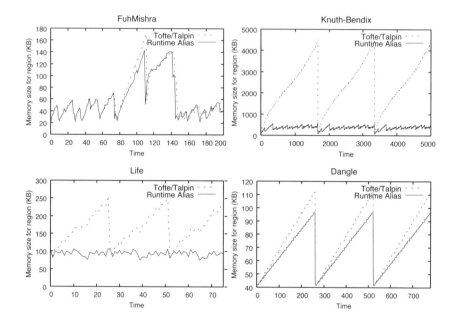

FIGURE 8.13.   Memory usage

larger, the difference of memory usage also becomes larger. There is no observable difference for two other benchmarks not shown here.

8.5   RELATED WORK

Aiken et al. [1](AFL) extended the Tofte/Talpin system, decoupling dynamic region allocation and deallocation from the introduction of region variables with the letregion construct. As a result, they realized better memory behavior and enabled the tail call optimization for more programs. The optimizations of AFL and SMA are orthogonal. Storage mode analysis "resets" the region at various times during its lifetime, and AFL allocates the region at some point before the dynamic lifetime (but later than the introduction of the region variable), and frees it at some point after the dynamic lifetime (earlier than the end of the letregion). Therefore these two optimizations do not conflict with each other.

Our method just resets the region at more times during its lifetime. So it doesn't conflict with AFL either. Sometimes the storage mode annotation with our optimization is effective, and sometimes AFL optimization is effective. However, there is still cases where both optimizations are not effective. Since our method doesn't deallocate regions themselves earlier, we cannot expect programs which keep allocating new regions during continuing function calls to be optimized, but we can expect more programs which keep adding objects in some regions to be optimized.

The AFL system uses an abstract region environment to analyze the lifetimes of regions, which has more precise information about region aliases than the region flow graph. Therefore we think that we can reduce the number of elements in the comparison set by using this kind of abstract region environment. Actually, in the example given in figure 8.1, if the first instantiation of f doesn't exist, ρ_1 and ρ_2 are never bound to the same region at the same time in any contexts. So when we are to create an object in a region bound to ρ_1, we need not to compare it with a region bound to ρ_2. Even if so, our method is still useful, because there are cases where there exists an instantiation in which two or more region variables are actually aliased in the program. Furthermore, programs are often compiled separately and when compiling, top level functions always have the possibility of problematic instantiations in other compilation modules.

8.6   FUTURE WORK

We currently give up translating to the extended `sat` directive in every case where the region we are to store an object is reachable starting a live effect variable in the region flow graph G (rule 8.7). Generally, it is impossible to generate enough set to exclude the possibility of problematic region aliases in these cases. However, there are several cases where we can generate enough set using region bindings within the current scope. Therefore improving memory usage further by treating these cases better is one of future work.

As we explained in section 8.5, the context where a region polymorphic function is instantiated determines whether region parameters of the function become aliases or not. So by specializing a function on alias relations of the region parameter, we expect that runtime checking of aliases can be reduced.

We haven't proved soundness of our algorithm, so giving a soundness proof is also one of our future work.

8.7   CONCLUSION

We proposed a technique to improve memory usage in systems using static regions as a method of managing memory. In our technique, objects can be created by overwriting at some points where overwriting was impossible by the original Tofte/Talpin system because of the possibility of aliases of the target region. We also implemented our technique to MLKit, which is a system with region inference and is compliant with a subset of Standard ML and confirmed that our technique really improves memory usage for some programs. By this fact, we expect more programs will run with reasonable memory usage.

REFERENCES

[1] Alexander Aiken, Manuel Fahndrich, and Raph Levien. Better static memory management: Improving region-based analysis of higher-order languages. In *SIGPLAN*

Conference on Programming Language Design and Implementation, pages 174–185, 1995.

[2] Lars Birkedal, Mads Tofte, and Jean-Pierre Talpin. From region inference to von neumann machines via region representation inference. In *the 23rd ACM SIGPLAN-SIGACT Symposium on Principles of Programming Languages*, pages 171–183. ACM Press, January 1996.

[3] Martin Elsman and Niels Hallenberg. An optimizing backend for the ml kit using a stack of regions. Technical report, Department of Computer Science, University of Copenhagen, July 1995.

[4] Robin Milner. A theory of type polymorphism in programming. *Journal of Computer and System Sciences*, 17:348–375, August 1978.

[5] Robin Milner, Mads Tofte, Robert Harper, and David MacQueen. *The Definition of Standard ML - Revised*. MIT Press, 1997.

[6] Mads Tofte and Lars Birkedal. A region inference algorithm. *ACM Trans. Program. Lang. Syst.*, 20(4):724–767, 1998.

[7] Mads Tofte, Lars Birkedal, Martin Elsman, Niels Hallenberg, Tommy Højfeld Olesen, and Peter Sestoft. Programming with regions in the ML Kit (for version 4). Technical report, IT University of Copenhagen, October 2001.

[8] Mads Tofte and Jean-Pierre Talpin. Implementing the call-by-value lambda-calculus using a stack of regions. In *the 21st ACM SIGPLAN-SIGACT Symposium on Principles of Programming Languages*, pages 188–201. ACM Press, January 1994.

Chapter 9

A Model of Functional Programming with Dynamic Compilation and Optimization

Martin Grabmüller[1]

Abstract: Modern virtual machines for object-oriented languages use dynamic (run-time) compilation in order to ensure fast execution while maintaining security and portability of program code. Several virtual machine implementations using this compilation model have been implemented and are successfully used in practice, but have rarely been used in the implementation of functional languages. This paper presents a framework for describing dynamically optimizing virtual machines in the context of purely functional programming languages.

9.1 INTRODUCTION

Using virtual machines to implement high-level programming languages is quite common today, as it promises several advantages when compared to traditional (static machine-code compiler) approaches. The code of programs is stored in a machine-independent format and the virtual machine provides a portable interface to the applications running on it, so that applications are automatically portable across different machine architectures and operating systems. Portability, together with the ability to load and link components at run-time enable highly dynamic and distributed applications. Another important aspect is security: the virtual machine has complete control over the applications it runs and may restrict their operation to conform to some security policy. This is especially important when

---

[1]Fakultät für Elektrotechnik und Informatik, Technische Universität Berlin; E-mail: magr@cs.tu-berlin.de

code from untrusted sources is to be executed, which is much more difficult for compiled systems.

The main drawback of virtual machines is, when naively implemented, their poor performance which results from safety verification of program codes and the overhead of interpreting the portable code representation. Reducing the cost of safety verification is not considered here, we concentrate on improving the execution of the code. A lot of work has been done on dynamic translation from portable to machine code at run-time (just-in-time, or JIT compilation). Virtual machines employ dynamic profiling and optimization in order to balance the time required for compilation with the performance benefits of optimized code.

Despite the wide application of dynamic compilation techniques in practice, they have only rarely been used in the implementations of functional languages. Even less work seems to have been done on the formalization of dynamic compilation and optimization. This paper therefore aims at providing a formal model of functional programming with dynamic compilation and optimization.

Contributions   This paper makes the following contributions:

- We present a formal model of dynamic translation, abstracted over source language, target language and execution model as well as the dynamic analysis and transformation algorithms.

- We establish properties of the virtual machine.

- In order to illustrate our model, we apply it to a well-known optimization, namely, dynamic profile-driven guarded inlining.

Outline   The rest of the paper is organized as follows: Section 9.2 gives an introduction to the principles of virtual machines and dynamic compilation. Section 9.3 describes our formal approach to dynamic analysis and transformation. We describe the components of the framework, their interplay and how existing transformations can be formulated in our terminology. In order to illustrate the use of the framework, section 9.4 describes how a well-known dynamic optimization can be expressed in the proposed notation. Section 9.5 compares to other work and section 9.6 outlines possible future extensions to the system. Finally, section 9.7 concludes.

9.2   VIRTUAL MACHINES AND DYNAMIC TRANSLATION

In this paper, we concentrate on virtual machines which do some kind of dynamic translation during the course of executing user programs. This section describes the principles of these machines and defines the terminology used throughout the paper.

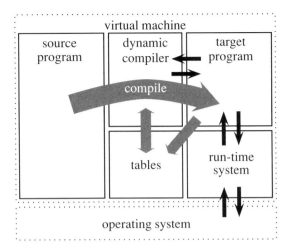

FIGURE 9.1.   Components of a virtual machine

9.2.1   Virtual Machines

Figure 9.1 shows the basic structure of a virtual machine and its interaction with the underlying operating system. Data flow is indicated using grey arrows and control flow with black arrows.

The *source program* is a program in some portable representation (e.g., Java bytecode [18] or CIL code [12]), whereas the *target program* consists of machine code which can be directly executed by the underlying machine architecture (e.g., IA-32 or SPARC machine code). The *dynamic compiler* translates source program parts (methods, functions, or basic blocks) from source to target language, storing it into the so-called *code cache*, which holds the target program fragments. The code fragments in the code cache are not required to correspond to the code fragments in the source program: the former may be superblocks made up of several source code basic blocks, for example. Note that the code cache in real implementations is limited in size, so that *code cache management* is necessary to act properly when the code cache overflows. Control is transferred from the target program to the dynamic compiler whenever some code is to be executed which has not yet been translated. The compiler then translates the corresponding source program part and continues execution in the newly created target code. The *tables* hold various information about the dynamic translation state, such as source-to-target address mappings or profiling information. This information is added both by the compiler and the target program when it has been instrumented to collect data about its own execution. This includes counts of function calls or loop iterations, for example. The compiler can base translation decisions on this analysis of the dynamic program behavior. The *run-time system* is responsible for virtualizing machine resources such as processes, files or network connections and provides the only interface to the operating system.

In general, virtual machines map from expected machines to actual machines. This includes both translation and the mapping of resources. This paper considers only translation, because the source language is expected to abstract over resource representations. Note that in this paper we concentrate on virtual machines which only execute target code after prior compilation. Settings where the virtual machine switches between interpretation and compilation/native execution [8, 20] are not covered.

9.2.2 Dynamic Compilation

Dynamic compilation translates the input to the virtual machine (source language) to the language actually executed (target language). This process naturally decomposes into two phases: *analysis* and *transformation*. In contrast to static (off-line) compilers, a dynamic (on-line) compiler has more information about the program, for example certain actual input values and dynamic execution profiles. An additional difference between static and dynamic compilers is that the former normally translate complete programs (or modules), while the latter can operate on much smaller parts of the program. This reduces compile times and therefore interruptions of the user program. It also reduces compilation to the parts of the program which are executed in the actual program run. For many programs, this is a big advantage, since no time is wasted on the compilation of unneeded program parts.

9.2.3 Feedback-driven Transformation

An important aspect in dynamic optimization is to find the parts of the program which are most often executed and which would therefore benefit from (possibly expensive) optimizations. In a *feedback-driven* optimization architecture, the target code is instrumented so that it maintains counters of how often each part of the program has been run. When a counter reaches some predefined threshold, the dynamic compiler is invoked to perform optimization on this program part. This can eventually happen several times through a single program run. Profiling information can also be gathered by sampling the active code blocks at regular intervals. This incurs less overhead than counting, but is less precise and requires support from the hardware and/or operating system.

A complete feedback-driven (also called *adaptive*) optimization architecture thus requires the collection of profiling data, a decision procedure for determining candidates for re-compilation and a run-time compiler supporting several modes of code generation: at different optimization levels and with or without code instrumentation.

9.3 FORMAL FRAMEWORK

Based on the terminology introduced in the previous section, we will now describe our formal framework in detail. The purpose of the machine model is to collect generally useful functionality in one place, so that different implementa-

tions of source or target languages and reduction strategies can concentrate on
the cases which cannot be fixed in a predefined framework. This goal is to be
achieved without fixing language features such as evaluation order or specific
language constructs. Therefore, we present a modular design in which the framework specifies requirements for both the source language and the target language
(both syntax and semantics) and we provide some concrete implementations of
functions which are independent of the source/target languages.

First, the virtual machine model will be introduced, including its components:
source program, target program, dynamic transformation and so on. After that, we
will provide details about the interplay between the various components and describe how the genericity of the framework is obtained by abstracting over source
and target languages as well as over the supported analyses and transformations.

In the following, we will use the following notation: a sequence of items (possibly empty) will be overlined, as in $\overline{D_t}$. The dot symbol $\cdot$ will be used for empty
sequences. The operation $\oplus$ adds an element to a sequence of definitions, overwriting any definition of the same name. The operation $\downarrow$ retrieves the expression
of a definition with a given name. We use the type **Maybe** t as an option type,
with the same semantics as in Haskell. Globally defined variables are written with
a hat ($\hat{x}$), local (λ-bound) variables without (x). For notational convenience, we
define *contexts*. Contexts are expressions which may contain *holes* (written $\bullet$).
Each hole stands for a position in the expression where another expression may
be placed. Filling the hole in a context C with an expression E is written as $C[E]$.
Contexts are used to select subexpressions for reduction and their grammar essentially defines the reduction order.

9.3.1   Source and Target Language

The framework requires the source language (the input to the machine) and the
target language (the language actually executed) to have the structure and to provide the functions shown in figure 9.2. Both source and target languages must be
defined as data types for expressions, together with a set of functions specifying
their semantics.

A program is a pair of a list of definitions and an expression. The expression
is the main program and the definitions are used to bind global variables to expressions. Definitions are mutually recursive. Both source and target expressions
must have at least references to global variables in their syntax, written as $\hat{x}$. One
other expression type is predefined for the target language and can be generated
by the translation function: the *count* primitive. This expression has a predefined
semantics, which simply increments a counter associated in the knowledge base
(see below) with the identifier in the *count* expression. The target language is
additionally required to provide a data type for contexts, which must at least have
a variant $\bullet$ (*hole*). Other cases of the context definition should reflect the desired
evaluation order of the language. Because the framework is independent of the
language and context definitions, two functions for converting between expressions and contexts are required: *decompose* splits an expression into a context

$$
\begin{array}{lll}
P_s & ::= & (\overline{D_s}, E_s) \qquad\qquad\qquad\text{source program} \\
D_s & ::= & \hat{x} = E_s \qquad\qquad\qquad\text{source definition} \\
E_s & ::= & \hat{x} \mid \ldots \qquad\qquad\qquad\text{source expression} \\[1em]
P_t & ::= & (\overline{D_t}, E_t) \qquad\qquad\qquad\text{target program} \\
D_t & ::= & \hat{x} = E_t \qquad\qquad\qquad\text{target definition} \\
E_t & ::= & \hat{x} \mid count\ I\ E_t \mid \ldots \qquad\text{target expression} \\[1em]
C_t & ::= & \bullet \mid \ldots \qquad\qquad\qquad\text{target reduction context} \\
decompose & : & E_t \to \mathsf{Maybe}\ (C_t \times E_t) \quad\text{redex decomposition} \\
compose & : & C_t \times E_t \to E_t \qquad\quad\text{expression composition} \\[1em]
K & ::= & \cdot \mid (I \mapsto \mathbb{N}), K \qquad\quad\text{knowledge base} \\
\oplus & : & K \times I \to K \\
k \oplus i & = & (i \mapsto 1), k \quad \text{if } i \notin k \\
k \oplus i & = & k_1, (i, n+1), k_2 \\
& & \quad \text{if } k = k_1, (i \mapsto n), k_2 \\
\downarrow & : & K \times I \to \mathbb{N} \\
k \downarrow i & = & 0 \quad \text{if } i \notin k \\
k \downarrow i & = & n \quad \text{if } (i \mapsto n) \in k \\
\rho & : & \overline{D_t} \times E_t \times K \to \overline{D_t} \times E_t \times K \quad\text{target reduction} \\
\tau & : & \overline{D_s} \times E_s \times K \to E_t \qquad\qquad\text{dynamic translation} \\
\sigma & : & P_s \times P_t \times K \to P_t \times K \qquad\text{strategy function}
\end{array}
$$

FIGURE 9.2.   Source and Target Language

and an expression (returning **Nothing** if no redex exists) and *compose* performs the reverse operation.

The knowledge base is a mapping from *identifiers* to natural numbers and collects profiling data generated by execution of *count* expressions. The domain of the mapping I is to be specified by the concrete language specifications. We define the operations $\oplus$ and $\downarrow$ on knowledge bases. The addition operation $\oplus$ adds a identifier/number pair to a knowledge base, setting the count to one if the identifier does not appear in the knowledge base and incrementing the count otherwise. The lookup operation $\downarrow$ retrieves the count for a given identifier and returns 0 if the identifier does not appear in the knowledge base. A knowledge base contains analysis results, both static (compile-time) as well as dynamic (run-time). Note that in this context, compile-time is actually part of the run-time of the user program and interleaved with user program execution, but we keep the classic distinction and use the term run-time for the actual (*productive*) execution of the user program and compile-time for the (*non-productive*) work performed by the dynamic compiler.

Program execution is based on three distinct operations: translation from source to target language (on an expression basis) called τ, reduction of a target expres-

$$\begin{aligned}
\rho(\overline{d_t}, \hat{x}, k) &= (\overline{d_t}, \overline{d_t} \downarrow \hat{x}, k) \\
\rho(\overline{d_t}, count\ i\ e_t, k) &= (\overline{d_t}, e_t, k \oplus i) \\
\tau(\overline{d_s}, \hat{x}, k) &= \hat{x} \\
\sigma((\overline{d_s}, e_s), (\overline{d_t}, C[\hat{x}]), k) &= ((\overline{d_t} \oplus (\hat{x} = \tau\ \overline{d_s}\ [\![\overline{d_s} \downarrow \hat{x}]\!]\ k), C[\hat{x}]), k) \\
&\quad \text{if } \hat{x} \notin \overline{d_t}
\end{aligned}$$

FIGURE 9.3.   Basic definitions of the reduction and strategy functions

sion called ρ and a strategy function which decides when to apply translations and/or optimization (called σ).

The context definition (together with the *decompose/compose* functions) and the reduction function ρ define how target programs are executed in the virtual machine, specifying the target language's operational semantics. The reduction function may return an altered set of definitions, which can be used to implement lazy (call-by-need) languages or ML-style reference cells.

The function τ defines the compilation of source to target expressions. This translation takes place in the context of the set of source definitions and the current knowledge base, so that optimization decisions can be made with respect to the program execution so far. The translation function τ together with the reduction function ρ defines the semantics of the source language.

The compilation strategy σ is a function which maps the virtual machine state to a target program. The strategy decides, based on the information contained in the knowledge base, which definitions should be re-compiled, that is, should be translated from the source to the target program, possibly replacing already compiled functions. Since the outcome of the decision might be to update (or reset) the knowledge base, the knowledge base is also an output of this function. Note that it would be possible to define this function as the identity, which means that no re-compilation would ever take place. The problem of code cache management mentioned in section 9.2 could also be modelled by appropriately defining the strategy function.

The framework provides the minimal functionality for the reduction, translation and strategy functions defined in figure 9.3. The given reduction rule replaces free variables in the target expression with their definition, and it executes *count* expressions by incrementing the counter associated with their identifier in the knowledge base. The translation rule translates source to target variables and the strategy rule detects when a free variable is in reduction context whose definition has not yet been compiled. The definition is then compiled on demand and added to the target definitions.

9.3.2   Program Evaluation

The execution of a user program p written in the source language is defined by the *eval* function in figure 9.4. Given a source program, the main source expression

$$eval(\overline{d_s}, e_s) \quad = \quad eval'((\overline{d_s}, e_s), (\cdot, \tau(\overline{d_s}, e_s, \cdot)), \cdot)$$

$$eval'(p_s, (\overline{d_t}, e_t), k) \quad = \quad \textbf{let } ((\overline{d_t'}, e_t'), k') = \sigma(p_s, (\overline{d_t}, e_t), k)$$
$$(\overline{d_t''}, e_t'', k'') = reduce(\overline{d_t'}, e_t', k')$$
$$\textbf{in if } e_t = e_t'' \wedge k = k''$$
$$\textbf{then } e_t$$
$$\textbf{else } eval'(p_s, (\overline{d_t''}, e_t''), k'')$$

$$reduce(\overline{d_t}, e_t, k) \quad = \quad \textbf{case } decompose \; e_t \textbf{ of}$$
$$\text{Just}(c, e) \rightarrow$$
$$\textbf{let } (\overline{d_t'}, e', k') = \rho(\overline{d_t}, e, k)$$
$$\textbf{in } (\overline{d_t'}, compose(c, e'), k')$$
$$\text{Nothing} \rightarrow (\overline{d_t}, e_t, k)$$

FIGURE 9.4.   Program evaluation

is translated to the target language. The target definitions and the knowledge base starts out empty. The function *eval'* then iteratively applies the strategy function, performing on-demand translation and other actions defined by the concrete languages, followed by a reduction step. This process terminates when both the main program expression and the knowledge base stop changing.

One reduction step is performed by the function *reduce*, also shown in figure 9.4. This function extends the target language reduction function ρ to complete target programs by first decomposing the program's main expression into a context and a redex, performing a target reduction on the redex and then recombining the context and the reduction result into a complete result expression.

The delayed compilation used in real virtual machines is thus modelled in our framework by the standard definition of the strategy function, which compiles a definition whenever it detects that a reference is made to a source program definition which has not yet been compiled. Section 9.4 (below) provides an example for re-compilation when the strategy function decides that a definition should be translated again in order to take advantage of the collected profiling data in the knowledge base.

A feature of the framework presented here is that it is able to model several levels of compilation and optimization. Many virtual machine implementations support a mixed mode of interpretation and compilation, so that the cost of compilation and the benefit of executing optimized code can be traded off. This can be supported by using a target language which is a superset of the source language. A kind of "interpreter" mode could be implemented by translating each source construct into the corresponding target construct, effectively interpreting it in the reduction function. For higher optimization levels, the translation can generate other target code expressions, which can be executed more efficiently. Section 9.4 gives an example of such a language.

9.3.3   Properties of the Virtual Machine Model

Since the model is simple and mainly serves as glue between the language definitions of the source and target language as well as analysis and transformation functions, most properties of the system depend heavily on the properties of the given languages. If properties like type preservation and progress hold for the language semantics, they will hold for the dynamically optimizing system as well, as long as the used transformations from source to target language also preserve these properties. Even though the structural and behavioral requirements of the source and target language are minimal, we can state some fundamental properties of the proposed virtual machine model:

Delayed translation will not change a program's meaning. Delayed translation may leave free variables and variables referring to not-yet translated definitions in target expressions. In order to preserve a program's meaning, a running program may never reference a free variable not present in the source program. This problem cannot arise, because whenever a reduction context determines that a global definition is needed, the strategy function recognizes the situation first and translates the corresponding source definition into the needed target definition.

The machine does not change termination behavior. That is, when the source program is translated into a target program, and this target program terminates when executing according to its context definition and reduction function, then it terminates when run in the virtual machine.

Only two actions are performed by the machine which are not determined by the language definitions: first, substitution of global definitions for global variable references. This is only done when the definition is in fact needed, because the target language context determines which references to substitute for. Second, evaluation of the *count* primitive. This is again only evaluated when needed and the reduction is terminating by definition.

Note that in general the number of translations may vary because of on-demand translation, but the number of reductions will only change when the concrete language implementations use optimizing transformations.

9.3.4   Modelling Common Transformations

Many commonly used program analyses and transformations can be defined using the framework described in this section. The strategy function plays several roles: first, it is responsible for detecting when a source definition needs to be compiled for the first time, that is, on the first invocation, or re-compiled when needed. Second, it has to decide at which optimization levels the compilation should proceed. The distinction of several optimization levels is common in real virtual machine implementations, because optimization is mainly a trade-off between fast compilation and slow execution on the one hand and slow compilation and fast execution

| | | reduction function | | |
		no reduction	reduce only	reduce and profile
strategy function	compile eagerly	static compiler	dynamic compiler	dynamic compiler + profiler
	compile on demand		incremental compiler	incremental compiler + profiler
	compile on demand and re-compile		incremental compiler	feedback-driven incremental compiler + profiler

TABLE 9.1.   Modelling common compilation techniques

on the other. Between the two extremes of compiling one definition at a time and compiling the whole program at once, it is also possible to compile several definitions at once so that possible initial start-up costs of the strategy function can be amortized over multiple definition compilations.

Table 9.1 shows the relation between various definitions of strategy and reduction functions and how they can be used to perform some classical kinds of compilers: when the strategy function compiles all definitions eagerly (at program start-up) and the reduction function is the identity, we get the equivalent of a static (off-line) compiler. The two on-demand compilation schemes only make sense when the reduction function performs useful work, therefore two of the table entries are left blank. By varying the strategy function to compile on demand and to allow re-compilation, and by letting the reduction function perform some useful work or even to gather profile information, the system is able to perform dynamic, incremental or even feedback-driven re-compilation.

9.4   CASE STUDY: GUARDED FEEDBACK-DRIVEN INLINING

Our claim is that the proposed virtual machine model is generic across multiple source and target languages as well as the analysis and transformation algorithms used. The machine execution is decoupled from all these aspects by requiring them to have some minimal structure and to be packaged up in the reduction, translation and strategy functions. Because this model is so abstract, it is not obvious how it can be used to model real-life applications of dynamic compilation techniques. This is the reason for presenting a concrete example in this section, where the model is instantiated with concrete languages and a concrete optimization.

The optimization realized here has been successfully used in practice: guarded feedback-driven inlining. *Inlining* (also called procedure integration) works by replacing a function application by the called function's definition, substituting the actual arguments for the formal parameters in the process. This optimization avoids the overhead of a function call and return and additionally allows other optimizations to work over larger parts of the code, thereby specializing the called function for the calling context. *Guarded inlining* additionally allows inlining when it is not possible to ensure that a given call site calls a specific function, but only that it is very likely that a specific function is called. This is often the case in functional languages where function arguments or results are called and a given call site might call one of several candidate functions. The guarded inlining optimization inlines one or more of the possible candidates and adds code which checks whether the assumption made by the optimizer was correct. If the actual call is to the inlined function, its body is executed, otherwise, a call is made to the actual function. This optimization makes the common case faster but adds overhead for checking the correctness of the optimizer's assumptions.

The notation $E_1[E_2/x]$ stands for the capture-free substitution of expression E_2 for variable x in expression E_1. The "lookup" operation $\downarrow$ on definitions is extended to take a λ label ℓ as an argument; in this case it returns the expression labelled ℓ.

Figure 9.5 contains the definitions of the source and target languages. For simplicity and in order to concentrate on the optimization used, the languages are nearly identical in this example. The language is an untyped λ-calculus extended with the operations zero, pred and succ as well as with a conditional expression (if0) which tests for equality to zero. The language is call-by-value and all expressions have their usual semantics. The λ expressions and the applications are labelled using unique markers. This is required for referencing application and λ expressions appearing in the source and target programs. The target language has one additional construct: a conditional function application. This construct contains a λ label, an application label and three subexpressions. It evaluates its first expression and checks whether the result is a λ expression with the same label as its first label component. When they are equal, the second subexpression is evaluated, otherwise the first is applied to the last expression.

The keys I for identifying entries in the knowledge base are pairs of labels, where the first label corresponds to a call site and the second to the λ expression which was actually called from this site.

Figure 9.5 also defines the reduction, strategy and translation functions for the example language. The reduction function performs profiling while reducing an expression: it counts applications of λ-expressions by inserting a *count* expression with the call site/abstraction label pair as the identifier argument.

Initial compilation and re-compilation is triggered by the general strategy function shown in figure 9.3 in the previous section. The function σ shown in figure 9.5 handles function applications by checking whether the call site is "hot", which means that it has called a specific function more than a predefined number of times T. If this is the case, the containing definition of the function application is re-compiled. The translation function is responsible for performing the actual inlining operation.

Most translations simply map from the source construct to the corresponding target construct, translating the components of a phrase recursively. The interesting cases are two possible translations of function application as shown in

$$E_s \quad ::= \quad \hat{x} \mid x \mid \lambda^\ell x. \, E_s \mid E_s @^\ell \, E_s \mid \texttt{zero} \mid \texttt{succ} \, E_s \mid \texttt{pred} \, E_s \mid \texttt{if0} \, E_s \, E_s \, E_s$$

$$E_t \quad ::= \quad \hat{x} \mid x \mid \lambda^\ell x. \, E_t \mid E_t @^\ell \, E_t \mid \texttt{zero} \mid \texttt{succ} \, E_t \mid \texttt{pred} \, E_t \mid \texttt{if0} \, E_t \, E_t \, E_t$$
$$\texttt{cond@} \, \ell \, (\ell) \, E_t \, E_t \, E_t$$

$$C_t \quad ::= \quad \bullet \mid \bullet @^\ell \, E_t \mid v @^\ell \bullet \mid \texttt{succ} \bullet \mid \texttt{pred} \bullet \mid \texttt{if0} \bullet E_t \, E_t$$
$$\texttt{cond@} \, \ell \, (\ell') \bullet E_t \, E_t \qquad \text{where } v ::= \texttt{zero} \mid \texttt{succ} \, v \mid \lambda^\ell x. \, E_s$$

$$I \quad ::= \quad (\ell, \ell')$$

$$\rho(\overline{d_t}, \texttt{if0 zero} \, e_{t1} \, e_{t2}, k) \quad = \quad (\overline{d_t}, e_{t1}, k) \qquad\qquad (r1)$$
$$\rho(\overline{d_t}, \texttt{if0 (succ} \, v) \, e_{t1} \, e_{t2}, k) \quad = \quad (\overline{d_t}, e_{t2}, k) \qquad\qquad (r2)$$
$$\rho(\overline{d_t}, \texttt{pred(succ} \, v), k) \quad = \quad (\overline{d_t}, v, k) \qquad\qquad (r3)$$
$$\rho(\overline{d_t}, (\lambda^{\ell'} x. \, e_{t1}) @^\ell \, v_2, k) \quad = \quad (\overline{d_t}, count \; (\ell, \ell')(e_{t1}[v_2/x]), k) \quad (r4)$$
$$\rho(\overline{d_t}, \texttt{cond@} \ell(\ell')(\lambda^\ell x. \, e_t) \, e_{t2} \, e_{t3}, k) \quad = \quad (\overline{d_t}, e_{t2}, k) \qquad\qquad (r5)$$
$$\rho(\overline{d_t}, \texttt{cond@} \ell(\ell')(\lambda^{\ell''} x. \, e_t) \, e_{t2} \, e_{t3}, k) \quad = \quad (\overline{d_t}, (\lambda^{\ell''} x. \, e_t) @^{\ell'} e_{t3}, k) \quad (r6)$$
$$\text{if } \ell \neq \ell''$$

$$\sigma((\overline{d_s}, e_s), (\overline{d_t}, e_t), k) \quad = \quad ((\overline{d_t} \oplus (\hat{x} = \tau \, \overline{d_s} \, [\![\overline{d_s} \downarrow \hat{x}]\!] \, k), e_t), k)$$
$$\text{where } e_t = C[(\lambda^{\ell'} y. \, e_2) @^\ell v_2],$$
$$\hat{x} \text{ contains } \ell \text{ and } k \downarrow (\ell, \ell') \geq T$$

$$\tau \, \overline{d_s} \, [\![e_{s1} @^\ell \, e_{s2}]\!] \, k \quad = \quad \texttt{cond@} \, \ell' \, (\ell) \, (\tau \, \overline{d_s} \, [\![e_{s1}]\!] \, k)$$
$$(\tau' \, [\![(\tau \, \overline{d_s} \, [\![e_s]\!] \, k) @^\ell \, (\tau \, \overline{d_s} \, [\![e_{s2}]\!] \, k)]\!]) \, (\tau \, \overline{d_s} \, [\![e_{s2}]\!] \, k)$$
$$\text{if } \exists \ell'.k \downarrow (\ell, \ell') \geq T \text{ and } \overline{d_s} \downarrow \ell' = e_s$$
$$\text{and inlined function is not recursive}$$
$$\tau \, \overline{d_s} \, [\![e_{s1} @^\ell \, e_{s2}]\!] \, k \quad = \quad (\tau \, \overline{d_s} \, [\![e_{s1}]\!] \, k) @^\ell \, (\tau \, \overline{d_s} \, [\![e_{s2}]\!] \, k) \quad \text{if } \forall \ell'.k \downarrow (\ell, \ell') < T$$

FIGURE 9.5.   Example source and target language

figure 9.5: if a call site has called a particular function for at least T times, its body is inlined, protected by a $\texttt{cond@}$ expression. The function τ' (not shown) simplifies an application expression when the function is a λ expression and the argument is a variable or constant by performing a β-substitution. If the call site is no candidate for inlining, it is simply translated to a target application expression.

Note that in this set-up, all optimizations are performed by the translation functions, whereas the necessary profile data collection is done by the reduction function and decisions concerning re-compilations are defined by the strategy function. This separation of concerns is not required and other uses of the formal framework could be defined differently, since the framework is sufficiently flexible to encode several policies. The distribution of responsibilities between the different components chosen here allows for modular extensions of the supported optimizations.

This example of using our framework for defining a dynamically optimizing system illustrates the flexibility of our approach. Other optimizations could be easily added by appropriately extending the strategy and/or translation functions. By adapting the reduction function, other profile data could be collected and used as the basis for optimizations.

9.5   RELATED WORK

A comprehensive description of virtual machines can be found in Smith and Nair [23], who treat both low-level (binary and hardware) and high-level language virtual machines. Examples of low-level virtual machines are binary translators [7], binary optimizers [17, 5] and co-designed hardware/software systems which execute machine code on different processor architectures using integrated translation software [11, 9]. High-level virtual machines provide additional services for user programs, such as abstraction over machine resources, garbage collection and multiple threads of execution [18, 12]. An earlier approach of portable code files and load-time compilation was that of Franz [13] for the Oberon system. The portable code files in Franz' system are actually compressed abstract syntax trees which are compiled when a module is loaded into the system. The Self system also relies heavily on dynamic compilation [14] and pioneered aggressive feedback directed optimizations. Self is a dynamically typed object-oriented language where all operations are dispatched dynamically, and thus requires good optimization in order to execute efficiently. For similar reasons, but not as aggressively, Deutsch and Schiffmann [10] have used dynamic compilation in their Smalltalk implementation.

The design of the formal model was inspired by several virtual machine architectures for the Java programming language. The Jalapeño virtual machine (later renamed to Jikes RVM) at IBM [6, 24] first introduced the notion of a *controller*, which is the component making optimization decisions based on a cost-benefit model of adaptive re-compilation. This component loosely corresponds to our strategy function and appears also in other Java VMs, such as the StarJIT system from Intel [1], where it is called *Profile Manager*.

Arnold et al. [3] propose a model-driven policy for detecting re-compilation opportunities which is used in the Jikes Research Virtual Machine. They model both expected re-compilation costs and the expected benefits of running optimized code, basing their heuristics on the compile times and profile data collected up to that point in execution. This seems to be the only published attempt to capture aspects of dynamic optimization systems formally. Several authors have aimed at formalizing the semantics of virtual machines, but as far as we know, they did not cover dynamic compilation and optimization (see, e.g., [2]).

Wakeling [25] used dynamic compilation of a lazy functional language in order to reduce the memory requirements of compiled code. In his system, Haskell source code is compiled to a compact intermediate format prior to execution and a dynamic compiler translates this code to machine code while the program is running. When the storage reserved for compiled code is exhausted, all compiled code is discarded and required code is re-generated (throw-away compilation [4]). Other uses of dynamic code generation in the context of functional languages include those in meta-programming, for example MetaML [22], which does not require but benefits from dynamic code generation. Lee and Leone [16] translate code written in a subset of ML into programs which automatically specialize programs at run-time. Run-time code generation as a user-level library was proposed by Lomov and Moscal [19]. They provide a library which allows the translation from abstract syntax trees to bytecode for the Caml system at run-time. This work on meta-programming differs from ours because we are dealing with performance improvement techniques which are invisible to the programmer, thus purely implementational.

Other work related to the presented model includes several works on defining language semantics which reflect aspects of evaluation such as the cost associated with each reduction step. Hope and Hutton [15] presented how a step-counting semantics can be derived from purely functional programs. Sands [21] investigated cost semantics for several languages, from simple first-order to higher-order languages.

9.6   FUTURE WORK

The work presented here can only be seen as a first step towards the formalization of dynamic optimization systems. Several topics for future work have been identified while developing the formal model and the example optimization presented here.

Modern virtual machines support dynamic loading of program code. This should be included in our framework by adding some primitive mechanism for replacing (parts of) the source program and triggering the re-compilation of replaced definitions.

An important aspect is whether other language constructs besides the concepts described here are useful enough across various source and target languages so that they should be included into the basic framework instead of being defined in the concrete languages used with the model. This would allow more work on the core framework to be applied to all possible source and target languages. One possible example is to define some general cost semantics which can be used across all (or at least most) reduction-based languages. The advantage is that the description of individual analyses and transformations is moved into the general framework, making the concrete language definitions smaller and easier to work with.

Another interesting path for future work is in lifting the restrictions on the current framework: we would like to allow languages with more complicated semantics than just reduction-based small-step semantics. Although we suppose lifting some of the restrictions will not impose major problems, we have not yet studied it in detail. We also plan to study the effect of dynamic optimization on the properties of the programs running on top of it. Though we expect no difficulties, since the machine is designed to be transparent to the running programs, it may be necessary to state specific requirements for the transformation and strategy functions used in order to ensure this transparency.

Finally, an empirical study of the effects of dynamic optimizations in the setting of functional programs should be performed, to assess the usefulness of this implementation technique for this programming paradigm.

9.7   CONCLUSION

In this paper, we have proposed a simple generic theoretical model of virtual machine execution with support for dynamic compilation and optimization for functional programs. The model is generic in that it does not prescribe specific source or target languages and gives freedom to the analysis and transformation algorithms used for dynamic compilation and optimization. Even though the model does not restrict the source and target languages to specific language constructs of evaluation strategy, we can state that their implementation on top of our machine model does not change their behavior.

Using the model, we have shown how to formulate a well-known optimization. The easy formulation of various optimizations in a unified formal model is expected to encourage the formal treatment of such transformations and to increase the understanding of dynamically optimizing systems in general.

ACKNOWLEDGMENTS

The criticism and the suggestions of the anonymous referees during the student feedback review round have significantly helped in improving the contents and the presentation of this paper and are greatly appreciated.

REFERENCES

[1] Ali-Reza Adl-Tabatabai, Jay Bharadwaj, Dong-Yuan Chen, Anwar Ghuloum, Vijay Menon, Brian Murphy, Mauricio Serrano, and Tatiana Shpeisman. The StarJIT compiler: A dynamic compiler for managed runtime environments. *Intel Technology Journal*, 7(1), February 2003.

[2] Jim Alves-Foss, editor. *Formal Syntax and Semantics of Java*, volume 1523 of *Lecture Notes in Computer Science*. Springer, 1999.

[3] Matthew Arnold, Stephen Fink, David Grove, Michael Hind, and Peter F. Sweeney. Architecture and policy for adaptive optimization in virtual machines. Research Report 23429, IBM Research, November 2004.

[4] P. J. Brown. Throw-away compiling. *Software Practice and Experience*, 6(4):423–434, 1976.

[5] Derek Bruening, Timothy Garnett, and Saman Amarasinghe. An infrastructure for adaptive dynamic optimization. In *CGO '03: Proceedings of the International Symposium on Code Generation and Optimization*, pages 265–275. IEEE Computer Society, 2003.

[6] M. Burke, J. Choi, S. Fink, D. Grove, M. Hind, V. Sarkar, M. Serrano, V. Sreedhar, H. Srinivasan, and J. Whaley. The Jalapeño dynamic optimizing compiler for Java. In *Proceedings ACM 1999 Java Grande Conference*, pages 129–141, San Francisco, CA, United States, June 1999. ACM Press.

[7] Anton Chernoff and Ray Hookway. Digital FX!32 – Running 32-Bit x86 Applications on Alpha NT. In *Proceedings of the USENIX Windows NT Workshop*, Seattle, Washington, August 1997.

[8] J. L. Dawson. Combining interpretive code with machine code. *Computer Journal*, 16(3):216–219, 1973.

[9] James C. Dehnert, Brian K. Grant, John P. Banning, Richard Johnson, Thomas Kistler, Alexander Klaiber, and Jim Mattson. The Transmeta Code Morphing™ Software: using speculation, recovery, and adaptive retranslation to address real-life challenges. In *CGO '03: Proceedings of the International Symposium on Code Generation and Optimization*, pages 15–24. IEEE Computer Society, 2003.

[10] L. Peter Deutsch and Allan M. Schiffman. Efficient implementation of the Smalltalk-80 system. In *Proceedings of the 11th ACM SIGACT-SIGPLAN Symposium on Principles of Programming Languages*, pages 297–302. ACM Press, 1984.

[11] Kemal Ebcioglu and Erik R. Altman. DAISY: Dynamic Compilation for 100% Architectural Compatibility. Technical Report 8502, IBM, 1996.

[12] ECMA International. *Standard ECMA-334: Common Language Infrastructure (CLI)*. 3rd edition, June 2005.

[13] Michael Steffen Oliver Franz. *Code-Generation On-the-fly: A Key to Portable Software*. PhD thesis, ETH Zürich, 1994.

[14] Urs Hölzle. *Adaptive optimization for Self: Reconciling High Performance with Exploratory Programming*. PhD thesis, Computer Science Department, Stanford University, 1994.

[15] Catherine Hope and Graham Hutton. Accurate step counting. In *Proceedings of the 17th International Workshop on Implementation and Application of Functional Languages*, Dublin, Ireland, 2005.

[16] Peter Lee and Mark Leone. Optimizing ML with run-time code generation. In *Proceedings of the ACM SIGPLAN 1996 Conference on Programming Language Design and Implementation*, pages 137–148. ACM Press, 1996.

[17] Mark Leone and R. Kent Dybvig. Dynamo: A staged compiler architecture for dynamic program optimization. Technical Report 490, Indiana University Computer Science Department, September 1997.

[18] T. Lindholm and F. Yellin. *The Java™ Virtual Machine Specification*. Sun Microsystems, 2nd edition, 1999.

[19] Dmitry Lomov and Anton Moscal. Dynamic Caml v. 0.2 – Run-Time Code Generation Library for Objective Caml. Available on the World Wide Web at `http://oops.tercom.ru/dml/files/dml-0.2.1.ps.gz`, last visited: 2006-10-20, May 2002.

[20] Michael Paleczny, Christopher Vick, and Cliff Click. The Java HotSpot™ Server Compiler. In *Proceedings of the Java™ Virtual Machine Research and Technology Symposium (JVM '01)*. USENIX Association, April 2001.

[21] D. Sands. *Calculi for Time Analysis of Functional Programs*. PhD thesis, Department of Computing, Imperial College, University of London, September 1990.

[22] Tim Sheard. Using MetaML: A Staged Programming Language. In S. Doaitse Swierstra, Pedro R. Henriques, and José N. Oliviera, editors, *Advanced Functional Programming*, volume 1608 of *Lecture Notes in Computer Science*, pages 207–239. Springer-Verlag, September 1998. Third International School, AFP'98.

[23] James E. Smith and Ravi Nair. *Virtual Machines – Versatile Platforms for Systems and Processes*. Morgan Kaufman, 2005.

[24] T. Suganuma, T. Ogasawara, M. Takeuchi, T. Yasue, M. Kawahito, K. Ishizaki, H. Komatsu, and T. Nakatani. Overview of the IBM Java Just-in-Time Compiler. *IBM Systems Journal*, 39(1):175–193, 2000.

[25] David Wakeling. The dynamic compilation of lazy functional programs. *Journal of Functional Programming*, 8(1):61–81, January 1998.

Chapter 10

Functional Concepts in C++

Rose H. Abdul Rauf[1], Ulrich Berger[2], Anton Setzer[2] [3]

Abstract: We describe a parser-translator program that translates typed λ-terms into C++ classes so as to integrate functional concepts. We prove the correctness of the translation of λ-terms into C++ with respect to a denotational semantics using a Kripke-style logical relation. We also introduce a general technique for introducing lazy evaluation into C++ and illustrate it by carrying out in C++ the example of computing the Fibonacci numbers efficiently using infinite streams and lazy evaluation.

10.1 INTRODUCTION

C++ is a general purpose language that supports object-oriented programming as well as procedural and generic programming, but unfortunately not directly functional programming. We have developed a parser-translator program that translates typed λ-terms into C++ statements so as to integrate functional concepts. The translated code uses the object oriented approach of programming that involves the creation of classes for the λ-term. By using inheritance, we achieve that the translation of a λ-abstraction is an element of a function type.

The paper is organised as follows: First, we introduce the translation and discuss how the translated code is executed including a description of the memory allocation (section 10.2). The correctness of our implementation is proved with respect to the usual (set-theoretic) denotational semantics of the simply typed λ-calculus and a mathematical model of a sufficiently large fragment of C++. The proof is based on a Kripke-style logical relation between C++ values and denotational values (section 10.3). In section 10.4 we introduce a general technique for

---

[1]Faculty of Information System and Quantitative Science, University of Technology MARA, 40450 Shah Alam, Selangor D.E., Malaysia; Email:
`hafsah@tmsk.uitm.edu.my`

[2]Department of Computer Science, University of Wales Swansea, Singleton Park, Swansea SA2 8PP, UK; Email: `{u.berger,a.g.setzer}@swansea.ac.uk`

[3]Supported by EPSRC grant GR/S30450/01

introducing lazy evaluation into C++ by introducing a data type of lazy elements of an arbitrary C++ type.

Related work. Several researchers [7], [8] have discovered that C++ can be used for functional programming by representing higher-order functions using classes. Our representation is based on similar ideas. There are other approaches that have made C++ a language that can be used for functional programming such as the FC++ library [9] (a very elaborate approach) as well as FACT! [19] (extensive use of templates and overloading) and [7] (creating macros that allow creation of single macro-closure in C++). The advantages of our solution are that it is very simple, it uses classes and inheritance in an essential way, it can be used for implementing λ-terms with side effects, and, most importantly, we have a formal correctness proof.

The approach of using denotational semantics and logical relations for proving program correctness has been used before by Plotkin [12], Reynolds [14] and many others. The method of logical relations can be traced back at least to Tait [20] and has been used for various purposes, for example, for proving normalization (Tait [20]), computational adequacy (Plotkin [12]) and completeness (Jung and Tiuryn [5], Statman [18], Plotkin [13]). To our knowledge the verification of the implementation of the λ-calculus in C++ (and related object-oriented languages) using logical relations is new.

There are other fragments of object-oriented languages in the literature which are used to prove the correctness of programs. A well-known example is Featherweight Java ([4]). The model for this language avoids the use of a heap, since methods do not modify instance variables. In contrast, our model of C++ does make use of a heap and is therefore closer to the actual implementation of C++. Although our fragment of C++ does not allow for methods with side effects, it could easily be extended this way and then used to verify programs in C++ using side effects. This could be used, for instance, to prove the efficiency of the Lazy construct introduced in section 10.4.

Lazy evaluation in C++ has been studied extensively in the literature (see e.g. [15], [9], [6]). To our knowledge, all implementations are restricted to lazy lists, whereas we introduce a general type of lazy elements of an arbitrary type, which not only corresponds to call-by-name (which is usually achieved by replacing a type A by $() \to A$), but also guarantees that elements are only evaluated once, as required by true lazy evaluation. Note as well that there is no need to add a new delay construct to C++ since our implementation of laziness makes use of the existing language of C++ only.

10.2   TRANSLATION OF TYPED λ-TERMS INTO C++

In this section we describe how to translate simply typed λ-terms into C++ using the object-oriented concepts of classes and inheritance.

The *simply typed λ-calculus*, *λ-calculus* for short, is given as follows: We assume a set basetype of base types $\rho, \sigma, \ldots$, and a set F of *basic functions* from base types to base types. Any native C++ type can be used as a base type, and any native C++ function without side effects can be used as a basic function. [4]

Types are elements of basetype, and function types $A \to B$ (if A, B are types). *Terms* are of the form x (variables), $\lambda x^A r$ (abstraction), $r\,s$ (application), $f[r_1, \ldots, r_n]$ (function application; $f \in \mathsf{F}$),[5] where r, s, r_i are terms. We treat constants, c, as basic functions with no arguments, and write in this case c instead of $c[\,]$.

A *context* is a finite set of pairs $\Gamma = x_1 : A_1, \ldots, x_n : A_n$ (all x_i distinct) which is, as usual, identified with a finite map.

We let Type, Var, Term, Context denote the set of types, variables, terms and contexts, respectively. The *typing rules* are as usual:

$$\Gamma, x : A \vdash x : A \qquad \frac{\Gamma, x : A \vdash r : B}{\Gamma \vdash \lambda x^A r : A \to B} \qquad \frac{\Gamma \vdash r : A \to B \qquad \Gamma \vdash s : A}{\Gamma \vdash r\,s : B}$$

$$\frac{\Gamma \vdash r_1 : \sigma_1 \ldots \Gamma \vdash r_k : \sigma_k}{\Gamma \vdash f[r_1, \ldots, r_k] : \rho} \quad (f \text{ a basic function of type } \sigma_1 \to \cdots \to \sigma_k \to \rho)$$

We now show how to translate λ-terms into C++. The translation is essentially the same as that given by the parsing function P introduced in section 10.3 – the only difference is that P will be developed in an abstract setting, whereas the translation given in the following generates genuine C++ code.

Our translation generates new identifiers, which we need to disambiguate; in order for this to work, we restrict ourselves to the translation of finitely many λ-terms and types at a time. We first define an identifier $\mathrm{name}(a) : \mathsf{String}$ for finitely many $a : \mathsf{Type}$. Here String is the set of strings.

- If A is a native C++-type, $\mathrm{name}(A)$ is a C++ identifier obtained from A. This is A, if A is already an identifier, and the result of removing blanks and modifying symbols not allowed in identifiers (e.g. replacing $*$ by x), in case A is a compound type like `long int` or $*A$.[6]

- $\mathrm{name}(A \to B) := \text{"C"}*\mathrm{name}(A)*\text{"\_"}*\mathrm{name}(B)*\text{"D"}$, where $*$ means concatenation. Here C stands for an open bracket, D for a closing bracket, and _ for the arrow in this identifier. By using these symbols we obtain valid C++-identifiers.[7]

---

[4]The translation given below makes sense as well for functions with side effects, including those which affect instance variables of the classes used. However, in this case we would go beyond the simply typed λ-calculus, and could not use the simple denotational semantics of the λ-calculus in order to express the correctness of the translation.

[5]Note that we do not have any product types and that native C++-functions are not necessarily objects – they can even be constants such as integers – therefore $f[r_1, \ldots, r_k]$ cannot be subsumed by the rule for $r\,s$.

[6]This modification might result in name clashes, in which case one adds some string like _n for some integer n in order to disambiguate the names. Since we are translating only finitely many λ-types at any time, this way of avoiding name clashes is always possible.

[7]Again, we might need to disambiguate the identifiers as it was done for native C++ types.

For instance, name(int $\rightarrow$ int) ="Cint_intD", name((int $\rightarrow$ int) $\rightarrow$ int) = "CCint_intD_intD". In the following, we write CA_BD instead of name($A \rightarrow B$) and CA_BD_aux instead of name($A \rightarrow B$)*"_aux" (this type will be introduced below), similarly for other types.

For every $A \in$ Type we introduce a series of class definitions, after which name(A) is a valid C++ type (assuming class definitions for any native C++ type used):

- For native C++-types the sequence of class definitions is empty.

- The sequence of class definitions for $A \rightarrow B$ consists of the class definitions of A, the class definitions of B not contained in the class definitions of A and additionally

```
class CA_BD_aux{
  public: virtual B operator () (A x)=0;};
typedef CA_BD_aux * CA_BD;
```

So, CA_BD_aux is a class with one virtual method used as application, which maps an element of type A to an element of type B. CA_BD is a pointer to an element of this class.

Now we define for every λ-term t a sequence of C++-class definitions and a C++-term t^{C++}, s.t. if $t : A$, then t^{C++} is of type name(A).[8]

- If x is a variable, then the class definitions for introducing x are empty and $x^{C++} := x$.

- Assume $A = E \rightarrow F$, $t = \lambda x^A.r$. Assume the free variables of t are of type $x_1 : A_1, \ldots, x_n : A_n$ and that t is a new identifier. Assume name(A_i) = Ai, xi is the C++-representation for x_i, name(E) = E, name(F) = F, and r^{C++} = r. The class definition for t consists of the class definition for r together with

```
class t : CE_FD_aux{
  public:
    A1 x1;
    ...
    An xn;
    t(A1 x1,A2 x2, ... , An xn){
        this->x1 = x1;
        ...
        this->xn = xn;}
    virtual F operator () (E x){
        return r;};};
```

---

[8]Strictly speaking, t^{C++} depends on the choice of identifiers for λ-types and C++-classes representing λ-terms. When defining the parse function P in section 10.3, this will be made explicit by having the dependency of this function on the context Γ and the class environment C. Since in our abstract setting λ-types are represented by themselves, P does not depend on the choice of identifiers for those types.

$t^{C++} := \text{new } t(\text{x1}, ..., \text{xn}).$

- Assume $t = r\,s$. Then the class definitions of t consist of the class definitions for r, and the class definitions for s (where the class definitions corresponding to λ-abstractions occurring in both r and s need to be introduced only once).[9] Furthermore $t^{C++} := (*(r^{C++}))(s^{C++})$.

- Assume $t = f[r_1, \ldots, r_n]$. Then the class definitions for t are the class definitions for r_i (again class definitions for λ-terms occurring more than once need only to be introduced once). Furthermore, $t^{C++} := f(r_1^{C++}, ..., r_n^{C++})$.

Note that a λ-abstraction is interpreted as a function of its free variables in the form $(\text{new } t(\text{x}_1, \ldots, \text{x}_n))$. Hence, the evaluation of a λ-abstraction in an environment for the free variables is similar to a "closure" in implementations of functional programming languages.

We have developed a program which parses λ-terms and translates them into C++. Our intention is to upgrade this to an extension of the language of C++ by λ-types and -terms together with a parser program which translates this extended language into native C++. For this purpose we introduce a syntax for representing λ-types and -terms in C++. We use functional style notation rather than overloading existing C++-notation, since we believe that this will improve readability and acceptability of our approach by functional programmers. In our extended language, we write A $->$ B for the function type A $\to$ B, r $\char94\char94$ s for the application of r to s,[10] and \A x.B s for $\lambda x^A.s$, if $s : B$. (If s is a term starting with λ, B will be omitted). For instance, the term

$$t = (\lambda f^{\text{int} \to \text{int}} \lambda x^{\text{int}}. f\,(f\,x))\,(\lambda x^{\text{int}}. x + 2)\,3$$

is written in our extended C++ syntax as

```
(\int->int f. \int x. int f^^(f^^x))^^(\int x. int x+2)^^3
```

We will use this extended syntax in our C++ implementation of lazy data structures (section 10.4).

As an example, we show how the translation program transforms the term t above into native C++ code. We begin with the class definitions for the λ-types:

```
class Cint_intD_aux
{ public : virtual int operator() (int x) = 0; };

typedef Cint_intD_aux*  Cint_intD;
```

---

[9] A λ-abstraction is represented as a new instance of its corresponding class. Even if the classes for two occurrences of the same λ-abstraction coincide, for each occurrence a new instance is created. Therefore there is no problem, if a variable occurs as the same name, but with different referential meaning in two identical λ-expressions.

[10] Note that we cannot $r(s)$ here, since this notation will not translate into application, but into $(*r)(s)$.

```
class CCint_intD_Cint_intDD_aux
{  public : virtual Cint_intD operator()
                              (Cint_intD x) = 0; };
```

```
typedef CCint_intD_Cint_intDD_aux*
        CCint_intD_Cint_intDD;
```

The class definition for $t_1 := \lambda x^{int}.f\ (f\ x)$ is

```
class t1 : public Cint_intD_aux{
 public :Cint_intD f;
 t1( Cint_intD f)  {    this-> f = f;};
 virtual int operator () (int x)
 { return (*(f))((*(f))(x)); };
};
```

and $t_1^{C++} = $ new t1(f). The class definitions for $t_0 := \lambda f^{int \to int} \lambda x^{int}.f(fx)$ and $t_2 := \lambda x^{int}.2 + x$ (using identifiers t0, t2) are as follows:

```
class t0 : public CCint_intD_Cint_intDD_aux{
 public :
 t0( ) { };
 virtual Cint_intD operator () (Cint_intD f)
 { return new  t1( f); }
};
```

```
 class t2 : public Cint_intD_aux{
 public :
 t2( ) { };
 virtual int operator () (int x)
 { return x + 2; };
};
```

Finally
$$t^{C++} := (*((*(\text{ new } t0( )))(\text{ new } t2( ))))(3);$$

When evaluating the expression t^{C++}, first the application of t0 to t2 is evaluated. To this end, instances 10, 12 of the classes t0 and t2 are created first. Then the operator() method of 10 is called. This call creates an instance 11 of t1, with the instance variable f set to 12. The result of applying t0 to t2 is 11.

The next step in the evaluation of t^{C++} is to evaluate 3, and then to call the operator() method of 11. This will first make a call to the operator method of f, which is bound to 12, and apply it to 3. This will evaluate to 5. Then it will call the operator method of f again, which is still bound to 12, and apply it to the result 5. The result returned is 7.

We see that the evaluation of the expression above follows the call-by-value evaluation strategy.[11] Note that 10, 11, 12 were created on the heap, but have

---

[11]Note that this computation causes some overhead, since for every subterm of the form $\lambda x.r$ a new object is created, which is in many cases used once, and can be thrown away

not been deleted afterwards. The deletion of 10, 11 and 12 relies on the use of a garbage collected version of C++, alternatively we could use smart pointers in order to enforce their deletion.

10.3 PROOF OF CORRECTNESS

We now prove the correctness of our C++ implementation of the λ-calculus. For notational simplicity we restrict ourselves to the base type int of integers. By "correctness" we mean that every closed term r of type int is evaluated by our implementation to a numeral which coincides with the *value* of r. The value of a term can be defined either *operationally* as the normal form w.r.t. β-reduction, $(\lambda x^A r)s \rightarrow_\beta r[s/x]$, and function reduction, $f[n_1, \ldots, n_k] \rightarrow_f n$ (n the value of f at $n_1, \ldots, n_k$), or, equivalently, *denotationally* as the natural value in a suitable domain of functionals of finite types. Since our calculus does not allow for recursive definitions, the details of the operational and denotational semantics do not matter: Operationally, any sufficiently complete reduction strategy (call-by-value, call-by-name, full normalisation) will do, and denotationally, any Cartesian closed category containing the type of integers can be used. For our purposes it is most convenient to work with a denotational model, for example, the naive set-theoretic hierarchy D of functionals of finite types over the integers[12] (setting $Z = \{\ldots, -2, -1, 0, 1, 2, \ldots\}$ and $X \rightarrow Y = \{f \mid f : X \rightarrow Y\}$):

$$D(\text{int}) = Z, \quad D(A \rightarrow B) = D(A) \rightarrow D(B), \quad D = \bigcup_{A \in \text{Type}} D(A)$$

A *functional environment* is a mapping $\xi : \text{Var} \rightarrow D$. FEnv denotes the set of all functional environments. If Γ is a context, then $\xi : \Gamma$ means $\forall x \in \text{dom}(\Gamma).\xi(x) \in D(\Gamma(x))$.

For every typed λ-term $\Gamma \vdash r : A$ and every functional environment $\xi : \Gamma$ the denotational value $[\![r]\!]\xi \in D(A)$ is defined by

i) $[\![n]\!]\xi = n$

ii) $[\![x]\!]\xi = \xi(x)$

iii) $[\![r\,s]\!]\xi = [\![r]\!]\xi([\![s]\!]\xi)$

iv) $[\![\lambda x^A.r]\!]\xi(a) = [\![r]\!]\xi[x \mapsto a]$

v) $[\![f[\vec{r}]]\!] = [\![f]\!]([\![\vec{r}]\!]\xi)$

where in the last clause $[\![f]\!]$ is the number-theoretic function denoted by f. Our implementation of the λ-calculus is modelled in a similar way as e.g. in [1] using functions eval and apply, but, in order to model the C++ implementation as

---

afterwards. One could optimize this, however at the price of having a much more complicated translation, and therefore a much more complex correctness proof of the translation.

[12]Recursion can be interpreted in a domain-theoretic model [12].

truthfully as possible, we make the pointer structures for the classes and objects explicit by letting the functions eval and apply modify these pointer structures via side effects.

We model only the fragment of C++ that we used in Section 10.2 to translate the simply typed λ-calculus into C++. Hence we assume that classes have instance variables, one constructor, and one method corresponding to the `operator()` method. The constructor has one argument for each instance variable and sets the instance variables to these arguments. No other code is performed. The method has one argument, and the body consists of an applicative term, where applicative terms are simplified C++ expressions in our model. So, a class is given by a context representing its instance variables, the abstracted variable of the method and its type, and an applicative term.

Applicative terms are numbers, variables, function terms applied to applicative terms, the application of one applicative term to another applicative term (which corresponds to the method call in case the first applicative term is an object), or a constructor applied to applicative terms.

When a constructor call of a class is evaluated, its arguments are first evaluated. Then, memory for the instance variables of this class is allocated on the heap, and these instance variables are set to the evaluated arguments. The address to this memory location is the result returned by evaluating this constructor call. The only other possible result of the evaluation of an applicative term is a number, so values are addresses or numbers. Hence, the data sets associated with our model of C++ classes are defined as follows (letting $X + Y$ and $X \times Y$ denote the disjoint sum and Cartesian product of X and Y, X^* the set of finite lists of elements in X and $X \to_{\mathsf{fin}} Y$ the set of finite maps from X to Y):

Addr	=	a set of numbers denoting addresses of classes on the heap
Constr	=	a set of strings denoting constructors, i.e. class names
Val	=	$\mathbb{Z} + \mathsf{Addr}$
F	=	a set of names for arithmetic C++ functions
App	=	$\mathbb{Z} + \mathsf{Var} + \mathsf{F} \times \mathsf{App}^* + \mathsf{App} \times \mathsf{App} + \mathsf{Constr} \times \mathsf{App}^*$
Context	=	$\mathsf{Var} \to_{\mathsf{fin}} \mathsf{Type}$
Class	=	$\mathsf{Context} \times \mathsf{Var} \times \mathsf{Type} \times \mathsf{App}$
VEnv	=	$\mathsf{Var} \to_{\mathsf{fin}} \mathsf{Val}$
Heap	=	$\mathsf{Addr} \to_{\mathsf{fin}} \mathsf{Constr} \times \mathsf{Val}^*$
CEnv	=	$\mathsf{Constr} \to_{\mathsf{fin}} \mathsf{Class}$

Applicative terms ($\in$ App), which we write as n, x, $f[a_1,\ldots,a_n]$, $(a\ b)$ and $c[a_1,\ldots,a_n]$, correspond to the C++ constructs n, x, f(a₁,...,aₙ), (*(a))(b) and new c(a₁,...,aₙ), while classes ($\in$ Class), written in the form $(\Gamma; x : A; b)$ with $\Gamma = x_1 : A_1,\ldots,x_n : A_n$, correspond to a C++ class definition of the form

```
class c : CA_BD_aux{
   public: A1 x1;
           ...
           An xn;
   c(A1 x1,A2 x2,  ... , An xn){
```

```
            this->x1 = x1;
            ...
            this->xn = xn;}
virtual B operator () (A x){
            return b;};};
```

The type B is omitted in $(\Gamma; x : A; b)$ since it can be derived, and the class name c is associated with the class through the class environment CEnv.

The fact that the parsing function as well as the functions eval and apply have side effects on the classes and the heap can be conveniently expressed using a *partial state monad* (the object part of which is)

$$\mathsf{M}_X(Y) := X \xrightarrow{\sim} Y \times X$$

where $X \xrightarrow{\sim} Y \times X$ is the set of partial functions from X to $Y \times X$. Elements of $\mathsf{M}_X(Y)$ are called *actions* and can be viewed as elements of Y that may depend on a current state $x \in X$ and also may change the current state. Monads are a category-theoretic concept whose computational significance was discovered by Moggi [10]. We need to work with partial instead of total functions because the operations eval and apply defined below do not yield defined results in general. We will however prove that for inputs generated by translating well-typed λ-terms the results will always be defined.

Using the monad terminology the functionalities of the parsing function P and the operations eval and apply can now be written as

$$
\begin{aligned}
\mathsf{P} : \quad & \mathsf{Context} \to \mathsf{Term} \to \mathsf{M}_{\mathsf{CEnv}}(\mathsf{App}) \\
\mathsf{eval} : \quad & \mathsf{CEnv} \to \mathsf{VEnv} \to \mathsf{App} \to \mathsf{M}_{\mathsf{Heap}}(\mathsf{Val}) \\
\mathsf{apply} : \quad & \mathsf{CEnv} \to \mathsf{Val} \to \mathsf{Val} \to \mathsf{M}_{\mathsf{Heap}}(\mathsf{Val})
\end{aligned}
$$

Hence, parsing has a side effect on the class environment, while eval and apply have side effects on the heap. The function P corresponds to the assignment $t \mapsto t^{C++}$ introduced in Section 10.2, but makes the dependencies on the context and the class environment explicit.

We use the following standard monadic notation (roughly following Haskell syntax): Suppose $e_1 : \mathsf{M}_X(Y_1)$, ..., $e_{k+1} : \mathsf{M}_X(Y_{k+1})$ are actions where e_i may depend on $y_1 : Y_1, \ldots, y_{i-1} : Y_{i-1}$. Then

$$\mathsf{do}\{y_1 \leftarrow e_1 ; \ldots ; y_k \leftarrow e_k ; e_{k+1}\} : \mathsf{M}_X(Y_{k+1})$$

is the action that maps any state $x_0 : X$ to (y_{k+1}, x_{k+1}) where $(y_i, x_i) \simeq e_i \, x_{i-1}$, for $i = 1, \ldots, k+1$ ($\simeq$ denotes the usual "partial equality"). We also allow let-expressions with pattern matching within a do-construct (with the obvious meaning). We adopt the convention that computations are "strict", i.e. the result of a computation is undefined if one of its parts is. Furthermore, we use the standard monadic notations

$$
\begin{aligned}
\mathsf{return} \quad &: \quad Y \to \mathsf{M}_X(Y) \qquad\qquad \mathsf{return} \, y \, x = (y, x) \\
\mathsf{mapM} \quad &: \quad (Z \to \mathsf{M}_X(Y)) \to Z^* \quad \mathsf{mapM} \, f \, \vec{a} = \mathsf{do}\{y_1 \leftarrow f \, a_1 ; \ldots \\
& \qquad\qquad \to \mathsf{M}_X(Y^*) \qquad\qquad \ldots ; y_k \leftarrow f \, a_k ; \mathsf{return} \, (y_1, \ldots, y_k)\}
\end{aligned}
$$

as well as

$$\text{read} : X \to \mathsf{M}_{X \to_{\text{fin}} Y}(Y), \quad \text{read } x\, m \simeq (m\, x, m)$$
$$\text{add} : Y \to \mathsf{M}_{X \to_{\text{fin}} Y}(X), \quad \text{add } y\, m \simeq (x, m[x \mapsto y]) \quad \text{where } x = \text{fresh}(m)$$

Here, fresh is a function with the property that if $m : X \to_{\text{fin}} Y$, then $\text{fresh}(m) \in X \setminus \text{dom}(m)$ [13]. With these notations the definitions of P, eval and apply read as follows

$$
\begin{aligned}
\mathsf{P}\,\Gamma\, u &= \text{return } u, \text{ if } u \text{ is a number or a variable} \\
\mathsf{P}\,\Gamma\, f[\vec{r}] &= \text{do}\{\vec{a} \leftarrow \text{mapM } (\mathsf{P}\,\Gamma)\,\vec{r}\,;\, \text{return } f[\vec{a}]\} \\
\mathsf{P}\,\Gamma\, (r\,s) &= \text{do}\{(a,b) \leftarrow \text{mapM } (\mathsf{P}\,\Gamma)\,(r,s)\,;\, \text{return } (a\,b)\} \\
\mathsf{P}\,\Gamma\, (\lambda x^A.r) &= \text{do}\{a \leftarrow \mathsf{P}\,\Gamma[x \mapsto A]\,r\,;\, c \leftarrow \text{add}(\Gamma; x : A; a)\,; \\
&\qquad \text{return } c[\text{dom}(\Gamma)]\}
\end{aligned}
$$

$$
\begin{aligned}
\text{eval } C\,\eta\, n &= \text{return } n \\
\text{eval } C\,\eta\, x &= \text{return } (\eta\, x) \\
\text{eval } C\,\eta\, f[\vec{a}] &= \text{do}\{\vec{n} \leftarrow \text{mapM } (\text{eval } C\,\eta)\,\vec{a}\,;\, \text{return } [\![f]\!](\vec{n})\} \\
\text{eval } C\,\eta\, (a\,b) &= \text{do}\{(v,w) \leftarrow \text{mapM}(\text{eval } C\,\eta)\,(a,b)\,;\, \text{apply } C\,v\,w\} \\
\text{eval } C\,\eta\, c[\vec{a}] &= \text{do}\{\vec{v} \leftarrow \text{mapM } (\text{eval } C\,\eta)\,\vec{a}\,;\, \text{add } (c,\vec{v})\} \\
\text{apply } C\,h\,v &= \text{do}\{(c,\vec{w}) \leftarrow \text{read } h\,;\, \text{let } (\vec{y} : \vec{B}; x : A; a) = C\,c\,; \\
&\qquad \text{eval } C\,[\vec{y}, x \mapsto \vec{w}, v]\,a\} \\
\text{apply } C\,n\,v &= \emptyset
\end{aligned}
$$

where $\emptyset$ is the undefined action, i.e. the partial function with empty domain [14].

Lemma 10.1. *(1)* $\mathsf{P}\,\Gamma\, r$ *is total and if* $\mathsf{P}\,\Gamma\, r\, C = (a, C')$*, then* $C \subseteq C'$*.*

(2) If $\text{eval } C\,\eta\, a\, H = (v, H')$*, then* $H \subseteq H'$*.*

(3) If $\text{apply } C\,v\,w\, H = (v', H')$*, then* $H \subseteq H'$*.*

Proof. Property (1) is direct by induction on the term r. Properties (2) and (3) can be proved by a straightforward simultaneous induction on the definitions of eval and apply, i.e. by "fixed point induction" [21].   □

Due to the complexity of C++ it would be a major task, which would require much more manpower than was available in our project, to formally prove that our mathematical model, given by eval and apply, coincides with the operational semantics of C++.[15] (Note that other models of fragments of object-oriented languages in the literature face the same problem and their correctness w.r.t. real

---

[13] In our applications X will be a space of addresses which we assume to be infinite, i.e. we assume that the allocation of a new address is always possible.

[14] It would be more appropriate to let apply $C\,n\,v$ result in an error, but, for simplicity, we identify errors with non-termination.

[15] The formalisation of the semantics of Java in [17] was a major project, and still this book excludes some features of Java like inner classes. Note that C++ is much more complex than Java.

languages is therefore usually not shown.) However, when going through the definitions we observe that the evaluation function eval is indeed defined in accordance with the expected behaviour of C++: An integer n is evaluated by itself, and a variable is evaluated by returning its value in the current environment η. The application of a native C++ function to arguments $a_1, \ldots, a_n$ is carried out by first evaluating $a_1, \ldots, a_n$ in sequence, and then applying the function f to those arguments. $(a\ b)$ corresponds in C++ to the construct $(*\ (a))(b)$. First a and b are evaluated. Because of type correctness, a must be an element of the type of pointers to a class, and the value of a will therefore be an address on the heap. On the heap the information about the class used and the values of the instance variables of that class are stored. Then $(*\ (a))(b)$ is computed by evaluating the body of the method of the class in the environment where the instance variables have the values as stored on the heap, and the abstracted variable has the result of evaluating b. This is what is computed by eval $C\ \eta\ (a\ b)$ (which makes use of the auxiliary function apply). The expression $c[\vec{a}]$, which stands for the C++ expression new $c(a_0, \ldots, a_n)$, is evaluated by first computing $a_0, \ldots, a_n$ in sequence. Then new storage on the heap is allocated. Note that in our simplified setting, the constructor of c simply assigns to the instance variables the values of $a_0, \ldots, a_n$. Consequently, the intended behaviour of C++ is that it stores on the heap the information about the class used and the result of evaluating $a_0, \ldots, a_n$, which is what is carried out by eval.

The formal correctness proof for the translated code with respect to our mathematical model of (a fragment of) C++ is based on a Kripke-style logical relation between a C++ value ($\in$ Val $\times$ Heap) and a denotational value ($\in$ D(A)). The relation is indexed by the class environment C and the type A of the term. The relation

$$\sim_A^C \subseteq (\text{Val} \times \text{Heap}) \times \text{D}(A),$$

where $A \in$ Type, $C \in$ CEnv, is defined by recursion on A as follows:

$$(v, H) \sim_{\text{int}}^C n \quad :\Longleftrightarrow \quad v = n$$
$$(v, H) \sim_{A \to B}^C f \quad :\Longleftrightarrow \quad \forall C' \supseteq C, \forall H' \supseteq H, \forall (w, d) \in \text{Val} \times \text{D}(A):$$
$$(w, H') \sim_A^{C'} d \Longrightarrow \text{apply } C'\ v\ w\ H' \sim_B^{C'} f(d)$$

Note that the formula apply $C'\ v\ w\ H' \sim_B^{C'} f(d)$ above states that apply $C'\ v\ w\ H'$ is defined and the result is in relation $\sim_B^{C'}$ with $f(d)$. The formula eval $C''\ \eta\ a\ H' \sim_A^{C''} [\![r]\!]\xi$ in the theorem below is to be understood in a similar way. We also set

$$(\eta, H) \sim_\Gamma^C \xi :\Leftrightarrow \text{dom}(\Gamma) \subseteq \text{dom}(\eta) \cap \text{dom}(\xi) \wedge \forall x \in \text{dom}(\Gamma)(\eta(x), H) \sim_{\Gamma(x)}^C \xi(x)$$

The main result below corresponds to the usual "Fundamental Lemma" or "Adequacy Theorem" for logical relations:

Theorem 10.2. *Assume* $\Gamma \vdash r : A$, P $\Gamma\ r\ C = (a, C')$, $C'' \supset C'$ *and* $\xi : \Gamma$. *Then for all* $(\eta, H) \in$ VEnv $\times$ Heap:

$$(\eta, H) \sim_\Gamma^{C''} \xi \Longrightarrow \text{eval } C''\ \eta\ a\ H \sim_A^{C''} [\![r]\!]\xi.$$

Proof. The proof is by induction on the typing judgement $\Gamma \vdash r : A$. In the proof we will use the properties (1) and (2) of Lemma 10.1 as well as the following property of the relation $\sim_A^C$, which is clear by definition, and which in the following will be referred to as "monotonicity":

If $(v, H) \sim_A^C d$ and $H \subseteq H'$ and $C \subseteq C'$, then $(v, H') \sim_A^{C'} d$.

We now consider the four possible cases of how $\Gamma \vdash r : A$ can be derived.

$\Gamma, x : A \vdash x : A$. We have $\mathsf{P}(\Gamma, x : A) \, x \, C = \mathrm{return} \, x \, C = (x, C)$. Assume $C' \supseteq C$, $\xi : (\Gamma, x : A)$ and $(\eta, H) \sim_{\Gamma, x:A}^{C'} \xi$. We need to show $\mathrm{eval} \, C' \, \eta \, x \, H \sim_A^{C'} [\![x]\!]\xi$. Since $\mathrm{eval} \, C' \, \eta \, x \, H = (\eta(x), H)$ and $[\![x]\!]\xi = \xi(x) \in \mathrm{D}(A)$, and the assumption $(\eta, H) \sim_{\Gamma, x:A}^{C'} \xi$ entails $(\eta(x), H) \sim_A^{C'} \xi(x)$, we are done.

$\Gamma \vdash \lambda x^A r : A \to B$, derived from $\Gamma, x : A \vdash r : B$. $\mathsf{P} \, \Gamma \, \lambda x^A r \, C = (c[\mathrm{dom}(\Gamma)], C')$ where $\mathsf{P}(\Gamma, x : A) \, r \, C = (a, C_1)$, with $C_1 \supseteq C$ by (1), $c = \mathrm{fresh}(C_1)$ and $C' = C_1[c \mapsto (\Gamma; x : A; a)]) \supseteq C$. Assume $C'' \supseteq C'$, $\xi : \Gamma$ and $(\eta, H) \sim_\Gamma^{C''} \xi$. We need to show $\mathrm{eval} \, C'' \, \eta \, c[\mathrm{dom}(\Gamma)] \, H \sim_{A \to B}^{C''} [\![\lambda x^A r]\!]\xi$. We have $\mathrm{eval} \, C'' \, \eta \, c[\mathrm{dom}(\Gamma)] \, H = (h, H_1)$ where $\vec{v} = \mathrm{map} \, \eta \, \mathrm{dom}(\Gamma)$ (the usual map function), $h = \mathrm{fresh}(H)$ and $H_1 = H[h \mapsto (c, \vec{v})])$. In view of the definition of $\sim_{A \to B}^{C''}$ we assume $C''' \supseteq C''$, $H' \supseteq H_1$ and $(w, H') \sim_A^{C'''} d$. We need to show $\mathrm{apply} \, C''' \, h \, w \, H' \sim_B^{C'''} [\![r]\!]\xi[x \mapsto d]$. Clearly, $\mathrm{apply} \, C''' \, h \, w \, H' = \mathrm{eval} \, C''' \eta_1 \, a \, H'$ where $\eta_1 = [\mathrm{dom}(\Gamma), x \mapsto \vec{v}, w]$. Furthermore, $(\eta_1, H') \sim_{\Gamma, x:A}^{C'''} \xi[x \mapsto d]$, by the assumptions $(\eta, H) \sim_\Gamma^{C''} \xi$ and $(w, H') \sim_A^{C'''} d$ and monotonicity. Using the induction hypothesis we obtain $\mathrm{eval} \, C''' \, \eta_1 \, a \, H' \sim_B^{C'''} [\![r]\!]\xi[x \mapsto d]$ since $\mathsf{P}(\Gamma, x : A) \, r \, C = (a, C_1)$ and $C_1 \supseteq C'''$.

$\Gamma \vdash r \, s : B$, derived from $\Gamma \vdash r : A \to B$ and $\Gamma \vdash s : A$. By (1), $\mathsf{P} \, \Gamma \, r \, C = (a, C_1)$ with $C \subseteq C_1$ and $\mathsf{P} \, \Gamma \, s \, C_1 = (b, C_2)$ with $C_1 \subseteq C_2$. Therefore, $\mathsf{P} \, \Gamma \, (r \, s) \, C = (a \, b, C_2)$. Assume $C' \supseteq C_2$, $\xi : \Gamma$ and $(\eta, H) \sim_\Gamma^{C'} \xi$. We need to show $\mathrm{eval} \, C' \, \eta \, (a \, b) \, H \sim_A^{C'} [\![r \, s]\!]\xi$. By induction hypothesis and (2), $\mathrm{eval} \, C' \, \eta \, a \, H = (v, H_1)$ for some $H_1 \supseteq H$ with $(v, H_1) \sim_{A \to B}^{C'} [\![r]\!]\xi$ and, using monotonicity, $\mathrm{eval} \, C' \, \eta \, a \, H_1 = (w, H_2)$ for some $H_2 \supseteq H_1$ with $(w, H_2) \sim_A^{C'} [\![s]\!]\xi$. Hence, $\mathrm{apply} \, C' \, v \, w \, H_2 \sim_B^{C'} [\![r]\!]\xi([\![s]\!]\xi)$ and we are done, since $\mathrm{eval} \, C' \, \eta \, (a \, b) \, H = \mathrm{apply} \, C' \, v \, w \, H_2$ and $[\![r \, s]\!]\xi = [\![r]\!]\xi([\![s]\!]\xi)$.

$\Gamma \vdash f[r_1, \ldots, r_k] : \mathrm{int}$, derived from $\Gamma \vdash r_i : \mathrm{int}$, $i = 1, \ldots, k$. By (1), $\mathsf{P} \, \Gamma \, r_1 \, C = (a_1, C_1)$ with $C \subseteq C_1$ and $\mathsf{P} \, \Gamma \, s \, C_{i+1} = (a_{i+1}, C_{i+1})$ with $C_i \subseteq C_{i+1}$, $i = 1, \ldots, k-1$. Hence, $\mathsf{P} \, \Gamma \, f[\vec{r}] \, C = (f[\vec{a}], C_k)$. Assume $C' \supseteq C_k$, $\xi : \Gamma$ and $(\eta, H) \sim_\Gamma^{C'} \xi$. We need to show $\mathrm{eval} \, C' \, \eta \, f[\vec{r}] \, H \sim_{\mathrm{int}}^{C'} [\![f[\vec{r}]]\!]\xi$. By induction hypothesis and (2), $\mathrm{eval} \, C' \, \eta \, a_1 \, H = (n_1, H_1)$ for some $n_1 \in \mathsf{Z}$ and $H_1 \supseteq H$ with $(n_1, H_1) \sim_{\mathrm{int}}^{C'} [\![r_1]\!]\xi$, i.e. $n_1 = [\![r_1]\!]\xi$. Similarly, using monotonicity and (2), for $i = 1, \ldots, k-1$ we have $\mathrm{eval} \, C' \, \eta \, a_{i+1} \, H_i = (n_{i+1}, H_{i+1})$ for some $n_{i+1} \in \mathsf{Z}$ and $H_{i+1} \supseteq H_i$ with $n_{i+1} = [\![r_{i+1}]\!]\xi$. It follows $\mathrm{eval} \, C' \, \eta \, f[\vec{r}] \, H = ([\![f]\!][\vec{n}], H_k) = ([\![f[\vec{r}]]\!]\xi, H_k)$. $\square$

Corollary 10.3 (Correctness of the implementation). *Assume* $\vdash r : \mathrm{int}$ *and let* $C \in \mathsf{CEnv}$. *Then* $\mathsf{P} \, \emptyset \, r \, C = (a, C')$ *for some* $C' \supseteq C$. *Furthermore, for any heap* H, *any environment* η *and any* $C'' \supseteq C'$ *we have*

$$\text{eval } C'' \, \eta \, a \, H = (n, H')$$

where n is the value of r and H' is some extension of H.

Remark. The proof of Theorem 10.2 is rather "low level" since it mentions and manipulates the class environment and the heap explicitly. It would be desirable, in particular with regard to a formalisation in a proof assistant, to lift the proof to the same abstract monadic level at which the functions P, eval and apply are defined. A framework for carrying this out might be provided by suitable versions of Moggi's Computational λ–Calculus, Pitts' Evaluation Logic [11] and special logical relations for monads [2].

10.4 LAZY EVALUATION IN C++

Haskell is famous for its programming techniques using infinite lists. A well-known example are the Fibonacci numbers, which are computed efficiently by using the following code:

```
fib = 1:1:(zipWith (+) fib (tail fib))
```

This example requires that we have infinite streams of natural numbers, and relies heavily on lazy evaluation. We show how to translate this code into efficient C++ code, by using lazy evaluation. The full code for the following example, in which we have translated λ-types and -terms into original C++, is available from [16].

The standard technique for replacing call-by-value by call-by-name is to delay evaluation by replacing types A by $() \to A$ where $()$ is the empty type (i.e. **void**). However, according to the slogan "lazy evaluation = call-by-name+sharing" (which we learnt from G. Hutton [3]) lazy evaluation means more than delaying evaluation: it means as well that a term is evaluated only once. In order to obtain this, we define a new type **Lazy(A)**. This type delays evaluation of an element of type A in such a way that, if needed, the evaluation is carried out – however, only once. Once the value is computed, the result is stored in a variable for later reuse. Note that this is a general definition, which is not restricted to lazy streams. The definition is as follows (we use the extended C++ syntax for λ-terms and -types introduced in section 10.2, esp. r `^^`t for application, \ for λ, and –> for →):

```
template<typename X> class lazy{
  bool is_evaluated;
  union {X       result;
         () -> X compute_function;};
public:
  lazy(()-> X compute_function){
    is_evaluated = false;
    this->compute_function = compute_function;};
  X eval(){
    if (not is_evaluated){
```

```
              result = compute_function ^^ ();
              is_evaluated = true;};
      return result;};};
#define Lazy(X) lazy<X>*
```

Note that without support by the extended syntax the code above would be much longer and considerably more complicated.

Using the class lazy we can now easily define lazy streams of natural numbers (lazy lists, i.e. possibly terminating streams, can be defined similarly, but require the usual technique based on the composite design pattern for formalising algebraic data types as classes by introducing a main class for the main type which has subclasses for each constructor, each of which stores the arguments of the constructor)

```
template<typename X>class lazy_stream{
    public: Lazy(X) head;
            Lazy(lazy_stream<X>*) tail;
            ... Constructor as usual ... }
#define Lazy_Stream(X) lazy_stream<X>*
```

We define an operation which takes a function of type $() \rightarrow X$ and returns the corresponding element of type $\text{Lazy}(X)$:

```
template<typename X> Lazy(X) create_lazy
    (()-> X compute_function){
                return new lazy<X>(compute_function);};
```

In order to deal with the example of the Fibonacci numbers, one needs to define the operators used in the above mentioned definition of fib:

- lazy_cons_lazy<X> computes the cons-operation on streams and returns lazily a lazy stream:

```
template<typename X>Lazy(Lazy_Stream(X)) lazy_cons_lazy
            (Lazy(X) head,
              Lazy(Lazy_Stream(X)) tail){
    return create_lazy
                (\ () x.new lazy_stream<X>(head,tail))};};
```

- lazy_tail<X> computes the tail of a stream lazily (we define here only its type):

```
Lazy(Lazy_Stream(X)) lazy_tail<X>
                    (Lazy(Lazy_Stream(X)) s)
```

- lazy_zip_with<X> computes the usual zip_with function (i.e. $\text{zip\_with}(f, [a, b, ..], [c, d, ..]) = [f\,a\,c, f\,b\,d, ...]$; we define here only its type):

```
Lazy(Lazy_Stream(X)) lazy_zip_with<X>
    (X -> X -> X f,
      Lazy(Lazy_Stream(X)) s0,
      Lazy(Lazy_Stream(X)) s1)
```

The definition of `lazy_tail` and `lazy_zip_with` is straightforward, once one has introduced a few combinators for dealing with `Lazy(X)`.

Now we can define the stream of Fibonacci numbers as follows (`plus` is $\lambda x, y.x + y$, `one_lazy` is the numeral 1 converted into an element of `Lazy(int)`, `create_lazy` transforms elements of type `()->A` into `Lazy(A)`, and `eval` evaluates an element of type `Lazy(A)` to an element of type A):

```
()-><Lazy_Stream(int)> fib_aux =
 \() x. Lazy_Stream(int)
      eval(
       lazy_cons_lazy(
         one_lazy,
         lazy_cons_lazy(
           one_lazy,
           lazy_zip_with(
             plus,
             create_lazy(this),
             lazy_tail(create_lazy(this))))));
Lazy_Stream(int) fib = eval(create_lazy(fib_aux))
```

Note that here we were using the keyword `this` in the definition of **fib_aux**. This is how a recursive call should be written. If we instead put **fib_aux** here, C++ will, when instantiating **fib_aux**, first instantiate **fib_aux** as an empty class, and then use this value when evaluating the right-hand side. Only when using `this` we obtain a truely recursive definition.

When evaluated, one sees that the nth element of **fib** computes to fib(n) and this computation is the efficient one in which previous calls of fib(k) are memoized. Replacing `Lazy(X)` by $() \mathbin{-}> X$, results in an implementation of the Fibonacci numbers which is still correct, but requires exponential space since memoization is lost (on our laptop we were not able to compute fib(25)).

Generalization. The above technique can easily be generalized to arbitrary algebraic types, in fact to all class structures available in C++. If, for example, one replaces in a tree structure all types by lazy types, then only a trunk of the tree structure is evaluated and kept in memory, namely the trunk which has been used already by any function accessing this structure.

10.5 CONCLUSION

In this paper we have shown how to introduce functional concepts into C++ in a provably correct way. The modelling and the correctness proof used monadic concepts as well as logical relations. We also have shown how to integrate lazy evaluation and infinite structures into C++.

This work lends itself to a number of extensions, for example, the integration of recursive higher-order functions, polymorphic and dependent type systems as well as the combination of larger parts of C++ with the λ-calculus. The accurate description of these extensions would require more sophisticated, e.g. domain-theoretic constructions and a more systematic mathematical modelling of C++. It would also be interesting to expand our fragment of C++ in order to deal with side effects. This would allow for instance to *prove* that our lazy construct actually gives rise to an efficient implementation of the Fibonacci function.

We believe that if our approach is extended to cover full C++, we obtain a language in which the worlds of functional and object-oriented programming are merged, and that we will see many examples, where the combination of both language concepts (e.g. the use of λ-terms with side effects) will result in interesting new programming techniques.

REFERENCES

[1] H. Abelson, G. J. Sussman, and J. Sussman. *Structure and interpretation of computer programs*. MIT Press, 1985.

[2] J. Goubault-Larrecq, S. Lasota, and D. Nowak. Logical relations for monadic types. In Julian C. Bradfield, editor, *Proceedings of the 16th International Workshop on Computer Science Logic (CSL'02)*, volume 2471 of *Lecture Notes in Computer Science*, pages 553–568, Edinburgh, Scotland, UK, September 2002. Springer.

[3] G. Hutton. *Programming in Haskell*. Cambridge University Press, Cambridge, UK, 2006.

[4] Atshushi Igarashi, Benjamin Pierce, and Philip Wadler. Featherweight Java: A minimal core calculus for Java and GJ. In Loren Meissner, editor, *Proceedings of the 1999 ACM SIGPLAN Conference on Object-Oriented Programming, Systems, Languages & Applications (OOPSLA'99)*, volume 34(10), pages 132–146, N. Y., 1999.

[5] A. Jung and J. Tiuryn. A new characterization of lambda definability. In M. Bezem and J. F. Groote, editors, *Typed Lambda Calculi and Applications*, volume 664 of *Lecture Notes in Computer Science*, pages 245–257. Springer, 1993.

[6] R. M. Keller. The Polya C++ Library. Version 2.0. Available via http://www.cs.hmc.edu/~keller/Polya/, 1997.

[7] O. Kiselyov. Functional style in C++: Closures, late binding, and lambda abstractions. In *ICFP '98: Proceedings of the third ACM SIGPLAN International conference on Functional programming*, page 337, New York, NY, USA, 1998. ACM Press.

[8] K. Läufer. A framework for higher-order functions in C++. In *COOTS*, 1995.

[9] B. McNamara and Y. Smaragdakis. Functional programming in C++. In *ICFP '00: Proceedings of the fifth ACM SIGPLAN international conference on Functional programming*, pages 118–129, New York, NY, USA, 2000. ACM Press.

[10] E. Moggi. Notions of computation and monads. *Information and Computation*, 93(1):55–92, 1991.

[11] A. M. Pitts. Evaluation logic. In G. Birtwistle, editor, *IVth Higher Order Workshop, Banff 1990*, Workshops in Computing, pages 162–189. Springer, 1991.

[12] G. D. Plotkin. LCF considered as a programming language. *Theoretical Computer Science*, 5:223–255, 1977.

[13] G. D. Plotkin. Lambda definability in the full type hierarchy. In R. Hindley and J. Seldin, editors, *To H.B. Curry: Essays in Combinatory Logic, lambda calculus and Formalisms*, pages 363 – 373. Academic Press, 1980.

[14] J. C. Reynolds. Types, abstraction and parametric polymorphism. In *IFIP'83*, pages 513–523. North-Holland, 1983.

[15] S. Schupp. Lazy lists in C++. *SIGPLAN Not.*, 35(6):47–54, 2000.

[16] A. Setzer. Lazy evaluation in C++. `http://www.cs.swan.ac.uk/ ~csetzer/articles/additionalMaterial/ lazyEvaluationCplusplus.cpp`, 2006.

[17] R. Stärk, J. Schmid, and E. Börger. *Java and the Java Virtual Machine – Definition, Verification, Validation.* Springer, 2001.

[18] R. Statman. Logical relations and the typed lambda-calculus. *Information and Control*, 65:85 – 97, 1985.

[19] J. Striegnitz. FACT! – the functional side of C++. http://www.fz-juelich.de/zam/FACT.

[20] W. W. Tait. Intensional interpretation of functionals of finite type. *Journal of Symbolic Logic*, 32:198 – 212, 1967.

[21] G. Winskel. *The formal semantics of programming languages: an introduction.* MIT Press, Cambridge, MA, USA, 1993.

Chapter 11

Resource-Based Web Applications

Sebastian Fischer[1]

Abstract: We present an approach to write web applications in the functional logic language Curry. Logic features are employed to provide type-based conversion combinators for arbitrary data types. With a restricted version of these combinators our library can also be implemented in a purely functional language.

The web applications we propose are directly based on the Hypertext Transfer Protocol (HTTP) – no additional protocol on top of HTTP is necessary. We provide a typed interface to HTTP that abstracts from the format used to transfer the data. Hence, we decouple a *resource* from its *representation* on the network.

11.1   INTRODUCTION

Present-day web applications are based on complex technologies (SOAP/WSDL) that are mastered by comprehensive frameworks in the mainstream programming worlds of .NET and Java. Inspired by [7], we show that it is possible to achieve similar goals with much simpler technology and less protocol overhead.

We develop a library for web applications based on simple HTTP message exchange without an additional protocol on top of HTTP. We provide functions to exchange arbitrary data as typed values, i.e., the user of our library is not concerned with error handling regarding data conversion. Most web applications use XML as platform independent format for data interchange and XML is tightly coupled with the web service frameworks mentioned above. With our library the representation of the transferred data is independent of the application itself. The programmer can plug in his own conversion functions into the framework. We even support multiple representations at once in a single web application. To simplify the definition of conversion functions, we provide type-based combinators to

---

[1]Institute of Computer Science, Christian-Albrechts-University of Kiel, Germany;
E-mail: `sebf@informatik.uni-kiel.de`

construct converters for standard data formats. Upcoming so-called AJaX[2] applications often use Javascript Object Notation (JSON)[3] instead of XML. It is more convenient to program with native objects instead of a representation of XML data on the client side of such applications. We primarily support different representation formats to be able to develop the server side of such applications using our library.

The remainder of this paper is structured as follows: Section 11.2 introduces key concepts of the Internet architecture and sketches different architectural styles to design web applications. In section 11.3 we present the API of our library and discuss an example how to use it in a client application. Section 11.4 focuses on data conversion and section 11.5 introduces the part of our library that supports server applications. In section 11.6 we give an overview of the implementation of our library. Related and future work is considered in section 11.7 before we conclude in section 11.8.

11.2   TRANSFER OF RESOURCE REPRESENTATIONS

A *resource* is any piece of information named by a Uniform Resource Identifier (URI). A web application provides access to internally stored information over the Internet or accesses such information provided by other web applications. Usually, (a representation of) this information is transferred using the Hypertext Transfer Protocol (HTTP) [8] – possibly employing some protocol on top of it. Note that we do not primarily consider applications running inside a web browser like [9, 12, 14].

HTTP provides different methods to access resources from which the most important are the GET and the POST method. GET is used to *retrieve* some information, e.g., web browsers use GET to ask for the content of web pages. POST is used to *send* information to be processed by a server, e.g., entries in a web form can be sent to the server using POST. While processing the request, the server can update its internally stored information and usually sends back a result of this process.

Web applications differ in their use of these two HTTP methods: RPC-style web applications are accessible through a single URI and communication is performed using the POST method. A representation of a procedure call is transferred to the server, which returns a representation of the result of this call as answer to the POST request. Note that both retrieval and update operations are performed using the POST method in RPC-style web applications and the interface of such applications is determined by the procedure calls that are understood by the server.

Fielding [7] proposes another architectural style for web applications: he proposes to use the POST method only to update the internal state of the server and to use the GET method to purely retrieve information. Consequently, everything

---

[2]**A**synchronous **J**avascript and **X**ML
[3]`http://www.json.org/`

that should be available for retrieval by clients needs to be identified by an own URI. This is a big difference to RPC-style web applications that are usually accessible through a single URI. In the architectural style proposed by Fielding, a client sends an HTTP GET request to retrieve a representation of the resource. To update a resource, the client sends a POST request to the URI that corresponds to the resource. Fielding calls this architectural style Representational State Transfer (REST).

The interface of a RESTful web application is given by the methods of HTTP and the URIs identifying the applications resources. In this work, we show how the interface given by the most important HTTP methods can be made available to functional (logic) programmers, hiding the details of HTTP communication. Hence, our framework is designed to support RESTful web applications. However, it can also be used to model web applications of different paradigms (e.g. RPC-style) since it provides an interface to arbitrary HTTP communication via the GET or POST method.

11.3   A RESOURCE API

We assume that the reader is familiar with the syntax of the programming language Haskell [13] or Curry [11]. Like the Internet architecture sketched in the previous section, our library is built around the concept of *resources*. In our approach, the programmer accesses resources as values of type `Resource a b c` which provide access to local or remote resources. For this purpose the operations

```
get    :: Resource a b c -> IO a
update :: Resource a b c -> b -> IO c
```

are provided. The type variable `a` denotes the type of the result of a resource retrieval. The type variables `b` and `c` denote the argument and return type of the operation updating a resource.

The operations shown above model the GET and POST methods of HTTP: the `get` operation is an IO action that takes a resource and returns the current state of this resource which is always of type `a`. To perform `get` on a remote resource, an HTTP GET request is sent to the corresponding URI and the response is converted into a value of type `a`. The `update` operation is an IO action that takes a resource along with a value of type `b` and returns a value of type `c` as result. To perform an `update` on a remote resource, a representation of the value of type `b` is sent to the corresponding URI using HTTP POST and the response to this request is converted into a value of type `c`. Access to a remote resource can be obtained by the function `remoteResource :: URI -> Resource a b c`. This signature is not completely honest, because in addition to the URI the programmer needs to specify how the transferred data has to be converted. For the moment, we skip the details of this conversion. The complete signature of `remoteResource` is given in section 11.4.1.

Note that specifying a resource is not an IO action as no communication with the outside world is necessary. Only *access* to resources is done using IO actions.

11.3.1   An Example: Access to a News Provider

In our framework we can model both RPC-style and RESTful web applications: the former would ignore the `get` operation and use `update` to send representations of procedure calls as values of type `b` to the server. As an example for the latter, we consider a news provider.

   To model an interface to news as algebraic data types, we define two data structures. The first represents a reference to the second and can be used in summaries. Note that these data types reflect the data transferred over the web. They are independent of the internal representation of news chosen by the server. Internally, the server does not need to distinguish news references from news items and can avoid redundant storage of headlines and dates.

```
data NewsRef  = NewsRef Headline Date URI
data NewsItem = NewsItem Headline Date Text [Comment]
```

If the news application provides a list of all headlines at the URI `www.example.net/news`, we can create a remote resource representing this list

```
newsList :: Resource [NewsRef] NewsItem NewsRef
newsList = remoteResource "www.example.net/news"
```

and retrieve a list of the currently available headlines by (`get newsList`) which could return something similar to[4]

```
[NewsRef "Italy wins world cup final"
  "2006/7/9" "www.example.net/news/final"]
```

The URI given as third argument of `NewsRef` is a link to the news item corresponding to the headline. We can also access this news item using a resource

```
final :: Resource NewsItem Comment NewsItem
final = remoteResource "www.example.net/news/final"
```

and retrieve the item by (`get final`) which could return

```
NewsItem "Italy wins world cup final" "2006/7/9"
  "The winner is ..." []
```

To add a comment to this news item, we can call

```
update final "What a great match!"
```

and would get

```
NewsItem "Italy wins world cup final" "2006/7/9"
  "The winner is ..." ["What a great match!"]
```

as the result of this call, which is equal to the result of an immediately[5] following call to (`get final`).

---

[4]For simplicity, we encode headlines, dates and URIs as strings.

[5]if no other client changes the item in between

Consider the three arguments of the type constructor `Resource` given in the definition of `final`: the first argument is `NewsItem` which means that if we call `get` on this resource we get a result of type `NewsItem`. The second and third arguments are `Comment` and `NewsItem`, respectively. So if we call `update` on this resource, we have to provide a value of type `Comment` and get a result of type `NewsItem`.

Now recall the corresponding types in the definition of `newsList`: we called `get` on this resource and got a list of `NewsRef`s which corresponds to the first type argument `[NewsRef]`. The other arguments are `NewsItem` and `NewsRef`, so we can call `update` on this resource with corresponding values:

```
update newsList
  (NewsItem "Next world cup in four years" "2006/7/10"
    "See you in four years ..." [])
```

As a response to this call, the server could add this news item to its internal news database and return a news reference with a newly created URI pointing to the new item:

```
NewsRef "Next world cup in four years"
  "2006/7/10" "www.example.net/news/next-wc"
```

In this example the different resources representing a list of news headlines and complete news items are connected by URIs. This is not an accident but typical for RESTful web applications. Just like ordinary web pages, resources can be interconnected by links, because everything that can be retrieved by clients is identified by a unique URI. If we want to take this idea one step further as we did in our example, we could include references to related news items in every news item.

The news provider may want to restrict the access to its internal news database. For example she could require an authentication to add comments to news items or create new items in the internal database. HTTP provides methods for authenticated communication and we integrate authenticated HTTP communication in our approach by a function `authResource` that is similar to `remoteResource`. The function has two additional arguments of type `String` to specify the user name and password that identify the client.

11.4   DATA AND ITS REPRESENTATION

In section 11.3 we omitted the details of data conversion for the transfer over the Internet. Unfortunately, Curry values cannot be transferred directly by HTTP but have to be converted. The payload of HTTP messages can be of arbitrary type, however, usually a textual representation is employed. So we need to be able to convert program data into a textual form. Curry provides functions to convert values into strings and vice versa, so we can use these functions to convert program data for HTTP transfer.

However, the direct representation of algebraic data types is language dependent. If we want to share information with as many other participants on the Internet as possible, we need to use an independent format. The standard format for data representation on the Internet is XML and this is where modern declarative languages expose an advantage: algebraic data types are tree-like structures that can be represented easily in XML [5, 15]. Although there are also XML language bindings for, e.g., object oriented languages, values of an algebraic data type are much closer to XML terms than objects.

JSON is another language independent data format which is sometimes preferred to XML because of its brevity. We support both XML and JSON in our approach and we want the user of our tool to be able to support other formats as well so we do not hide data conversion completely. The user should also be able to support more than one format in a single web application by allowing the clients to choose the format according to their needs. We use HTTP content negotiation for this purpose, where the client sends a list of content types that he is willing to accept in the header of an HTTP request.

11.4.1 Content-Type-based Conversion

The function `remoteResource` mentioned in section 11.3 has additional arguments that control data conversion:

```
remoteResource ::
  Conv a -> Conv b -> Conv c -> URI -> Resource a b c
```

The type `Conv a` is defined as

```
type Conv a      = [(ContentType, ReadShow a)]
data ContentType = Plain | Xml | Json |...| CT String
type ReadShow a  = (String -> Maybe a, a -> String)
```

Values of type `ContentType` represent content types that are specified in the header of HTTP messages. To access a remote resource, the converters are used as follows:

- When `get` is called on a resource, an HTTP GET request is sent to the corresponding URI and the response is parsed with the read function that is associated with the content type of the response in the list of type `Conv a`. The read function returns a value of type `Maybe a` and should indicate malformed data by returning `Nothing`.

- When `update` is called on a resource and a value of type `b`, this value is converted using the first show function in the list of type `Conv b` and sent to the corresponding URI using HTTP POST. The result of this request is parsed with the read function that is associated with the content type of the response in the list of type `Conv c`. If the POST request fails, the other show functions are tried successively.

We provide a function `plainConv`[6] that converts values of arbitrary first-order type[7]:

```
plainConv :: Conv a
plainConv = [(Plain, (safeRead, showQTerm))]

safeRead :: String -> Maybe a
safeRead s = case readsQTerm s of
                  [(x,"")] -> Just x
                  _ -> Nothing
```

11.4.2 Type-based Construction of Converters

The implementation of `plainConv` is very simple. However, for applications that communicate with other applications - possibly written in different programming languages - over the Internet, we need to convert data into a language independent format. Implementing these converters by hand is a complex, error prone and usually tedious task. Hence, we provide a framework to concisely construct such converters using a run-time type specification of type `ConvSpec` a as part of our library. We provide primitive specification functions

```
cInt    :: String -> ConvSpec Int
cString :: String -> ConvSpec String
cBool   :: String -> String -> ConvSpec Bool
```

to construct converters for values of type `Int`, `String` and `Bool`. The arguments of type `String` specify labels that are used for the conversion. For values of type `Bool` one label for each `True` and `False` is specified. More complex converters can be built by combinators like

```
cList   :: String -> ConvSpec a -> ConvSpec [a]
cMaybe  :: String -> String -> ConvSpec a
           -> ConvSpec (Maybe a)
cPair   :: String -> ConvSpec a -> ConvSpec b
           -> ConvSpec (a,b)
cTriple :: String
           -> ConvSpec a -> ConvSpec b -> ConvSpec c
           -> ConvSpec (a,b,c)
...
cEither :: String -> String
           -> ConvSpec a -> ConvSpec b
           -> ConvSpec (Either a b)
```

---

[6]Here we represent content types as strings for simplicity.

[7]`readsQTerm` and `showQTerm` are standard Curry functions to read and show qualified data.

Since all first-order data types can be mapped to values of types covered by the presented combinators, these are sufficient to build converters for such data types. We provide a function

```
cAdapt :: (a->b) -> (b->a) -> ConvSpec a -> ConvSpec b
```

to construct a converter for a type that is not covered by the presented combinators. The first two arguments convert between this data type and another data type with converter specification of type `ConvSpec a`.

We provide implementations of these combinators in Curry to construct converters for XML, JSON and both XML and JSON at the same time. For example, to support XML conversion we define

```
type ConvSpec a = (XmlExp -> a,a -> XmlExp)
```

and `cPair` could be defined as

```
cPair tag (rda,sha) (rdb,shb) = (rd,sh)
 where
  rd (XElem t [] [a,b]) | t==tag = (rda a,rdb b)
  sh (a,b) = XElem tag [] [sha a,shb b]
```

In fact, we can employ the concept of function patterns [4] and provide more general combinators to construct converters for arbitrary record types directly. Function patterns extend the notion of patterns by applications of defined operation symbols. Note, that we employ the logic features of Curry to provide more convenient combinators. However, the expressiveness of the combinators is not changed, since similar converter specifications could be constructed using `cAdapt`.

A generalization of `cPair` is defined as part of our library using function patterns as[8]:

```
c2Cons  :: (a -> b -> c) -> String
        -> ConvSpec a -> ConvSpec b
        -> ConvSpec c
c2Cons cons tag (rda,sha) (rdb,shb) = (rd,sh)
 where
  cf a b = cons a b
  rd (xml t [a,b])
    | t==tag  = cons (rda a) (rdb b)
  sh (cf a b) = xml tag [sha a,shb b]
```

Similar converters are defined for constructors that take one (`cCons`) or more (`c3Cons`, `c4Cons`, ...) arguments. As another logic feature of Curry we employ nondeterminism to specify converters for data types with multiple constructors. For example a converter specification for binary trees can be defined as:

---

[8]`xml tag xs = XElem tag [] xs` describes an XML element with empty attribute list.

```
data Tree = Leaf Int | Branch Tree Tree

cTree :: ConvSpec Tree
cTree = cCons Leaf "leaf" (cInt "value")
cTree = c2Cons Branch "branch" cTree cTree
```

In Curry multiple rules are not applied in a top-down approach. Instead every matching rule is applied nondeterministically.

We provide a function

```
conv :: ConvSpec a -> Conv a
```

that generates a converter from a specification. The programmer can decide to create different kinds of converters by importing different modules. The modules are designed such that only import declarations and no other code has to be changed in order to change the generated converters.

As an example application of the provided combinators, consider converter specifications for the news data types presented in section 11.3.1:

```
cNewsRef :: ConvSpec NewsRef
cNewsRef = c3Cons NewsRef "ref"
 (cString "headline") (cString "date") (cString "uri")

cNewsRefs :: ConvSpec [NewsRef]
cNewsRefs = cList "refs" cNewsRef

cNewsItem :: ConvSpec NewsItem
cNewsItem = c4Cons NewsItem "item"
 (cString "headline") (cString "date")
 (cString "text") (cList "comments" cComment)

cComment :: ConvSpec Comment
cComment = cString "comment"
```

This is everything we need to define to get conversion functions for both the XML and JSON format!

The presented combinators construct complex converter functions from concise definitions. Thus, they eliminate a source of subtle errors and release the programmer from the burden to write such converters by hand. The programmer only has to give a specification that resembles a type declaration augmented with labels, that identify components of complex data types.

11.5 SERVER APPLICATIONS

In the previous sections we always considered the access of remote resources. In this section we describe how to provide local resources through a web-based interface. An interface to a local resource is created by the function

```
localResource :: IO a -> (b -> IO c) -> Resource a b c
```

that takes two IO actions performing the `get` and `update` operations of the created resource. The details of accessing a local resource are hidden inside the resource data type. The resource operations `get` and `update` provide a uniform interface to both local resources and remote resources available via HTTP. The programmer can access a remote resource in the same way she accesses local resources and does not need to deal with the details of communication.

To provide a web-based interface to a (not necessarily) local resource, the programmer can use the functions:

```
provide :: ConvSpec a -> ConvSpec b -> ConvSpec c
        -> Resource a b c -> Handler

cgi :: (Path -> IO (Maybe Handler⁹)) -> IO ()
```

These functions associate a resource with a URI to provide remote access. The function `provide` takes converter specifications for the types `a`, `b` and `c`, a resource of type `Resource a b c` and returns a value of the abstract type `Handler` that handles GET and POST requests. The function `cgi` takes an IO-action that computes an optional handler corresponding to path information and returns an IO-action that acts as a CGI program. Both functions will be discussed in more detail in section 11.6 after we reconsider the news example.

11.5.1 Example Continued: The News Provider

In section 11.3.1 we introduced a client to a news provider. In this section we show how the provider itself can be implemented using our framework. Suppose we have a local news database that supports the following operations:

```
getNewsPaths    :: IO [Path]
getNewsList     :: IO [NewsRef]
getNewsItem     :: Path -> IO NewsItem
addNewsItem     :: NewsItem -> IO Path
addNewsComment  :: Path -> Comment -> IO ()
```

With these operations we can implement the news provider introduced in section 11.3.1. We define a function `newsProvider` that dispatches requests to appropriate handler functions:

```
newsProvider :: Path -> IO (Maybe Handler)
newsProvider p
  | p == "" = return (Just newsList)
  | otherwise = do
    ps <- getNewsPaths
    if elem p ps then return (Just (newsItem p))
     else return Nothing
```

---

⁹The type `Handler` is defined in section 11.6.1.

```
newsList :: Handler
newsList = provide cNewsRefs cNewsItem cNewsRef
  (localResource getNewsList addItem)

newsItem :: Path -> Handler
newsItem path = provide cNewsItem cComment cNewsItem
  (localResource (getNewsItem path) (addComment path))
```

We need to provide functions `addItem` and `addComment` based on the database operations given above:

```
addItem :: NewsItem -> IO NewsRef
addItem item@(NewsItem headline date _ _) = do
  path <- addNewsItem item
  return (NewsRef headline date (myLocation++path))
```

The string `myLocation` represents the URI pointing to the CGI program serving the requests. The function `addComment` returns the updated news item:

```
addComment :: Path -> Comment -> IO NewsItem
addComment path comment = do
  addNewsComment path comment
  getNewsItem path
```

We have shown the complete implementation of a news server that provides access to an internal news database via an XML-, JSON- and plain-text-based interface. Clients communicate with the database via HTTP GET and POST requests which are served by a CGI program.

11.6 IMPLEMENTATION

In this section we discuss the library functions introduced above in more detail. We discuss the implementation of the GET and POST handler functions and explain what errors are handled automatically within our framework.

We represent HTTP messages as algebraic data type `Http`. Since its definition is not important to understand the rest of this section, we do not discuss this data type here.

11.6.1 Common Gateway Interface

The easiest way to build a server application for a resource is to create an executable CGI program. Such a program takes inputs from *stdin* and the environment and sends its output to *stdout*. The details of this communication are defined in the Common Gateway Interface and are completely hidden by our library. It would also be possible to create an application that directly connects to a port and acts as a server. However, we did not consider this possibility, because a server is more complex to use as well as to implement than a CGI program that can be used together with existing web server software.

Since RESTful web applications provide URIs for everything that can be retrieved by clients, one resource is usually not enough to model the application. In fact, every path extending[10] the location of the created CGI program points to a new resource. Unlike [12], we explicitly handle multiple URIs with a single CGI program. The most obvious type for a function that creates a CGI program from different resources associated with paths would be

```
cgi :: (Path -> Resource a b c) -> IO ()
```

This function would take a dispatcher mapping paths to resources and return an IO action that act as CGI program. Unfortunately, such a dispatcher cannot be defined. The value of type `Path` has no information about the type of the resource to be returned. Probably, existential quantification could be employed to use a list of paths associated to resources of arbitrary type instead of the dispatcher. Fortunately, we can define a similar `cgi` function without this feature: instead of returning a typed resource, the dispatcher supplied as argument to `cgi` maps paths to GET and POST handler functions:

```
cgi :: (Path -> IO (Maybe Handler)) -> IO ()
```

A request to the created CGI program is dispatched to the appropriate handler functions by the given mapping which is applied to the path that identifies the requested resource. The dispatcher returns an optional handler to be able to indicate invalid path arguments. Also, it may perform IO actions to determine whether the path is valid or to compute an appropriate resource.

We now discuss how untyped handler functions can be created from typed resources. We need to define functions that handle GET and POST requests:

```
type GetHandler = [ContentType] -> IO Http

type PostHandler =
  ContentType -> String -> [ContentType] -> IO Http

handleGet :: Conv a -> Resource a b c -> GetHandler

handlePost ::
  Conv b -> Conv c -> Resource a b c -> PostHandler
```

The presented handler functions proceed as follows:

- `handleGet` performs the operation `get` on the supplied resource and the result is converted into a textual representation using a show function in the list of type `Conv a`. This representation is wrapped in an HTTP message that can be sent back to the client. If the request accepts only specific content types for the response an appropriate show function is selected.

---

[10]Such paths are provided in the environment variable PATH_INFO available to CGI programs.

- `handlePost` parses the given string with the read function in the list of type `Conv b` that is determined by the given content type. The resulting value is supplied to the operation `update` along with the resource and the result of this operation is converted into an appropriate textual representation by a show function in the list of type `Conv c`. Again, this representation is wrapped in an HTTP message to be sent back to the client.

We provide a shortcut for creating both a GET and a POST handler for a resource at the same time:

```
type Handler = (GetHandler, PostHandler)

handle :: Conv a -> Conv b -> Conv c
          -> Resource a b c -> Handler
```

For convenience, we also provide a function that computes a `Handler` from `ConvSpec`'s instead of `Conv`'s:

```
provide :: ConvSpec a -> ConvSpec b -> ConvSpec c
           -> Resource a b c -> Handler
```

So, in order to be able to define a dispatcher function as argument of `cgi`, we need to compute handlers that abstract from the types of the resource. A handler computes untyped HTTP messages using the converters that match the types of the associated resource. The higher-order features of the implementation language are essential for the described modeling of handler functions and dispatchers.

11.6.2 Error Handling

There are several situations, where the server should deliver an error message in response to a clients request. For example, if a resource specified by the client is not available on the server, the server should indicate this with an *Not Found* status in the response message. This error is the reason for the `Maybe` type in the declaration of the function `cgi` given above: if the supplied IO-action returns `Nothing` for a given path, the CGI program generates a *Not Found* error message.

The functions `handle` and `provide` generate both GET and POST handlers for a given resource. However, if the HTTP method of the request is neither GET nor POST the computed handler generates a *Method Not Allowed* error message. We also provide the functions

```
handleGetOnly ::
  Conv a -> Resource a b c -> Handler

provideGetOnly ::
  ConvSpec a -> Resource a b c -> Handler
```

to create a handler that handles only GET requests and

```
handlePostOnly ::
  Conv b -> Conv c -> Resource a b c -> Handler

providePostOnly ::
  ConvSpec b -> ConvSpec c -> Resource a b c
  -> Handler
```

to handle only POST requests. These functions generate a *Method Not Allowed* error message for other methods.

The type `Conv` a that specifies data conversion was defined in section 11.4.1 as follows:

```
type Conv a = [(ContentType, ReadShow a)]
```

This list contains one pair for every content type supported by the application. If

1. the client uses the *Accept* header field to specify which content type she accepts in the response message and

2. none of the accepted content types is supported by the application

the CGI program generates a *Not Acceptable* error message as response to the request. The type `ReadShow` a was defined as

```
type ReadShow a = (String -> Maybe a, a -> String)
```

The read function returns a value of type `Maybe` a and should return `Nothing` if the given string cannot be parsed. When handling a POST request, the CGI program uses such a read function to parse the message body of the request. If the result is `Nothing` it generates a *Bad Request* error message as response.

In this section we sketched the implementation of a library for web applications implemented in the functional logic programming language Curry. Our library is directly based on HTTP and uses the logic features of Curry only for the type-based conversion combinators presented in section 11.4.2. Since data conversion is explicit in our framework, resources can be transferred in arbitrary representations. The implementation employs higher-order features of Curry to provide a declarative interface for describing server applications.

11.7 RELATED AND FUTURE WORK

Hanus [9], Meijer [12] and Thiemann [14] provide frameworks to build server side web applications based on HTML forms that run inside a web browser. Although [12] abstracts from network communication, it uses strings as references to input fields, which is a source of possible errors. [9, 14] abstract also from such references, which not only prevents typing-errors but also enables the programmer to compose different web forms without the risk of name clashes. Recently, Hanus [10] presented an approach to concisely describe type-based web user interfaces (WUIs), based on [9].

Our approach differs from the mentioned approaches because we do not aim at web-based *user* interfaces through HTML forms but provide a framework for web-based interfaces that transfer *raw data*. Such interfaces can be used for machine-to-machine communication or in the upcoming Web 2.0 applications based on asynchronous HTTP transfer using Javascript. The transferred data can be in a variety of formats (e.g., XML, JSON, or almost anything else) and we provide a mechanism to support multiple formats at once in a single web application. A client could even send a request in XML and receive the response in JSON format. The type-based combinators we presented to specify how data has to be converted are inspired by the WUI combinators presented by Hanus [10]. In fact they are so similar, that we plan to integrate both approaches in the future.

The type-based conversion combinators have a strong generic programming flavor although they do not rely on special features for generic programming. Conversion between XML and typed data using generic Haskell is explored in [5]. Our approach is different because it supports user-defined data types instead of using a fixed one. However, generic programming features [3] can also be employed to map between user-defined types and XML data [6] – as it is done for GUI components in [1]. The conversion in [5] is more general than our approach because it supports arbitrary XML data. For example, we do not support attributes. Such limitations will be the subject of future work.

Since the logic features of Curry are only employed for data conversion which could be realized using generic programming in Clean, our library could be ported to Clean by replacing monadic IO with explicit passing of unique environments [2] – similar to the explicit passing of resources in our approach.

11.8 CONCLUSIONS

We presented an approach to write resource-based web applications in the declarative programming language Curry. We provide a data type `Resource a b c` and library functions `get` and `update` to create a uniform interface to local and remote resources. Remote resources are directly accessed via HTTP and we provide operations to create a CGI program that makes local resources available over the Internet. Using our library both the client and server side of web applications can be implemented without knowledge of the details of HTTP communication. Hence, the programmer can concentrate on the application logic which is separated from network communication.

Since our library is directly based on HTTP, it involves considerably less protocol overhead than SOAP-based web applications. Moreover, our approach to web applications differs from others in that it does not determine the format used to transfer data. We build upon the concept of *resources* and abstract from their *representations* in a type-safe way using explicit conversion functions. Our library even supports different formats in a single web application with content negotiation. For clients of a web application it is very convenient to be able to choose between different representations. While typical clients probably use XML data, Javascript-based web sites may prefer data in JSON format because it can be parsed directly into Javascript values. In a local setting, a platform dependent textual representation may be preferred for efficiency reasons. We provide type-based combinators to concisely construct XML and JSON converters and integrate them seamlessly into our framework. Hence, for standard formats the conversion functions need not be implemented by hand. Moreover, we implement authenticated communication over HTTP and integrate it transparently into our framework, i.e., hiding the details from the programmer of web applications.

We see two main advantages in using a declarative programming language for writing web applications: algebraic data types are tree-like structures and therefore well suited to represent hierarchically structured data, e.g., in XML format. If the type-based conversion combinators are used, the strongly typed messages help to find errors in advance, which is very important in applications publicly available over the Internet. Even if custom parsers are employed, there remains the advantage that these can be developed and tested separately. Due to the type-based conversion combinators and the built-in error handling mechanism, the programmer of a web application always gets type-correct inputs from clients. She is therefore released from the burden to write complex and error-prone code that is not primarily concerned with the application itself.

REFERENCES

[1] P. Achten, M. v. Eekelen, R. Plasmeijer, and A. v. Weelden. Programming Generic Graphical User Interfaces. Technical report, Nijmegen Institute for Computing and Information Sciences, Faculty of Science, University of Nijmegen, 2005.

[2] P. Achten, J. H. G. v. Groningen, and R. Plasmeijer. High Level Specification of I/O in Functional Languages. In *Proceedings of the 1992 Glasgow Workshop on Functional Programming*, pages 1–17, London, UK, 1993. Springer-Verlag.

[3] A. Alimarine and M. J. Plasmeijer. A Generic Programming Extension for Clean. In *IFL '02: Selected Papers from the 13th International Workshop on Implementation of Functional Languages*, pages 168–185, London, UK, 2002. Springer-Verlag.

[4] S. Antoy and M. Hanus. Declarative Programming with Function Patterns. In *Proceedings of the International Symposium on Logic-based Program Synthesis and Transformation (LOPSTR'05)*, pages 6–22. Springer LNCS 3901, 2005.

[5] F. Atanassow, D. Clarke, and J. Jeuring. UUXML: A type-preserving XML Schema-Haskell data binding. In Bharat Jayaraman, editor, *Proceedings of the 6th International Symposium on Practical Aspects of Declarative Languages, PADL'04*, volume 3057 of *LNCS*, pages 71–85. Springer-Verlag, 2004.

[6] F. Atanassow and J. Jeuring. Inferring Type Isomorphisms Generically. In Dexter Kozen, editor, *Proceedings of the 7th International Conference on Mathematics of Program Construction, MPC'04*, volume 3125 of *LNCS*, pages 32–53. Springer-Verlag, 2004.

[7] R. Fielding. *Architectural Styles and the Design of Network-based Software Architectures*. PhD thesis, University of California, Irvine, 2000.

[8] R. Fielding, J. Gettys, J. Mogul, H. Frystyk, L. Masinter, P. Leach, and T. Berners-Lee. Hypertext Transfer Protocol — HTTP/1.1. June 1999.

[9] M. Hanus. High-Level Server Side Web Scripting in Curry. In *Proc. of the Third International Symposium on Practical Aspects of Declarative Languages (PADL'01)*, pages 76–92. Springer LNCS 1990, 2001.

[10] M. Hanus. Type-Oriented Construction of Web User Interfaces. Technical report, Technical Report, CAU Kiel, 2006.

[11] M. Hanus (ed.). Curry: An Integrated Functional Logic Language (Vers. 0.8). Available at `http://www.informatik.uni-kiel.de/~curry`, 2003.

[12] E. Meijer. Server Side Web Scripting in Haskell. *Journal of Functional Programming*, 10(1):1–18, 2000.

[13] S. Peyton Jones, editor. *Haskell 98 Language and Libraries—The Revised Report*. Cambridge University Press, 2003.

[14] P. Thiemann. WASH/CGI: Server-side Web Scripting with Sessions and Typed, Compositional Forms. In *4th International Symposium on Practical Aspects of Declarative Languages (PADL 2002)*, pages 192–208. Springer LNCS 2257, 2002.

[15] M. Wallace and C. Runciman. Haskell and XML: Generic Combinators or Type-Based Translation? In *International Conference on Functional Programming (ICFP'99)*, September 1999.

Chapter 12

Extensible and Modular Generics for the Masses

Bruno C. d. S. Oliveira[1], Ralf Hinze[2], Andres Löh[2]

Abstract: A *generic function* is a function that is defined on the structure of data types: with a single definition, we obtain a function that works for many data types. In contrast, an *ad-hoc polymorphic* function requires a separate implementation for each data type. Previous work by Hinze on *lightweight generic programming* has introduced techniques that allow the definition of generic functions directly in Haskell. A severe drawback of these approaches is that generic functions, once defined, cannot be extended with ad-hoc behaviour for new data types, precluding the design of an extensible and modular generic programming library based on these techniques. In this paper, we present a revised version of Hinze's *Generics for the masses* approach that overcomes this limitation. Using our new technique, writing an extensible and modular generic programming library in Haskell 98 is possible.

12.1 INTRODUCTION

A *generic*, or *polytypic*, function is a function that is defined over the structure of types: with a single definition, we obtain a function that works for many data types. Standard examples include the functions that can be derived automatically in Haskell [14], such as *show*, *read*, and '==', but there are many more.

By contrast, an *ad-hoc polymorphic* function [15] requires a separate implementation for each data type. In Haskell, we implement ad-hoc polymorphic functions using type classes. Here is an example, a binary encoder:

---

[1]Oxford University Computing Laboratory, Wolfson Building, Parks Road, Oxford OX1 3QD, UK, bruno@comlab.ox.ac.uk

[2]Institut für Informatik III, Universität Bonn, Römerstraße 164, 53117 Bonn, Germany, {ralf,loeh}@informatik.uni-bonn.de

class *Encode t* **where**
  $encode :: t \rightarrow [Bit]$

instance *Encode Char* **where**
  $encode = encodeChar$

instance *Encode Int* **where**
  $encode = encodeInt$

instance *Encode a* $\Rightarrow$ *Encode* $[a]$ **where**
  $encode\,[\,] \quad\;\; = [0]$
  $encode\,(x:xs) = 1:(encode\,x + \! + encode\,xs)$

The **class** construct introduces an overloaded function with a type parameter t, and the **instance** statements provide implementations for a number of specific types. An instance for lists of type $[a]$ can only be given if an instance for a exists already. The function *encode* thus works on characters, integers, and lists, and on data types that are built from these types. If we call *encode*, the compiler figures out the correct implementation to use, or, if no suitable instance exists, reports a type error.

We assume that primitive bit encoders for integers and characters are provided from somewhere. Lists are encoded by replacing an occurrence of the empty list $[\,]$ with the bit 0, and occurrences of the list constructor $(:)$ with the bit 1 followed by the encoding of the head element and the encoding of the remaining list.

The following example session demonstrates the use of *encode* on a list of strings (where strings are lists of characters in Haskell).

$Main\rangle\; encode\,[\,"\mathtt{xy}"\,,\,"\mathtt{x}"\,]$
$[1,1,0,0,0,1,1,1,1,1,1,0,0,1,1,1,1,0,1,1,0,0,0,1,1,1,1,0,0]$

The function *encode* can be extended at any time to work on additional data types. All we have to do is write another instance of the *Encode* class. However, each time we add a new data type and we want to encode values of that data type, we need to supply a specific implementation of encode for it.

In "Generics for the Masses" (GM) [4] a particularly lightweight approach to generic programming is presented. Using the techniques described in that paper we can write generic functions directly in Haskell 98. This contrasts with other approaches to generic programming, which usually require significant compiler support or language extensions.

In figure 12.1, we present a generic binary encoder implemented using the GM technique. We will describe the technical details, such as the shape of class *Generic*, in section 12.2. Let us, for now, focus on the comparison with the ad-hoc polymorphic function given above. The different methods of class *Generic* define different cases of the generic function. For characters and integers, we assume again standard definitions. But the case for lists is now subsumed by three generic cases for unit, sum and product types. By viewing all data types in a uniform way, these three cases are sufficient to call the encoder on lists, tuples, trees, and several more complex data structures – a new instance declaration is not required.

newtype *Encode a* = *Encode* { *encode′* :: *a* → [*Bit*] }

instance *Generic Encode* **where**

$$
\begin{array}{ll}
\textit{unit} & = \textit{Encode} \,(\textit{const} \,[\,]) \\
\textit{plus a b} & = \textit{Encode} \,(\lambda x \to \textbf{case} \; x \; \textbf{of} \; \textit{Inl} \; l \; \to 0 : \textit{encode′} \; a \; l \\
& \qquad\qquad\qquad\qquad\qquad\quad \textit{Inr} \; r \to 1 : \textit{encode′} \; b \; r) \\
\textit{prod a b} & = \textit{Encode} \,(\lambda(x \times y) \to \textit{encode′} \; a \; x \mathbin{+\!\!+} \textit{encode′} \; b \; y) \\
\textit{char} & = \textit{Encode} \; \textit{encodeChar} \\
\textit{int} & = \textit{Encode} \; \textit{encodeInt} \\
\textit{view iso a} & = \textit{Encode} \,(\lambda x \to \textit{encode′} \; a \; (\textit{from iso x}))
\end{array}
$$

FIGURE 12.1.   **A generic binary encoder**

However, there are situations in which a specific case for a specific data type – called an *ad-hoc case* – is desirable. For example, lists can be encoded more efficiently than shown above: instead of encoding each constructor, we can encode the length of the list followed by encodings of the elements. Or, suppose that sets are represented as trees: The same set can be represented by multiple trees, so a generic equality function should not compare sets structurally, and therefore we need an ad-hoc case for sets.

Defining ad-hoc cases for ad-hoc polymorphic functions is trivial: we just add an **instance** declaration with the desired implementation. For the generic version of the binary encoder, the addition of a new case is, however, very difficult. Each case of the function definition is implemented a method of class *Generic*, and adding a new case later requires the modification of the class. We say that generic functions written in this style are not *extensible*, and that the GM approach is not *modular*, because non-extensibility precludes writing a generic programming library. Generic functions are more concise, but ad-hoc polymorphic functions are more flexible.

While previous foundational work [2, 7, 3, 9] provides a very strong basis for generic programming, most of it only considered non-extensible generic functions. It was realized by many authors [5, 4, 8] that this was a severe limitation.

This paper makes the following contributions:

- In section 12.3, we give an encoding of extensible generic functions directly within Haskell 98 that is modular, overcoming the limitations of GM while retaining its advantages. An extensible generic pretty printer is presented in section 12.4.

- In section 12.5, we show that using a type class with two parameters, a small extension to Haskell 98, the notational overhead can be significantly reduced further.

- The fact that an extensible and modular generic programming library requires the ability to add both new generic functions and new ad-hoc cases is related to the expression problem [18]. We establish this relation and present other related work in section 12.6.

But let us start with the fundamentals of the GM approach, and why extensibility in this framework is not easy to achieve.

12.2 GENERICS FOR THE MASSES

In this section we will summarize the key points of the GM approach.

12.2.1 A class for generic functions

In the GM approach to generic programming, each generic function is an instance of the class *Generic*:

```
class Generic g where
  unit      :: g 1
  plus      :: g a → g b → g (a + b)
  prod      :: g a → g b → g (a × b)
  constr    :: Name → Arity → g a → g a
  constr _ _ = id
  char      :: g Char
  int       :: g Int
  view      :: Iso b a → g a → g b
```

Our generic binary encoder in figure 12.1 is one such instance. The idea of *Generic* is that g represents the type of the generic function and each method of the type class represents a case of the generic function. Haskell 98 severely restricts the type terms that can appear in instance declarations. To fulfil these restrictions, we have to pack the type of the encoder in a data type *Encode*. For convenience, we define *Encode* as a record type with one field and an accessor function $encode' :: Encode\ a → (a → [Bit])$.

The first three methods of class *Generic* are for the unit, sum and product types that are defined as follows:

```
data 1    = 1
data a + b = Inl a | Inr b
data a × b = a × b
```

The types of the class methods follow the kinds of the data types [3], where kinds are types of type-level terms. Types with values such as *Int*, *Char*, and 1 have kind $*$. The parameterized types $+$ and $×$ have kind $* → * → *$, to reflect the fact that they are binary operators on types of kind $*$. The functions *plus* and *prod* correspondingly take additional arguments that capture the recursive calls of the generic function on the parameters of the data type.

The binary encoder is defined to encode the unit type as the empty sequence of bits. In the sum case, a 0 or 1 is generated depending on the constructor of the input value. In the product case, we concatenate the encodings of the left and right component.

If our generic functions require information about the constructors (such as the name and arity), we can optionally provide a definition for the function *constr*. Otherwise – such as for the binary encoder – we can just use the default implementation, which ignores the extra information.

Cases for the primitive types *Char* and *Int* are defined by providing the functions *char* and *int*, respectively.

The *view* function is the key to genericity: given an isomorphism (between the data type and a sum of products) and a representation for the isomorphic type, returns a representation for the original data type. Let us look at lists as an example. A list of type $[a]$ can be considered as a binary sum (it has two constructors), where the first argument is a unit (the $[]$ constructor has no arguments) and the second argument is a pair (the $(:)$ constructor has two arguments) of an element of type a and another list of type $[a]$. This motivates the following definitions:

data $Iso\ a\ b = Iso\ \{from :: a \rightarrow b, to :: b \rightarrow a\}$

$isoList :: Iso\ [a]\ (\mathbb{1} + (a \times [a]))$
$isoList = Iso\ fromList\ toList$

$fromList :: [a] \rightarrow \mathbb{1} + (a \times [a])$
$fromList\ [] \qquad = Inl\ \mathbb{1}$
$fromList\ (x:xs) = Inr\ (x \times xs)$

$toList :: \mathbb{1} + (a \times [a]) \rightarrow [a]$
$toList\ (Inl\ \mathbb{1}) \qquad = []$
$toList\ (Inr\ (x \times xs)) = x:xs$

In order to use generic functions on a data type, the programmer must define such an isomorphism once. Afterwards, all generic functions can be used on the data type by means of the *view* case. The function *rList* – also within the programmer's responsibility – captures how to apply *view* in the case of lists:

$rList :: Generic\ g \Rightarrow g\ a \rightarrow g\ [a]$
$rList\ a = view\ isoList\ (unit\ `plus`\ (a\ `prod`\ rList\ a))$

The first argument of *view* is the isomorphism for lists defined above. The second argument reflects the list-isomorphic type $\mathbb{1} + (a \times [a])$. Using *rList*, we can apply any generic function to a list type, by viewing any list as a sum of products and then using the generic definitions for the unit, sum and product types.

The *view* case of the encoder applies the *from* part of the isomorphism to convert the type of the input value and then calls the encoder recursively on that value. Generally, functions such as the encoder where the type variable appears only in the argument position are called generic *consumers* and require only the *from* part of the isomorphism. Functions that *produce* or *transform* values generically make also use of the *to* component.

We have demonstrated that a fixed amount of code (the isomorphism and the *view* invocation) is sufficient to adapt all generic functions to work on a new data type. This is a huge improvement over ad-hoc polymorphic functions, which have to be extended one by one to work on an additional data type.

12.2.2 Using generic functions

In order to call a generic function such as *encode'*, we have to supply a suitable value of type *Encode*. As a simple example, suppose that we want to call the function *encode'* on a pair of an integer and a character. We then use *prod int char* to build the desired value of type *Encode* (*Int × Char*), and use *encode'* to extract the function:

> *Main⟩ encode' (prod int char)* (1 × 'x')
> [1,0,0,0,0,0,0,0,0,0,0,0,0,0,0,0,0,0,0,0,0,1,1,1,1]

Similarly, if we want to encode a list of strings, we can make use of function *rList* to build the argument to *encode'*:

> *Main⟩ encode' (rList (rList char))* ["xy","x"]
> [1,1,0,0,0,1,1,1,1,1,1,0,0,1,1,1,1,0,1,1,0,0,0,1,1,1,1,0,0]

The argument to *encode'* is dictated by the type at which we call the generic function. We can therefore use the type class *Rep*, shown in figure 12.2, to infer this so-called *type representation* automatically for us. We call such a type class a *dispatcher*, because it selects the correct case of a generic function depending on the type context in which it is used. Note that the dispatcher works for any *g* that is an instance of *Generic*. Therefore, it needs to be defined only once for all generic functions. With the dispatcher, we can define *encode* as follows:

> *encode* :: *Rep t* ⇒ *t* → [*Bit*]
> *encode* = *encode' rep*

Here, the type representation is implicitly passed via the type class. The function *encode* can be used with the same convenience as any ad-hoc overloaded function, but it is truly generic.

12.3 EXTENSIBLE GENERIC FUNCTIONS

This section consists of two parts: in the first part, we demonstrate how the non-extensibility of GM functions leads to non-modularity. In the second part, we show how to overcome this limitation.

12.3.1 The modularity problem

Suppose that we want to encode lists, and that we want to use a different encoding of lists than the one derived generically: a list can be encoded by encoding its length, followed by the encodings of all the list elements. For long lists, this

class *Rep a* **where**
  rep :: (*Generic g*) $\Rightarrow$ *g a*
instance *Rep* $\mathbb{1}$ **where**
  rep = *unit*
instance *Rep Char* **where**
  rep = *char*
instance *Rep Int* **where**
  rep = *int*
instance (*Rep a*, *Rep b*) $\Rightarrow$ *Rep* (*a* + *b*) **where**
  rep = *plus rep rep*
instance (*Rep a*, *Rep b*) $\Rightarrow$ *Rep* (*a* $\times$ *b*) **where**
  rep = *prod rep rep*
instance *Rep a* $\Rightarrow$ *Rep* [*a*] **where**
  rep = *rList rep*

FIGURE 12.2.   A generic dispatcher

encoding is more efficient than to separate any two subsequent elements of the lists and to mark the end of the list.

The class *Generic* is the base class of all generic functions, and its methods are limited. If we want to design a generic programming library, it is mandatory that we constrain ourselves to a limited set of frequently used types. Still, we might hope to add an extra case by introducing subclasses:

  class *Generic g* $\Rightarrow$ *GenericList g* **where**
    list :: *g a* $\rightarrow$ *g* [*a*]
    list = *rList*

This declaration introduces a class *GenericList* as a subclass of *Generic*: we can only instantiate *GenericList* for type *g* that are also instances of class *Generic*. The subclass contains a single method *list*. By default, *list* is defined to be just *rList*. However, the default definition of *list* can be overridden in an instance declaration. For example, here is how to define the more efficient encoding for lists:

  instance *GenericList Encode* **where**
    list a = *Encode* ($\lambda x \rightarrow$ *encodeInt* (*length x*) ++ *concatMap* (*encode'* *a*) *x*)

Our extension breaks down, however, once we try to adapt the dispatcher: the method *rep* of class *Rep* has the type *Generic g* $\Rightarrow$ *g a*, and we cannot easily replace the context *Generic* with something more specific without modifying the *Rep* class. Therefore, the only methods of a type class depending on the type

class *RepEncode t* **where**
  repEncode :: *Encode t*
instance *RepEncode* 𝟙 **where**
  repEncode = *Encode* (*encode′ unit*)
instance *RepEncode Int* **where**
  repEncode = *Encode* (*encode′ int*)
instance *RepEncode Char* **where**
  repEncode = *Encode* (*encode′ char*)
instance (*RepEncode a*,*RepEncode b*) ⇒ *RepEncode* (*a* + *b*) **where**
  repEncode = *Encode* (*encode′* (*plus repEncode repEncode*))
instance (*RepEncode a*,*RepEncode b*) ⇒ *RepEncode* (*a* × *b*) **where**
  repEncode = *Encode* (*encode′* (*prod repEncode repEncode*))

FIGURE 12.3.   An ad-hoc dispatcher for binary encoders

variable *g* that we can use at the definitions of *rep* are those of *Generic* – any uses
of methods from subclasses of *Generic* will result in type errors. In particular, we
cannot adapt the instance of *Rep* for lists to make use of *list* rather than *rList*.

Consequently, generic functions in the GM approach are not extensible. This
rules out modularity: all cases that can appear in a generic function must be turned
into methods of class *Generic*, and as we have already argued, this is impossible:
it may be necessary to add specific behaviour on user-defined or abstract types
that are simply not known to the library writer.

12.3.2   Ad-hoc dispatchers

The problem with the GM approach is that the generic dispatcher forces a specific
dispatching behaviour on all generic functions. A simple solution to this problem
is to specialize the dispatcher *Rep* to the generic function in question. This means
that we now need one dispatcher for each generic function, but it also means
that extensibility is no longer a problem. Figure 12.3 shows what we obtain by
specializing *Rep* to the binary encoder. In the instances, we use *encode′* to extract
the value from the **newtype** and redirect the call to the appropriate case in *Generic*.
The specialized dispatcher can be used just as the general dispatcher before, to
define a truly generic binary encoder:

  encode :: *RepEncode t* ⇒ *t* → [*Bit*]
  encode = *encode′ repEncode*

It is now trivial to extend the dispatcher to new types. Consider once more the
ad-hoc case for encoding lists, defined by providing an **instance** declaration for
GenericList Encode. The corresponding dispatcher extension is performed as follows:

instance *RepEncode a* ⇒ *RepEncode* [*a*] **where**
  repEncode = *Encode* (*encode'* (*list repEncode*))

Let us summarize. By specializing dispatchers to specific generic functions, we obtain an encoding of generic functions in Haskell that is just as expressive as the GM approach and shares the advantage that the code is pure Haskell 98. Additionally, generic functions with specialized dispatchers are extensible: we can place the type class *Generic* together with functions such as *encode* in a library that is easy to use and extend by programmers.

12.4   EXAMPLE: AN EXTENSIBLE GENERIC PRETTY PRINTER

In this section we show how to define a *extensible generic pretty printer*. This example is based on the non-modular version presented in GM (originally based on Wadler's work [19]).

12.4.1   A generic pretty printer

In figure 12.4 we present an instance of *Generic* that defines a generic pretty printer. The pretty printer makes use of Wadler's pretty printing combinators. These combinators generate a value of type *Doc* that can be rendered into a string afterwards. For the structural cases, the *unit* function just returns an empty document; *plus* decomposes the sum and pretty prints the value; for products, we pretty print the first and second components separated by a line. For base types *char* and *int* we assume existing pretty printers *prettyChar* and *prettyInt*. The *view* case just uses the isomorphism to convert between the user defined type and its structural representation. Finally, since pretty printers require extra constructor information, the function *constr* calls *prettyConstr*, which pretty prints constructors.

Suppose that we add a new data type *Tree* for representing labelled binary trees. Furthermore, the nodes have an auxiliary integer value that can be used to track the maximum depth of the subtrees.

  data *Tree a* = *Empty* | *Fork Int* (*Tree a*) *a* (*Tree a*)

Now, we want to use our generic functions with *Tree*. As we have explained before, what we need to do is to add a subclass of *Generic* with a case for the new data type and provide a suitable *view*.

  class *Generic g* ⇒ *GenericTree g* **where**
    tree :: *g a* → *g* (*Tree a*)
    tree a = *view isoTree* (*constr* "`Empty`" 0 *unit* `plus`
                  constr "`Fork`" 4
                    (*int* `prod` (*rTree a* `prod` (*a* `prod` *rTree a*)))))

(We omit the boilerplate definition of *isoTree*). Providing a pretty printer for *Tree* amounts to declaring an empty instance of *GenericTree* – that is, using the default definition for *tree*.

newtype *Pretty a = Pretty* {*pretty′ :: a → Doc*}
instance *Generic Pretty* **where**
    unit   = *Pretty* (*const empty*)
    char   = *Pretty* (*prettyChar*)
    int   = *Pretty* (*prettyInt*)
    plus a b   = *Pretty* (λ*x* → **case** *x* **of** *Inl l* → *pretty′ a l*
                                   Inr r → *pretty′ b r*)
    prod a b   = *Pretty* (λ(*x* × *y*) → *pretty′ a x* ⋄ *line* ⋄ *pretty′ b y*)
    view iso a   = *Pretty* (*pretty′ a* ∘ *from iso*)
    constr n ar a = *Pretty* (*prettyConstr n ar a*)
prettyConstr n ar a x = **let** *s = text n* **in**
  if *ar* == 0 **then** *s*
           else *group* (*nest* 1 (*text* " (" ⋄ *s* ⋄ *line* ⋄ *pretty′ a x* ⋄ *text* ") "))

FIGURE 12.4.   A generic pretty printer

Main⟩ **let** *t = Fork* 1 (*Fork* 0 *Empty* 'h' *Empty*) 'i' (*Fork* 0 *Empty* '!' *Empty*)
Main⟩ *render* 80 (*pretty′* (*tree char*) *t*)
(*Fork* 1 (*Fork* 0 *Empty* 'h' *Empty*) 'i' (*Fork* 0 *Empty* '!' *Empty*))
Main⟩ **let** *i = Fork* 1 (*Fork* 0 *Empty* 104 *Empty*) 105 (*Fork* 0 *Empty* 33 *Empty*)
Main⟩ *render* 80 (*pretty′* (*tree* (*Pretty* (λ*x* → *text* [*chr x*]))) *i*)
(*Fork* 1 (*Fork* 0 *Empty h Empty*) *i* (*Fork* 0 *Empty* ! *Empty*))
Main⟩ *render* 80 (*pretty t*)
(*Fork* 1 (*Fork* 0 *Empty* 'h' *Empty*) 'i' (*Fork* 0 *Empty* '!' *Empty*))

FIGURE 12.5.   A sample interactive sesssion

   instance *GenericTree Pretty*

   We now demonstrate the use of generic functions, and the pretty printer in particular, by showing the outcome of a console session in figure 12.5.

   The first use of *pretty′* prints the tree *t* using the generic functionality given by *tree* and *char*. More interestingly, the second example (on a tree of integers), shows that we can override the generic behaviour for the integer parameter by providing a user-defined function instead of *int* – in this case, we interpret an integer as the code of a character using the function *chr*.

   Whenever the extra flexibility provided by the possibility of overriding the generic behaviour is not required (as in the first call of *pretty′*), we can provide a dispatcher such as the one presented in figure 12.6 and just use the convenient *pretty* function.

class *RepPretty a* **where**
  repPretty   :: *Pretty a*
  repPrettyList :: *Pretty* [*a*]
  repPrettyList = *Pretty* (*pretty′* (*list repPretty*))

instance *RepPretty* $\mathbb{1}$ **where**
  repPretty   = *Pretty* (*pretty′ repPretty*)

instance *RepPretty Char* **where**
  repPretty   = *Pretty* (*pretty′ char*)
  repPrettyList = *Pretty prettyString*

instance *RepPretty Int* **where**
  repPretty   = *Pretty* (*pretty′ int*)

instance (*RepPretty a*, *RepPretty b*) $\Rightarrow$ *RepPretty* (*a* + *b*) **where**
  repPretty   = *Pretty* (*pretty′* (*plus repPretty repPretty*))

instance (*RepPretty a*, *RepPretty b*) $\Rightarrow$ *RepPretty* (*a* × *b*) **where**
  repPretty   = *Pretty* (*pretty′* (*prod repPretty repPretty*))

instance *RepPretty a* $\Rightarrow$ *RepPretty* (*Tree a*) **where**
  repPretty   = *Pretty* (*pretty′* (*tree repPretty*))

pretty :: *RepPretty t* $\Rightarrow$ *t* → *Doc*
pretty = *pretty′ repPretty*

FIGURE 12.6.   An ad-hoc dispatcher for pretty printers

12.4.2 Showing lists

For user-defined types like *Tree*, our generic pretty printer can just reuse the generic functionality and the results will be very similar to the ones we get if we just append **deriving** *Show* to our data type definitions. However, this does not work for built-in lists. The problem with lists is that they use a special mix-fix notation instead of the usual alphabetic and prefix constructors. Fortunately, we have seen in section 12.3 that we can combine ad-hoc polymorphic functions with generic functions. We shall do the same here: we define an instance of *GenericList Pretty* but, deviating from *GenericTree Pretty*, we override the default definition.

    instance *GenericList Pretty* **where**
      list p = *Pretty* (λ*x* →
        case *x* **of** [ ]   → *text* " [ ] "
                 (*a* : *as*) → *group* (*nest* 1 (*text* " [" ◇ *pretty′ p a* ◇ *rest as*)))
        where *rest* [ ]   = *text* "] "
              rest (*x* : *xs*) = *text* " , " ◇ *line* ◇ *pretty′ p x* ◇ *rest xs*

We can now extend the dispatcher in figure 12.6 with an instance for lists that uses Haskell's standard notation.

> **instance** *RepPretty a* ⇒ *RepPretty* [*a*] **where**
>   *pretty* = *pretty'* (*list repPretty*)

Unfortunately, we are not done yet. In Haskell there is one more special notation involving lists: strings are just lists of characters, but we want to print them using the conventional string notation. So, not only do we need to treat lists in a special manner, but we also need to handle lists of characters specially. We thus have to implement a nested case analysis on types. We anticipated this possibility in figure 12.6 and included a function *repPrettyList*. The basic idea is that *repPrettyList* behaves as expected for all lists except the ones with characters, where it uses *prettyString*.This is the same as Haskell does in the *Show* class. Finally, we modify *RepPretty* [*a*] to redirect the call to *prettyList* and we are done.

> **instance** *RepPretty a* ⇒ *RepPretty* [*a*] **where**
>   *repPretty* = *repPrettyList*

In the pretty printer presented in GM, supporting the list notation involved adding an extra case to *Generic*, which required us to have access to the source code where *Generic* was originally declared. In contrast, with our solution, the addition of a special case for lists did not involve any change to our original *Generic* class or even its instance for *Pretty*.

The additional flexibility of ad-hoc dispatchers comes at a price: while in GM the responsibility of writing the code for the dispatchers was on the library writer side, now this responsibility is on the user of the library, who has to write additional boilerplate code. Still, it is certainly preferable to define an ad-hoc dispatcher than to define the function as an ad-hoc polymorphic function, being forced to give an actual implementation for each data type. Yet, it would be even better if we could somehow return to a single dispatcher that works for all generic functions and restore the definition of the dispatcher to the library code.

In the next section we will see an alternative encoding that requires a single generic dispatcher only and still allows for modular and extensible functions. The price to pay for this is that the code requires a small extension to Haskell 98.

12.5 MAKING AD-HOC DISPATCHERS LESS AD-HOC

In this section we present another way to write extensible generic functions, which requires only one generic dispatcher just like the original GM approach. It relies, however, on an extension to Haskell 98: multi-parameter type classes, which are widely used and supported by the major Haskell implementations.

Recall the discussion at the end of section 12.3.1. There, we have shown that the problem with GM's dispatcher is that it fixes the context of method *rep* to the class *Generic*. This happens because the type variable *g*, which abstracts over the "generic function", is universally quantified in the class method *rep*. However,

instance $Generic\ g \Rightarrow GRep\ g\ \mathbb{1}$ **where**
  $grep = unit$

instance $Generic\ g \Rightarrow GRep\ g\ Int$ **where**
  $grep = int$

instance $Generic\ g \Rightarrow GRep\ g\ Char$ **where**
  $grep = char$

instance $(Generic\ g, GRep\ g\ a, GRep\ g\ b) \Rightarrow GRep\ g\ (a+b)$ **where**
  $grep = plus\ grep\ grep$

instance $(Generic\ g, GRep\ g\ a, GRep\ g\ b) \Rightarrow GRep\ g\ (a \times b)$ **where**
  $grep = prod\ grep\ grep$

instance $(GenericList\ g, GRep\ g\ a) \Rightarrow GRep\ g\ [a]$ **where**
  $grep = list\ grep$

instance $(GenericTree\ g, GRep\ g\ a) \Rightarrow GRep\ g\ (Tree\ a)$ **where**
  $grep = tree\ grep$

FIGURE 12.7. A less ad-hoc dispatcher.

since we want to use subclasses of *Generic* to add additional cases to generic functions, the context of *rep* must be flexible. We therefore must be able to abstract from the specific type class *Generic*. Our solution for this problem is to change the quantification of g: instead of universally quantifying g at the method *rep* we can quantify it on the type class itself.

  class $GRep\ g\ a$ **where**
    $grep :: g\ a$

The type class $GRep\ g\ a$ is a variation of $Rep\ a$ with the proposed change of quantification. The fact that g occurs at the top level gives us the extra flexibility that we need to provide more refined contexts to the method *grep* (which corresponds to the method *rep*).

In figure 12.7 we see how to use this idea to capture all ad-hoc dispatchers in a single definition. The instances of *GRep* look just like the instances of *Rep* except that they have the extra parameter g at the top level. The structural cases $\mathbb{1}$, $+$ and $\times$ together with the base cases *int* and *char* are all handled in *Generic*, therefore we require g to be an instance of *Generic*. However, for $[a]$ and *Tree a* the argument g must be constrained by *GenericList* and *GenericTree*, respectively, since these are the type classes that handle those types. The remaining constraints, of the form $GRep\ g\ a$, contain the necessary information to perform the recursive calls. Now, we can just use this dispatcher to obtain an extensible *encode* by specializing the argument g to *Encode*:

  $encode :: GRep\ Encode\ t \Rightarrow t \rightarrow [Bit]$
  $encode = encode'\ grep$

For pretty printers we can just use the same dispatcher, but this time using *Pretty* instead of *Encode*:

$$pretty :: GRep\ Pretty\ t \Rightarrow t \rightarrow Doc$$
$$pretty = pretty'\ grep$$

This approach avoids the extra boilerplate of the solution with ad-hoc dispatchers presented in sections 12.3 and 12.4 requiring a similar amount of work to the original GM technique. Still it is modular, and allows us to write a generic programming library.

In a previous version of this paper [13] we used a trick proposed by Hughes [6] and also used by Lämmel and Peyton Jones [8] that simulated abstraction over type classes using a class of the form:

class *Over t* **where**
    over :: *t*

While the same effect could be achieved using *Over* instead of *GRep*, this would be more demanding on the type system since the instances would not be legal in Haskell 98: For example, the instance for *GRep g Int* would become *Over (g Int)*. The former is legal in Haskell 98, the latter is not. Moreover, *GRep* is also more finely typed allowing us to precisely specify the kind of the "type class" that we are abstracting from.

Since the publication of the original version of this paper, Sulzmann and Wang [16] have shown how to add extensible superclasses to the Haskell language, which would constitute another solution to the extensibility problem for GM generic functions.

12.6 DISCUSSION AND RELATED WORK

In this section we briefly relate our technique to the *expression problem* [18] and discuss some other closely related work.

12.6.1 Expression problem

Wadler [18] identified the need for extensibility in two dimensions (adding new variants *and* new functions) as a problem and called it the expression problem. According to him, a solution for the problem should allow the definition of a data type, the addition of new variants to such a data type as well as the addition of new functions over that data type. A solution should not require recompilation of existing code, and it should be statically type safe: applying a function to a variant for which that function is not defined should result in a compile-time error. Our solution accomplishes all of these for the particular case of generic functions. It should be possible to generalize our technique in such a way that it can be applied to other instances of the expression problem. For example, the work of Oliveira and Gibbons [11], which generalizes the GM technique as a design pattern, could be recast using the techniques of this paper.

Let us analyze the role of each type class of our solution in the context of the expression problem. The class *Generic* plays the role of a data type definition and declares the variants that *all* functions should be defined for. The subclasses of *Generic* represent extra variants that we add: not all functions need to be defined for those variants, but if we want to use a function with one of those, then we need to provide the respective case. The instances of *Generic* and subclasses are the bodies of our extensible functions. Finally, the dispatcher allows us to encode the dispatching behaviour for the extensible functions: if we add a new variant and we want to use it with our functions, we must add a new instance for that variant.

12.6.2   Other related work

Generic Haskell (GH) [9] is a compiler for a language extension of Haskell that supports generic programming. The compiler can generate Haskell code that can then be used with a Haskell compiler. Like our approach, GH uses sums of products for viewing user-defined types. GH can generate the boilerplate code required for new data types automatically. With our approach we need to manually provide this code, but we could employ an additional tool to facilitate its generation. However, our generic functions are *extensible*; at any point we can add an extra ad-hoc case for some generic function. We believe this is of major importance since, as we have been arguing, extensible functions are crucial for a modular generic programming library. This is not the case for GH since all the special cases need to be defined at once. Also, since GH is an external tool it is less convenient to use. With our approach, all we have to do is to import the modules with the generic library.

"Derivable Type Classes" (DTCs) [5] is a proposed extension to Haskell that allows us to write generic default cases for methods of a type class. In this approach, data types are viewed as if constructed by binary sums and binary products, which makes it a close relative of both our approach and GM. The main advantage of DTCs is that it is trivial to add ad-hoc cases to generic functions, and the isomorphisms between data types and their structural representations (see section 12.2.1) are automatically generated by the compiler. However, the approach permits only generic functions on unparameterized types (types of kind $\star$), and the DTC implementation lacks the ability to access constructor information, precluding the definition of generic parsers or pretty printers. The generic extension to Clean [1] uses the ideas of DTCs and allows the definition of generic functions on types of any kind.

Lämmel and Peyton Jones [8] present another approach to generic programming based on type classes. The idea is similar to DTCs in the sense that one type class is defined for each generic function and that default methods are used to provide the generic definition. Overriding the generic behaviour is as simple as providing an instance with the ad-hoc definition. The approach shares DTC's limitation to generic functions on types of kind $\star$. One difference to our approach is that data types are not mapped to a common structure consisting of sums and products. Instead, generic definitions make use of a small set of combinators. Another difference is that their approach relies on some advanced extensions to the type class system, while our approach requires only a multi-parameter type class or even just Haskell 98.

Löh and Hinze [10] propose an extension to Haskell that allows the definition of extensible data types and extensible functions. With the help of this extension, it is also possible to define extensible generic functions, on types of any kind, in Haskell. While their proposed language modification is relatively small, our solution has the advantage of being usable right now. Furthermore, we can give more safety guarantees: in our setting, a call to an undefined case of a generic function is a static error; with open data types, it results in a pattern match failure.

Vytiniotis and others [17] present a language where it is possible to define extensible generic functions on types of any kind, while guaranteeing static safety. While it is not a novelty that we can define such flexible generic functions, we believe it is the first time that a solution with all these features is presented in Haskell, relying solely on implemented language constructs or even solely on Haskell 98.

12.7 CONCLUSIONS

In the GM approach defining generic functions in Haskell 98 is possible but it is impossible to extend them in a modular way. The ability to define extensible generic function is very important since, in practice, most generic functions have ad-hoc cases. In this paper we presented two variations of GM that allow the definition of generic functions that are both extensible and modular. The first variation, like the original GM, can be encoded using Haskell 98 only but requires extra boilerplate code not present in the original approach. The second variation requires a multi-parameter type class, an extension to Haskell 98 that is supported by the major Haskell implementations. This variation still allows extensibility and does not add any significant boilerplate over the original GM. One important aspect of the GM and our encoding is that dispatching generic functions is resolved statically: calling a generic function on a case that is not defined for it is a compile-time error.

Based on the results of this paper, we are currently in the process of assembling a library of frequently used generic functions. For the interested reader, the Haskell source code for this paper can be found online [12].

ACKNOWLEDGMENTS

We would like to thank Jeremy Gibbons and Fermín Reig for valuable suggestions and discussions about this work. We would also like to thank the anonymous referees whose reviews greatly contributed for improving the presentation of this paper. This work was partially funded by the *EPSRC Datatype-Generic Programming* and the *DFG "A generic functional programming language"* projects.

REFERENCES

[1] Artem Alimarine and Marinus J. Plasmeijer. A generic programming extension for Clean. In *Implementation of Functional Languages*, pages 168–185, 2001.

[2] Richard Bird, Oege de Moor, and Paul Hoogendijk. Generic functional programming with types and relations. *Journal of Functional Programming*, 6(1):1–28, 1996.

[3] Ralf Hinze. Polytypic values possess polykinded types. In Roland Backhouse and J. N. Oliveira, editors, *Proceedings of the Fifth International Conference on Mathematics of Program Construction, July 3–5, 2000*, volume 1837 of *Lecture Notes in Computer Science*, pages 2–27. Springer-Verlag, 2000.

[4] Ralf Hinze. Generics for the masses. In *ICFP '04: Proceedings of the ninth ACM SIGPLAN international conference on Functional programming*, pages 236–243. ACM Press, 2004.

[5] Ralf Hinze and Simon Peyton Jones. Derivable type classes. In Graham Hutton, editor, *Proceedings of the 2000 ACM SIGPLAN Haskell Workshop*, volume 41.1 of Electronic Notes in Theoretical Computer Science. Elsevier Science, August 2001. The preliminary proceedings appeared as a University of Nottingham technical report.

[6] J. Hughes. Restricted data types in Haskell. In E. Meijer, editor, *Proceedings of the 1999 Haskell Workshop*, number UU-CS-1999-28, 1999.

[7] Patrik Jansson. *Functional Polytypic Programming*. PhD thesis, Chalmers University of Technology, May 2000.

[8] Ralf Lämmel and Simon Peyton Jones. Scrap your boilerplate with class: extensible generic functions. In *Proceedings of the ACM SIGPLAN International Conference on Functional Programming (ICFP 2005)*, pages 204–215. ACM Press, September 2005.

[9] Andres Löh. *Exploring Generic Haskell*. PhD thesis, Utrecht University, 2004.

[10] Andres Löh and Ralf Hinze. Open data types and open functions. Technical Report IAI-TR-2006-3, Institut für Informatik III, Universität Bonn, February 2006.

[11] B. Oliveira and J. Gibbons. Typecase: A design pattern for type-indexed functions. In *Haskell Workshop*, pages 98–109, 2005.

[12] Bruno Oliveira, Ralf Hinze, and Andres Löh. Source code accompanying "Extensible and modular generics for the masses".
Available from http://web.comlab.ox.ac.uk/oucl/work/bruno.oliveira/.

[13] Bruno Oliveira, Ralf Hinze, and Andres Löh. Generics as a library. In *Seventh Symposium on Trends in Functional Programming*, 2006.

[14] Simon Peyton Jones, editor. *Haskell 98 Language and Libraries: The Revised Report*. Cambridge University Press, 2003.

[15] Christopher Strachey. Fundamental concepts in programming languages. Lecture Notes, International Summer School in Computer Programming, Copenhagen, August 1967. Reprinted in *Higher-Order and Symbolic Computation*, 13(1/2), pp. 1–49, 2000.

[16] Martin Sulzmann and Meng Wang. Modular generic programming with extensible superclasses. In *WGP '06: Proceedings of the 2006 ACM SIGPLAN workshop on Generic programming*, pages 55–65. ACM Press, 2006.

[17] Dimitrios Vytiniotis, Geoffrey Washburn, and Stephanie Weirich. An open and shut typecase. In *TLDI '05: Proceedings of the 2005 ACM SIGPLAN international workshop on Types in languages design and implementation*, pages 13–24, New York, NY, USA, 2005. ACM Press.

[18] Philip Wadler. The expression problem. Java Genericity Mailing list, November 1998.

[19] Philip Wadler. A prettier printer. In Jeremy Gibbons and Oege de Moor, editors, *The Fun of Programming*, pages 223–244. Palgrave Macmillan, 2003.

Chapter 13

When is an Abstract Data Type a Functor?

Pablo Nogueira[1]

Abstract: A parametric algebraic data type is a functor when we can apply a function to its data components while satisfying certain equations. We investigate whether parametric *abstract* data types can be functors. We provide a general definition for their map operation that needs only satisfy one equation. The definability of this map depends on properties of interfaces and is a sufficient condition for functoriality. Instances of the definition for particular abstract types can then be constructed using their axiomatic semantics. The definition and the equation can be adapted to determine, necessarily and sufficiently, whether an ADT is a functor for a given implementation.

13.1 INTRODUCTION

The application of a function to the data components of a data type has been recognised as a fundamental operation at least since the *maplist* function of LISP [11]. A data type that supports the operation while satisfying certain equations is said to be 'mappable' and its formal characterisation is provided by the category-theoretic concept of *functor*. The functor concept is also important because it is preliminary to the concept of *natural transformation* [3] which provides a formal characterisation of parametrically polymorphic functions between mappable data types and is central to the notion of parametricity [19].

In functional languages, mappable algebraic data types are recognised as functors. Such types are free algebras: there are no equations among their value constructors and therefore construction and observation (pattern matching) are inverse operations. In contrast, *abstract* data types (ADTs) may not be free algebras and therefore construction and observation may not be inverses. ADTs are

---

[1]School of Computer Science and Information Technology, University of Nottingham; E-mail: `pni@cs.nott.ac.uk`

defined in terms of ordinary functions and equations, in particular among constructors, that specify the axiomatic semantics of the type [13, 10].

We investigate the functoriality of unary parametric ADTs such as queues,
stacks, ordered sets, sets, bags, etc. More precisely, we provide a general definition for their map operation that needs only satisfy one equation. The definability
of this operation depends on properties of interfaces and is a sufficient condition
for functoriality. Instances of the definition for particular abstract types can then
be constructed using their axiomatic semantics. The definition and the equation
can be adapted to determine, necessarily and sufficiently, whether an ADT is a
functor for a given implementation.

13.2 CATEGORIES AND FUNCTORS

A category $\mathbf{C}$ is an algebraic structure consisting of a collection $\mathrm{Obj}(\mathbf{C})$ of *objects*
(entities with structure) and a collection $\mathrm{Arr}(\mathbf{C})$ of *arrows* (structure-preserving
maps between objects) such that there is a binary arrow-composition operator,
written ∘, that is closed (yields an arrow in $\mathrm{Arr}(\mathbf{C})$), is associative, and has unique
left and right neutral element (the identity arrow) for every object. Every arrow
has only one *source* and one *target* object. We write $f :: a \rightarrow b$ to denote the arrow
f with source a and target b, and write $id_a :: a \rightarrow a$ to denote the unique identity
arrow for a.

A *functor* $F :: \mathbf{C} \rightarrow \mathbf{D}$ maps all objects and arrows in category $\mathbf{C}$ respectively
to objects and arrows in category $\mathbf{D}$ while preserving the categorical structure.[2]
More precisely, F denotes a pair of total maps $F :: \mathrm{Obj}(\mathbf{C}) \rightarrow \mathrm{Obj}(\mathbf{D})$ (the object-
level map) and $F :: \mathrm{Arr}(\mathbf{C}) \rightarrow \mathrm{Arr}(\mathbf{D})$ (the arrow-level map) such that source, target, composition, and identities are preserved. Given an arrow $f :: a \rightarrow b$ we have
$F f :: F a \rightarrow F b$ and F distributes over composition and preserves identities:

$$\begin{array}{rcl} F(g \circ f) & = & F g \circ F f \\ F \, id_a & = & id_{Fa} \end{array}$$

We refer to the equations as *functorial laws*. Notice that the symbol F is heavily
overloaded. A functor $F :: \mathbf{C} \rightarrow \mathbf{C}$ is called an *endofunctor*.

13.3 CATEGORIES AND TYPES

A connection between functional programming (e.g., Haskell) and category theory is the category **Type** where, broadly, objects are monomorphic types and
arrows are functional programs involving those types. Arrow composition is
function composition (which is closed and associative) and identity arrows are
instances of the polymorphic identity function for monomorphic types [3]. A
polymorphic function $f :: a \rightarrow b$ is a collection of arrows of $\mathrm{Arr}(\mathbf{Type})$, but we
informally refer to f as 'an' arrow.

---

[2]We use a double colon when writing the source and target categories because functors
are also arrows in functor categories [3].

A unary parametrically polymorphic algebraic data type F is an endofunctor $F :: \textbf{Type} \rightarrow \textbf{Type}$ when at the object level F maps monomorphic types to monomorphic types and at the arrow level $mapF$ satisfies the functorial laws. The categorical convention is to write F for $mapF$. For example, the list type is a typical functor. At the object level, the type constructor [] maps monomorphic types (e.g., *Bool*) to monomorphic types (e.g., [*Bool*]). At the arrow level, the list function *map* satisfies the functorial laws. The categorical convention is to write *List* for *map*.

There are two important points. First, *map* respects the structure or *shape* of the list, mapping only the data or *payload*—from now on we refer to the type-argument of a data type as its payload. Second, *map*'s definition follows the structure of the list type and the proof that it satisfies the functorial laws proceeds by structural induction on lists [13].

In this paper we are only concerned with unary first-order data types. Mappable algebraic data types of arbitrary arity and order can be recognised as functors with the help of other categorical devices such as product and functor categories [3].

We conclude the section with a non-functor example: $Fix \, a = (a \rightarrow a) \rightarrow a$ is the type of the fixed-point combinator $fix \, f = f \, (fix \, f)$. It is not possible to write a map function for Fix that satisfies the functorial laws. Unfortunately, proving this formally is beyond the scope of this paper [3].

13.3.1 Subcategories and type classes

In Haskell, algebraic data types can be constrained in their type-argument range by type-class membership. For example:

$$data \; Ord \; a \Rightarrow Tree \; a = Empty \; | \; Node \; a \; (Tree \; a) \; (Tree \; a)$$

This is the type of binary trees whose nodes contain values of types in class *Ord*. Constrained data types are often used in the implementation of ADTs. For example, *Tree* can be used in the implementation of binary search trees, ordered bags, ordered sets, priority queues, etc. [16].

A *subcategory* $\textbf{S}$ of a category $\textbf{C}$ is such that $\text{Obj}(\textbf{S}) \subseteq \text{Obj}(\textbf{C})$, $\text{Arr}(\textbf{S})$ contains all the arrows in $\text{Arr}(\textbf{C})$ involving only $\textbf{S}$-objects, and composition and identities in $\text{Arr}(\textbf{S})$ are those in $\text{Arr}(\textbf{C})$ involving only $\textbf{S}$-objects [3].

Mappable constrained data types are functors $F :: \textbf{S} \rightarrow \textbf{Type}$, where $\textbf{S}$ is a subcategory of $\textbf{Type}$. For example, in $\textbf{Ord}$ objects are types in *Ord* and arrows are functions on those objects. An overloaded function $f :: (Ord \, a, Ord \, b) \Rightarrow a \rightarrow b$ is a collection of arrows of $\text{Arr}(\textbf{Ord})$, but we informally refer to f as 'an' arrow.

13.3.2 Algebras, Coalgebras, and Bialgebras

Free algebras are neatly characterised as the least fixed point of the functor expression determined by their constructors [12]. To illustrate this, we need to introduce $\triangledown$, the case eliminator for sums, and $\triangle$, the lifted pair constructor (we occasionally deviate from Haskell notation and write $a \times b$ for the product type and 1 for the unit type):

$$\nabla :: (a \rightarrow c) \rightarrow (b \rightarrow c) \rightarrow a + b \rightarrow c$$
$$(f \nabla g) \; (Inl \; x) = f \; x$$
$$(f \nabla g) \; (Inr \; y) = g \; y$$
$$\triangle :: (c \rightarrow a) \rightarrow (c \rightarrow b) \rightarrow c \rightarrow a \times b$$
$$(f \triangle g) \; x = (f \; x, \; g \; x)$$

Take the list type, for example. Let us write the type signatures of list constructors slightly differently as $[\,] :: 1 \rightarrow [a]$ and $(:) :: a \times [a] \rightarrow [a]$. The 'nil' constructor is lifted to a function from the unit type and the 'cons' constructor is uncurried. The list type $[a]$ is characterised as the least fixed point of the functor $Fx = 1 + a \times x$ determined by the list constructors: $([\,]\nabla(:)) :: F[a] \rightarrow [a]$.

In a category $\mathbf{C}$, the pair consisting of an object X and an arrow $\alpha :: FX \rightarrow X$ is called an F-algebra. The pair consisting of an object Y and an arrow $\beta :: Y \rightarrow FY$ is called an F-coalgebra. In **Type**, the pair consisting of the algebraic data type Pa and the arrow $\alpha :: F(Pa) \rightarrow Pa$ is an F-algebra. Because Pa is free, observation can be characterised either by the inverse F-coalgebra $\alpha^{-1} :: Pa \rightarrow F(Pa)$ which formalises pattern matching or, alternatively, by the G-coalgebra $\beta :: Pa \rightarrow G(Pa)$, where $\alpha^{-1} = cond \circ \beta$ and $\beta^{-1} = \alpha \circ cond$. Function $cond :: Gx \rightarrow Fx$ formalises discriminated (guarded) selection [12]. The pair (α, β) is called an FG-bialgebra. For example, in the case of lists we have:

$$
\begin{array}{lll}
Gx & = & Bool \times a \times x \\
\beta & = & (null \triangle head \triangle tail) \\
cond & :: & (Bool \times a \times x) \rightarrow (1 + a \times x) \\
cond(p,t,e) & = & if \; p \; then \; Inl \; () \; else \; Inr \; (t,e)
\end{array}
$$

The following equation follows from $cond$'s definition:

$$((f \nabla g) \circ cond \circ (h \triangle i \triangle j)) \; x \; = \; if \; h \; x \; then \; f() \; else \; g(i \; x, \; j \; x)$$

13.4 ABSTRACT DATA TYPES

ADTs are typically specified in terms of function interfaces. In Haskell, the type-class system is employed for this purpose. For example, below type class $OrdSet$ specifies the interface of ordered sets and type class $Queue$ the interface of FIFO queues:[3]

```
class OrdSet s where                    class Queue q where
  emptyS   :: Ord a ⇒ s a                 emptyQ   :: q a
  insert   :: Ord a ⇒ a → s a → s a       enq      :: a → q a → q a
  isEmptyS :: Ord a ⇒ s a → Bool          isEmptyQ :: q a → Bool
  min      :: Ord a ⇒ s a → a             front    :: q a → a
  remove   :: Ord a ⇒ a → s a → s a       deq      :: q a → q a
  member   :: Ord a ⇒ a → s a → Bool
```

---

[3]Strictly speaking, $OrdSet$ and $Queue$ are so-called *constructor* classes.

The nullary constructors *emptyS* and *emptyQ* return respectively an empty or-dered set and an empty queue. Constructor *insert* inserts an element into a given ordered set whereas *enq* enqueues a value at the rear of a queue. Func-tions *isEmptyS* and *isEmptyQ* discriminate respectively whether an ordered set or a queue is empty. Function *min* returns the minimum element in an ordered set and *front* returns the front element in a queue. Function *deq* dequeues the front element in a queue and *remove* removes a specified element from an ordered set. Finally, *member* performs a membership test.

ADTs are not formally defined by interfaces alone but also by a set of (con-ditional) equations among their operators that specify the axiomatic semantics of the type [13, 10]. There may be equations among constructors, in which case con-struction and observation are not inverses (e.g., queue values are inserted at the rear of the queue but selected from the front). Equations are necessary to *imple-ment* and *reason about* ADTs. The following is a sample of *Queue*'s and *OrdSet*'s equations:

$$(isEmptyQ\ q)\ \Rightarrow\ deq\ (enq\ x\ q) = q$$
$$\neg\ (isEmptyQ\ q)\ \Rightarrow\ deq\ (enq\ x\ q) = enq\ x\ (deq\ q)$$
$$member\ x\ s\ \Rightarrow\ insert\ x\ s = s$$

Programmers supply implementations by providing an implementation type and definitions for the operators that satisfy the equations. For example, ordered sets can be implemented using lists. Below, the standard functions *sort* and *nub* re-spectively sort and remove duplicates from a list:

```
instance OrdSet [] where
  emptyS   =  []
  min      =  head
  insert x =  sort ∘ nub ∘ (x:)
  ...
```

An abstract type can be characterised by an FG-bialgebra (γ, ν) for some functors F and G. In the case of queues, for example, we have $\gamma = (emptyQ\ \triangledown\ enq)$ and $\nu = (isEmptyQ\ \triangle\ front\ \triangle\ deq)$, where F and G are the same functors of the list bialgebra of section 13.3.2. For queues, however, the equations $\gamma^{-1} = cond \circ \nu$ and $\nu^{-1} = \gamma \circ cond$ do not hold.

13.4.1 Payload, clutter, representation invariant, and repair function

ADTs arise because programmers cannot express their imagined types as free al-gebras. The values of an ADT Aa are represented (simulated) by a subset of the values of an algebraic data type Ia. The subset is characterised formally by a *rep-resentation invariant* [6], that is, a predicate $rep :: Ia \rightarrow Bool$ such that $rep(i)$ holds iff the value i of type Ia represents a value of Aa. Interface operators maintain the equations of the ADT and maintain the representation invariant by implement-ing a conceptual function $\phi :: Ia \rightarrow Ia$ such that $\forall i.rep(\phi(i))$. We call ϕ a *repair function* because it re-establishes the representation invariant.

The type Ia contains payload data and may also contain *clutter*, i.e., extra data used for efficiency or structuring purposes. Clutter data is either of a fixed monomorphic type or is parametric on the payload type (otherwise, Ia would have to be parametric on the same types as the clutter). Examples of clutter are the colour of nodes in Red-Black Trees (monomorphic), the height of a sub-tree in a heap (monomorphic), the cached front list in a physicists' implementation of FIFO queues (payload-parametric), etc. [16]. Clutter is more the norm than the exception: data (space) will be used to improve operator speed (time).

13.5   ABSTRACT DATA TYPES AND FUNCTORS

In order to establish the connection between ADTs and functors we need to define source and target categories and the object-level and arrow-level mappings that satisfy the functorial laws. To identify the categories, we classify ADTs into *sensitive* or *insensitive* depending on whether the internal arrangement of payload elements is, respectively, dependent or independent of properties of the payload type. We assume properties of the payload type are expressed via type-class constraints (e.g., the payload type has equality if it is an instance of Eq).

Examples of insensitive ADTs are FIFO queues, double-ended queues, arrays, matrices, etc. The order of insertion is determined by the operators (e.g., *enq* enqueues payload at the rear), and the ADTs can be characterised by the number and logical position of payload elements in the abstract structure.

Examples of sensitive ADTs are sets, bags, ordered sets, ordered bags, binary search trees, heaps, priority queues, hash tables, dictionaries, etc. In a set, payload position is irrelevant and cannot be used in the characterisation of the type. Sets require payload types in Eq to define the membership operator. Ordered sets require payload in Ord, etc.

We recognise mappable ADTs as functors $F :: \mathbf{S} \rightarrow \mathbf{ADT}$. The source category $\mathbf{S}$ is a subcategory of **Type** to account for constraints. There are ADTs for which we cannot characterise $\mathbf{S}$. We postpone this discussion until section 13.6.2 and concentrate for the moment on ADTs where the characterisation is possible. We cannot take **Type** as the target category for the reasons given in section 13.4.1. Instead, **ADT** is the category whose objects are monomorphic ADTs (e.g., *Queue Char*, *OrdSet Int*) and arrows are functions on those ADTs. The category can be formalised in various ways which make use of representation invariants or equational laws to pin down the type [3, 5].

The arrow-level part of the functor is the ADT's map operation that satisfies the functorial laws. To the programmer, the operation can be defined *internally* for the implementation type (map is part of the interface), or *externally*, in terms of interface operators. In the internal approach, the operation must satisfy the functorial laws and preserve representation invariants. If this is the case, it can only be claimed that A implemented as I is a functor. The external approach is independent of implementations, but there are several obstacles. First, programmers have to find a definition that satisfies the functorial laws and the equations of the ADT. Second, structural induction cannot be deployed in proofs. Take for example *OrdSet* :: **Ord** → **ADT**.[4] The following is a sensible definition for its map operation:

ordSet :: (*Ord a*, *Ord b*, *OrdSet s*) ⇒ (*a* → *b*) → *s a* → *s b*
ordSet f s = *if isEmptyS s then emptyS else*
           let (*m*,*r*) = (*min s*,*remove m s*) *in insert* (*f m*) (*ordSet f r*)

Haskell functions must start with lowercase letters so we use *ordSet* instead of *OrdSet* as the name for the map. Function *ordSet* must satisfy the functorial laws and the equations of the ADT. For example, the following equation must hold:

$$member\ x\ s\ \Rightarrow\ ordSet\ f\ (insert\ x\ s)\ =\ ordSet\ f\ s$$

Because of this equation, the map operation does not respect the shape of the ordered set. An expression such as *ordSet* (*const* 0) {1,2,3} must yield the value {0}. We should not be deceived into thinking that, for this reason, *ordSet* is not a valid map operation. The functoriality condition is that *ordSet* satisfies the functorial laws, and this may be the case regardless of whether it satisfies extra equations. Unfortunately, we cannot deploy structural induction in proofs. For example, given a non-empty ordered set *insert x s*, function *ordSet* is defined in terms of observers *min* and *remove*, with the recursive call involving *m* and *r*, not *x* and *s*. To deploy induction we have to prove intermediate lemmas such as $\neg(isEmptyS\ s) \wedge \neg(member\ m\ r) \Rightarrow insert\ m\ r = s$.

13.6 FUNCTORIAL LAWS FOR ADTS

In this section we provide a general definition for the map operation of ADTs whose interfaces satisfy certain properties made precise below. The definition needs only satisfy one equation that makes use of the notion of payload and re-pair function. Instances of the definition for particular ADTs can be constructed using their axiomatic semantics. The definability of the operation is a sufficient condition for functoriality (section 13.6.2).

Let *Aa* be an abstract data type and *Pa* be an algebraic data type. Let us assume that *P* is a functor and that it is possible to define an *extraction* function ε :: *Aa* → *Pa* and an *insertion* function ι :: *Pa* → *Aa* such that $\iota \circ \varepsilon = id_{Aa}$. The intuition is that ε ignores clutter and collects the payload in *Pa* maintaining the logical positioning, whereas ι enforces the equations of the ADT for the given payload and sets up the clutter. Because *A* satisfies equations, ε may not be surjective and ι may not be injective. Consequently, ε ∘ ι need not be the identity for *Pa*. (For example, we may not get the same list when inserting the elements into an ordered set and then extracting them back to a list.) Notice that ε ∘ ι corresponds to ϕ_P :: *Pa* → *Pa*, the behaviour of the repair function φ on the payload. (For example, the resulting list will be ordered and without repetitions.)

Assuming the above premises, we can write a definition for the map operation, namely, $Af = \iota \circ Pf \circ \varepsilon$. It is easy to prove that it preserves identities:

---

[4]Do not confuse *OrdSet* with a functor *F* :: **Poset** → **Poset**, where **Poset** is the category of partially ordered sets [3].

$$A\ id_a$$
$$=\qquad \{\ \text{def. of } A\ \}$$
$$\iota \circ P\ id_a \circ \varepsilon$$
$$=\qquad \{\ P\ \text{functor}\ \}$$
$$\iota \circ id_{Pa} \circ \varepsilon$$
$$=\qquad \{\ id_{Pa} \circ \varepsilon = \varepsilon\ \}$$
$$\iota \circ \varepsilon$$
$$=\qquad \{\ \iota \circ \varepsilon = id_{Aa}\ \}$$
$$id_{Aa}$$

We obtain a functorial law when attempting to prove that the map distributes over composition:

$$A\ (g \circ f) = Ag \circ Af$$
$$=\qquad \{\ \text{def. of } A\ \}$$
$$\iota \circ P\ (g \circ f) \circ \varepsilon = \iota \circ Pg \circ \varepsilon \circ \iota \circ Pf \circ \varepsilon$$
$$=\qquad \{\ P\ \text{functor and } \varepsilon \circ \iota = \phi_P\ \}$$
$$\iota \circ Pg \circ Pf \circ \varepsilon = \iota \circ Pg \circ \phi_P \circ Pf \circ \varepsilon$$

We call the last equation a *repair law*. The key element is the presence of the intermediate ϕ_P. Read from left to right, the law states that extracting payload, then distributing P over the composition, and finally inserting back payload must yield the same value as extracting payload, distributing P over the composition with an intermediate repair, and finally inserting payload. Due to the presence of ϕ_P, the equations $Af \circ \iota = \iota \circ Pf$ and $\varepsilon \circ Ag = Pg \circ \varepsilon$ do not hold (expand Af by its definition).[5]

Let Aa be characterised by the FG-bialgebra (γ, ν) where $\gamma :: F(Aa) \to Aa$ and $\nu :: Aa \to G(Aa)$. Definitions for ι and ε can be constructed for a Pa characterised by the FG-bialgebra (α, β), where $\alpha :: F(Pa) \to Pa$ and $\beta :: Pa \to G(Pa)$, as indicated by the following diagram:

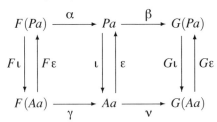

Because F and G are functors, we have:

$$\iota \circ \alpha\ =\ \gamma \circ F\iota$$
$$\beta \circ \varepsilon\ =\ G\varepsilon \circ \nu$$

From these equations we can obtain definitions for ι and ε using the fact that Pa is a free algebra:

$$\iota\ =\ \gamma \circ F\iota \circ cond \circ \beta$$
$$\varepsilon\ =\ \alpha \circ cond \circ G\varepsilon \circ \nu$$

---

[5]In other words, ε and ι are not natural transformations.

The definitions must also satisfy $\iota \circ \varepsilon = id_{Aa}$. Unfortunately, this is not the case when $\alpha^{-1} = cond \circ \beta$ and $\beta^{-1} = \alpha \circ cond$ because it leads to $\gamma \circ cond \circ \nu = id_{Aa}$ which does not hold in general (section 13.4).

Notice, however, that α does not occur in ι's definition and β does not occur in ε's definition. Thus, for *insensitive* ADTs we can use for Pa an FG-bialgebra (α, β') for extraction and another (α', β) for insertion where α and β' are inverses and so are α' and β.

Formally, the pair (α', β') is to be obtained from (γ, ν) by an FG-bialgebra homomorphism $\Sigma(\gamma, \nu) = (\alpha', \beta')$. The intuition is that the operators in (α', β') are those that make P behave like A or, in other words, P is *viewed* as an A. In practice, the programmer is to find (α', β') by searching for (or programming) Pa operators that satisfy the same equations as those operators in (γ, ν). Then, α and β are defined as the inverses of β' and α', that is, $\alpha = cond \circ \beta'$ and $\beta = \alpha' \circ cond$.

For example, let A be *Queue*. We have $Fx = 1 + a \times x$, $Gx = Bool \times a \times x$, and $(\gamma, \nu) = (emptyQ \triangledown enq, isEmptyQ \vartriangle front \vartriangle deq)$. The obvious choice of P is the list type. We have the following:

$$
\begin{aligned}
(\alpha', \beta') &= ([\,] \triangledown snoc,\ null \vartriangle head \vartriangle tail) \\
(\alpha, \beta) &= ([\,] \triangledown (:),\ null \vartriangle last \vartriangle init)
\end{aligned}
$$

(α', β') views lists as queues. Function $snoc :: a \times [a] \to [a]$ is the dual of 'cons'. It inserts an element at the rear of a list, e.g., $snoc\ x\ xs = xs\,{+}{+}\,[x]$.

Knowing β, we can obtain the definition of $\iota :: Queue\ q \Rightarrow [a] \to q\ a$ from the equation $\iota = \gamma \circ F\iota \circ cond \circ \beta$:

$$
\begin{aligned}
&\iota\,x \\
={}&\quad \{\ \text{def. of } \iota\ \} \\
&\gamma\,(F\iota\,(cond\,(\beta\,x))) \\
={}&\quad \{\ \text{def. of } \beta\ \} \\
&\gamma\,(F\iota\,(cond\,(null\,x,\ last\,x,\ init\,x))) \\
={}&\quad \{\ \text{def. of } cond\ \} \\
&\gamma\,(F\iota\,(if\ null\,x\ then\ Inl\,()\ else\ Inr\,(last\,x,\ init\,x))) \\
={}&\quad \{\ F\ \text{functor}\ \} \\
&\gamma\,(if\ null\,x\ then\ Inl\,()\ else\ Inr\,(last\,x,\ \iota\,(init\,x))) \\
={}&\quad \{\ \text{def. of } \gamma\ \} \\
&if\ null\,x\ then\ emptyQ\,()\ else\ enq\,(last\,x,\ \iota\,(init\,x)) \\
={}&\quad \{\ \text{isomorphism } emptyQ\,() \simeq emptyQ\ \text{and curry } enq\ \} \\
&if\ null\,x\ then\ emptyQ\ else\ enq\,(last\,x)\,(\iota\,(init\,x))
\end{aligned}
$$

Knowing α, we can obtain the definition of $\varepsilon :: Queue\ q \Rightarrow q\ a \to [a]$ from the equation $\varepsilon = \alpha \circ cond \circ G\varepsilon \circ \nu$:

$$
\begin{aligned}
&\varepsilon\,x \\
={}&\quad \{\ \text{def. of } \varepsilon\ \} \\
&\alpha\,(cond\,(G\varepsilon\,(\nu\,x))) \\
={}&\quad \{\ \text{def. of } \nu\ \} \\
&\alpha\,(cond\,(G\varepsilon\,(isEmptyQ\,x,\ front\,x,\ deq\,x)))
\end{aligned}
$$

$$=\qquad \{\ G\ \text{functor}\ \}$$
$$\alpha\ (cond\ (isEmptyQ\ x,\ front\ x,\ \varepsilon\ (deq\ x)))$$
$$=\qquad \{\ \text{def. of } cond\ \}$$
$$\alpha\ (if\ isEmptyQ\ x\ then\ Inl\ ()\ else\ Inr\ (front\ x,\ \varepsilon\ (deq\ x)))$$
$$=\qquad \{\ \text{def. of } \alpha\ \}$$
$$if\ isEmptyQ\ x\ then\ [\,]\ ()\ else\ (:)\ (front\ x,\ \varepsilon\ (deq\ x))$$
$$=\qquad \{\ \text{isomorphism}\ [\,]\ ()\simeq[\,]\ \text{and curry } (:)\ \}$$
$$if\ isEmptyQ\ x\ then\ [\,]\ else\ (front\ x)\ :\ \varepsilon\ (deq\ x)$$

Other list operators are to be used in the case of stacks. More precisely, $(\alpha',\beta')=([\,]\triangledown(:),\ null\bigtriangleup head\bigtriangleup tail)$ and $(\alpha,\beta)=([\,]\triangledown(:),\ null\bigtriangleup head\bigtriangleup tail)$:

$$\iota\ ::\ Stack\ s\ \Rightarrow\ [a]\ \rightarrow\ s\ a$$
$$\iota\ x\ =\ if\ null\ x\ then\ emptyStack\ else\ push\ (head\ x)\ (\iota\ (tail\ x))$$
$$\varepsilon\ ::\ Stack\ s\ \Rightarrow\ s\ a\ \rightarrow\ [a]$$
$$\varepsilon\ x\ =\ if\ isEmptyStack\ x\ then\ [\,]\ else\ (top\ x)\ :\ \varepsilon\ (pop\ x)$$

For *insensitive* ADTs, we can use the same FG-bialgebra for Pa for insertion and extraction because the observers in ν place payload in Pa at fixed positions but the constructors in γ place them according to the semantics of the type. For example, payload from an ordered set is extracted into an ordered list, but an arbitrary list is inserted into an ordered set. Thus, we can have:

$$(\gamma,\nu)\quad =\quad (emptyS\ \triangledown\ insert,\ isEmptyS\ \bigtriangleup\ min\ \bigtriangleup\ (\lambda s\ \rightarrow\ remove\ (min\ s)\ s))$$
$$(\alpha,\beta)\quad =\quad ([\,]\ \triangledown\ (:),\ null\ \bigtriangleup\ head\ \bigtriangleup\ tail)$$

and the following definitions for ι and ε are obtained from their respective equations:

$$\iota\ ::\ (OrdSet\ s,\ Ord\ a)\ \Rightarrow\ [a]\ \rightarrow\ s\ a$$
$$\iota\ x\ =\ if\ null\ x\ then\ emptyS\ else\ insert\ (head\ x)\ (\iota\ (tail\ x))$$
$$\varepsilon\ ::\ (OrdSet\ s,\ Ord\ a)\ \Rightarrow\ s\ a\ \rightarrow\ [a]$$
$$\varepsilon\ x\ =\ if\ isEmptyS\ x\ then\ [\,]\ else\ (min\ x)\ :\ \varepsilon\ (remove\ (min\ x)\ x)$$

Alternatively, we could have used the same (α,β) we used for queues and still satisfy $\iota\circ\varepsilon=id_{Aa}$.

The reader can verify that the repair law is satisfied and FIFO queues, stacks, and ordered sets are functors. In insensitive ADTs, ϕ_P does not reshuffle payload (constructors place payload in fixed positions). We conjecture that the repair law is always satisfied and therefore insensitive ADTs are functors. Other characterisations of insensitive ADTs also recognise them as functors (section 13.8). In sensitive ADTs, ϕ_P may reshuffle payload, even remove some. The repair law need not hold. We conjecture that the repair law is broken only in a particular case of payload removal (section 13.6.2).

13.6.1   Functorial laws for ADT implementations

The definition of Af can be adapted to define If, the map operation for the implementation type, where now $\varepsilon::Ia\rightarrow Pa$ and $\iota::Pa\rightarrow Ia$. Let us define $If=\phi\circ\sigma f$, where $\phi = \iota$ and $\sigma f = Pf \circ \varepsilon$. The repair law is now written:

$$\phi \circ \sigma (g \circ f) = \phi \circ \sigma g \circ \phi \circ \sigma f$$

However, If can be defined directly without using interface operators; that is, we need not be concerned with functors F and G, and we can define ϕ and σ directly in terms of the implementation type, not in terms of ι and ε.

More precisely, we can define Pa as the type in Ia that holds the payload. Function ϕ takes a value of Pa and creates a value of Ia by enforcing ϕ_P and creating the clutter. Function $\sigma :: (a \rightarrow b) \rightarrow Ia \rightarrow Pb$ is a 'selection' function that ignores clutter and maps over the payload.

Consider FIFO queues, for example. The so-called physicists' representation is a reasonably efficient way of implementing queues [16]:

data PhysicistQueue a = PQ [a] Int [a] Int [a]

The implementation type consists of three lists and two integers. The first integer is the length of the second list, which contains the front elements, and the second integer is the length of the third list, which contains the rear elements in reverse order. Elements are moved from the rear list to the front list when the length of the former is less than the length of the latter. In a lazy language the move is computed on demand so a prefix of the front list (10 elements, say) is cached for efficiency. The first list is such prefix.

The second and third lists make up the payload type. The cached front list and the lengths are clutter. We have:

type P a = ([a],[a])
$\sigma :: (a \rightarrow b) \rightarrow PhysicistQueue\ a \rightarrow P\ b$
$\sigma\ f\ (PQ\ \_\ \_\ fs\ \_\ rs) = (map\ f\ fs\ ,\ map\ f\ rs)$
$\phi :: P\ a \rightarrow PhysicistQueue\ a$
$\phi\ (fs,rs) = PQ\ (init\ 10\ fs)\ (length\ fs)\ fs\ (length\ rs)\ rs$
$queue :: (a \rightarrow b) \rightarrow PhysicistQueue\ a \rightarrow PhysicistQueue\ a$
$queue\ f = \phi \circ \sigma\ f$

Notice that by fusing ϕ and σ we obtain the definition for *queue* that the programmer would have written. The repair law can be proved directly from the fact that the list type is a functor:

$\quad \phi\ (\sigma g\ (\phi\ (\sigma f\ (PQ\ cs\ lf\ fs\ lr\ rs))))$
$=\qquad \{\ \text{def. of } \sigma\ \}$
$\quad \phi\ (\sigma g\ (\phi\ (map\ f\ fs\ ,\ map\ f\ rs)))$
$=\qquad \{\ \text{def. of } \phi \text{ where } mf = map\ f\ fs \text{ and } mr = map\ f\ rs\ \}$
$\quad \phi\ (\sigma g\ (PQ\ (init\ 10\ mf)\ mf\ (length\ mf)\ mr\ (length\ mr)))$
$=\qquad \{\ \text{def. of } \sigma\ \}$
$\quad \phi\ (map\ g\ mf\ ,\ map\ g\ mr)$
$=\qquad \{\ \text{def. of } mf \text{ and } mr, \text{ and list is functor}\ \}$
$\quad \phi\ (map\ (g \circ f)\ fs,\ map\ (g \circ f)\ rs)$
$=\qquad \{\ \text{def. of } \sigma\ \}$
$\quad \phi\ (\sigma\ (g \circ f)\ (PQ\ cs\ lf\ fs\ lr\ rs))$

Now consider ordered sets. Suppose they are implemented in terms of lists:

$type\ SetList\ a\ =\ [a]$

There is no clutter in this implementation and the payload type is $Pa = [a]$:

$\sigma\ ::\ (Ord\ a,\ Ord\ b)\ \Rightarrow\ (a\ \rightarrow\ b)\ \rightarrow\ SetList\ a\ \rightarrow\ P\ b$
$\sigma\ =\ map$
$\phi\ ::\ Ord\ a\ \Rightarrow\ P\ a\ \rightarrow\ SetList\ a$
$\phi\ =\ sort\ \circ\ nub$
$set\ ::\ (Ord\ a,\ Ord\ b)\ \Rightarrow\ (a\ \rightarrow\ b)\ \rightarrow\ SetList\ a\ \rightarrow\ SetList\ b$
$set\ f\ =\ \phi\ \circ\ \sigma\ f$

Fusing ϕ and σ gives the definition the programmer would have written. The repair law is:

$$sort\ \circ\ nub\ \circ\ map\ (g\ \circ\ f)\ =\ sort\ \circ\ nub\ \circ\ map\ g\ \circ\ sort\ \circ\ nub\ \circ\ map\ f$$

which can be proved by induction on lists.

13.6.2 Non-functors

The definition of Af and its repair law are conditional on the definability of ι and ε such that $\iota \circ \varepsilon = id_{Aa}$. The definability of Af that satisfies the repair law is therefore a sufficient condition for functoriality in our source and target categories.

There are examples of ADTs for which either ι or ε are not definable but whose functoriality can be established internally for particular implementations (section 13.6.1). Examples are ordinary (unordered) sets and bags where membership test, cardinality, and number of element occurrences in bags are the only observers. The definability of ε is conditional upon the existence of operators that enable the observation of everything that is constructed. In the case of sets, $\gamma = (emptyS \bigtriangledown insert)$ where $insert :: Set\ s \Rightarrow a \times s\ a \rightarrow s\ a$, but we cannot find $\nu = (isEmptyS \bigtriangleup x \bigtriangleup y)$ such that $(x \bigtriangleup y) :: Set\ s \Rightarrow s\ a \rightarrow a \times s\ a$. However, if sets are implemented as lists then $\phi = nub$, $\sigma = map$, and the repair law of section 13.6.1 is satisfied.

In general, if an ADT is a functor for a given implementation type then it should be a functor for alternative implementation types. Otherwise, the implementation types would not implement the same ADT. More work is needed to formalise this claim. For example, let k be a type of keys and v be a type of keyed values. Association lists $[(k,v)]$ and finite functions $k \rightarrow v$ can be used to implement dictionaries. However, with finite functions we cannot define the empty dictionary, nor remove a key-value pair from a dictionary, and remain total.

We have mentioned in section 13.5 that it may not be possible to identify a mappable ADT with a functor $F :: \mathbf{S} \rightarrow \mathbf{C}$ where $Obj(\mathbf{S})$ are monomorphic Haskell types. For example, let $OrdSetP$ be the type of ordered sets with positive numbers. The equation $x < 0 \Rightarrow insert\ x\ s = s$ is part of its axiomatic semantics. Type class Num contains types Int, $Integer$, $Float$, and $Double$, but we cannot define the class of positive numbers as a subclass of Num. In particular, we cannot define the type *Nat* of positive integers as a subtype of *Int*. At most we can define an algebraic data type for natural numbers, e.g., *data Nat = Zero | Succ Nat*, and provide mappings *in* :: *Int → Nat* and *out* :: *Nat → Int*. This is the idea behind *views* for ADTs [18], a deprecated approach with serious drawbacks [17]. (Notice the similarity with section 13.4.1, where instead of *rep* and types *I* and *A* we have a property and type classes *S* and *Num*. We might define **S** as a subcategory of **ADT**.)

Despite the limitation, we can use the repair law to disprove that *OrdSetP* is a functor from **Num** to **ADT**. A counter-example is provided by $g(x) = x^2$ and $f(x) = -x$. Notice that g is not an arrow of Arr(**S**). The negative payload is removed by ϕ_P in $Pg \circ \phi_P \circ Pf$ whereas in $Pg \circ Pf$, function g 'corrects' f and the negative payload becomes positive. The resulting sets may have different cardinality. A particular way of determining whether the repair law is broken is to look for counter-examples in which the two sides of the equation produce ADTs with different sizes.

13.7   CONCLUSION

We have investigated the connection between first-order parametric ADTs and functors. At the object level, ADTs map objects in subcategories of the category of types to objects in the category of monomorphic ADTs. At the arrow-level we have presented a general definition for their map operation that needs only satisfy a repair law which makes the connection between functorial laws and representation invariants explicit. The definability of such a map is a sufficient condition for functoriality. We have shown how instances of the operation for particular ADTs can be constructed using the latter's axiomatic semantics. We have shown that the definition can be adapted to construct the map for an ADT with a particular implementation. Finally, we have discussed situations in which ADTs are not functors.

13.8   RELATED WORK

The C++ Standard Template Library [14] classifies containers with iterators into sequences and collections which are, respectively, insensitive and sensitive ADTs. We prefer to use terminology that highlights the role of parametricity.

Functions ι and ε are structurally polymorphic (or polytypic [8]) on the structure of so-called *F*-views [15] which are, roughly, a way of representing the operators and the functors of *FG*-bialgebras. Polytypic functions on ADTs can be programmed in terms of polytypic ι, polytypic ε, and polytypic functions on algebraic data types. In particular, *Af* can be programmed polytypically where *Pf* is the polytypic map for algebraic data types.

Functors and *F*-algebras provide a variable-free characterisation of free algebras. A variable-free characterisation of non-free algebras is presented in [5] where equations are expressed as pairs of transformers, i.e., mappings from dialgebras to dialgebras that satisfy certain properties. An *FG-di*algebra is a mapping

$\varphi :: Fx \rightarrow Gx$. However, homomorphisms in the category of such dialgebras cannot map to dialgebras with less equations or would not be uniquely defined.

Bialgebras are used in [4] to define catamorphisms (folds) for ADTs as 'metamorphisms' where the F-algebra of the target ADT is composed with the G-coalgebra of the source ADT. Functions ι and ε can be expressed as metamorphisms. There are notable differences with our approach. First, the notion of ADT is artificial and not aimed at hiding representations. For example, a queue is an FG-bialgebra (α, ν) where α is the list F-algebra and ν is the observer F-coalgebra where dequeuing reverses the list, gets the tail, and returns the reverse of the tail. Second, there is no discussion of maps or of the satisfiability of functorial laws apart from the mention of 'invertible' ADTs for which $F = G$ and $\beta \circ \alpha = id$. Invertibility is a stronger requirement than our repair law. Finally, although metamorphisms are defined as the least solutions of an equation, it is not shown how to arrive at the solutions.

A container type is defined in [7] as a relator with membership. The result is presented in the context of allegory theory. The discussion of section 13.6.2 suggests f and g must preserve some sort of membership test in order for the repair law to hold. More work is needed to understand a possible connection.

A container type is defined in [1] as a dependent pair type $(s \in S) \times Ps$ where S is a set of shapes and for every $s \in S$, Ps is a set of positions. Containers can characterise algebraic data types and insensitive ADTs. The semantics of a container is a functor $F :: \mathbf{C} \rightarrow \mathbf{C}$ where $\mathbf{C}$ is the category giving meaning to shapes (e.g., types) and where at the object level $Fx = (s \in S) \times (Ps \rightarrow x)$. In words, F sends a type x to the dependent pair type where the first component s is a type and the second component is a function 'labelling' the positions over s with values in x. The authors have extended the container definition with *quotient* containers (containers with an equivalence relation on positions) which capture a few sensitive ADTs such as bags [2]. This work is related to Joyal's combinatorial species [9] where types are described combinatorially in terms of the power series of the arrangements of payload and shapes in an implementation type.

ACKNOWLEDGMENTS

The author is grateful to Roland Backhouse, Jeremy Gibbons, Henrik Nilsson, Conor McBride, and the anonymous reviewers for their invaluable feedback and bibliographic pointers. This work has been partially funded by EPSRC grant GR/S27078/01.

REFERENCES

[1] Michael Abott, Thorsten Altenkirch, and Neil Ghani. Containers - constructing strictly positive types. *Theoretical Computer Science*, 342:3–27, September 2005.

[2] Michael Abott, Thorsten Altenkirch, Neil Ghani, and Conor McBride. Constructing polymorphic programs with quotient types. In *International Conference on Mathematics of Program Construction (MPC'04)*, 2004.

[3] Michael Barr and Charles Wells. *Category Theory for Computing Science*. Prentice-Hall, 1990.

[4] Martin Erwig. Categorical programming with abstract data types. In *International Conference on Algebraic Methodology and Software Technology (AMAST'98)*, pages 406–421. Springer-Verlag, 1999.

[5] Maarten M. Fokkinga. Datatype laws without signatures. *Mathematical Structures in Computer Science*, 6:1–32, 1996.

[6] C. A. R. Hoare. Proofs of correctness of data representations. *Acta Informatica*, 1:271–281, 1972.

[7] Paul F. Hoogendijk and Oege de Moor. Container types categorically. *Journal of Functional Programming*, 10(2):191–225, 2000.

[8] Johan Jeuring and Patrik Jansson. Polytypic programming. In *Advanced Functional Programming*, number 1129 in LNCS, pages 68–114. Springer-Verlag, 1996.

[9] André Joyal. Foncteurs analytiques et espèces de structures. In G. Labelle and P. Leroux, editors, *Combinatoire énumérative: Proc. of "Colloque de Combinatoire Énumérative", Univ. du Québec à Montréal, 28 May–1 June 1985*, volume 1234 of *Lecture Notes in Mathematics*, pages 126–159. Springer-Verlag, Berlin, 1986.

[10] Ricardo Peña Marí. *Diseño de Programas, Formalismo y Abstracción*. Prentice-Hall, 1998.

[11] John McCarthy. History of LISP. *SIGPLAN Notices*, 13(8), August 1978.

[12] Erik Meijer, Maarten Fokkinga, and Ross Paterson. Functional programming with bananas, lenses, envelopes and barbed wire. In *Functional Programming Languages and Computer Architecture (FPCA'91)*, volume 523 of *LNCS*. Springer-Verlag, 1991.

[13] John C. Mitchell. *Foundations for Programming Languages*. MIT Press, 1996.

[14] David R. Musser and Atul Saini. *STL Tutorial and Reference Guide*. Addison-Wesley, Reading, Mass., 1996.

[15] Pablo Nogueira. *Polytypic Functional Programming and Data Abstraction*. PhD thesis, School of Computer Science and IT, University of Nottingham, UK, 2006.

[16] Chris Okasaki. *Purely Functional Data Structures*. Cambridge University Press, 1998.

[17] Pedro Palao Gostanza, Ricardo Peña, and Manuel Núñez. A new look at pattern matching in abstract data types. In *International Conference on Functional Programming (ICFP'96)*, pages 110–121. ACM Press, 1996.

[18] Philip Wadler. Views: A way for pattern matching to cohabit with data abstraction. In *Principles of Programming Languages (POPL'87)*, pages 307–312. ACM Press, 1987.

[19] Philip Wadler. Theorems for free! In *Functional Programming Languages and Computer Architecture (FPCA'89)*, pages 347–359. ACM Press, 1989.